SOCIAL THEMES OF THE CHRISTIAN YEAR

SOCIAL THEMES
OF THE
CHRISTIAN YEAR

A Commentary on the Lectionary

Edited by
DIETER T. HESSEL

THE GENEVA PRESS
Philadelphia

BOOK DESIGN BY DOROTHY ALDEN SMITH

Published by The Geneva Press®
Philadelphia, Pennsylvania

PRINTED IN THE UNITED STATES OF AMERICA
9 8 7 6 5 4 3

Library of Congress Cataloging in Publication Data

Main entry under title:

Social themes of the Christian year.

    Includes bibliographical references.
    1. Bible—Liturgical lessons, English. I. Hessel,
Dieter T.
BS391.2.H45   1983   264'.34   83–1504
ISBN 0–664–24472–6 (pbk.)

CONTENTS

CONTRIBUTORS

JAMES H. ADAMS AND MARGARET G. ADAMS are full-time co-pastors of the Rockville Presbyterian Church, Rockville, Maryland, and coauthors of *Developing Leadership for the Church's Teaching Ministry* (Griggs, 1978). Margaret also leads workshops on intergenerational Christian Education and is president of Church Employed Women. Jim is a leader of young pastors seminars and author of several units of adult Bible study curriculum.

HORACE T. ALLEN, JR., is Assistant Professor of Worship at Boston University School of Theology and author of *A Handbook for the Lectionary* (Geneva Press, 1980). He is former director of the Presbyterian Joint Office of Worship, and chairperson of the North American Consultation on Common Texts.

RICHARD K. AVERY is pastor of the First Presbyterian Church of Port Jervis, New York, where he has served for twenty-three years. Together with Donald Marsh he has written over 200 songs and choral works for churches, leads workshops in worship and music, and publishes a monthly letter, *In the Worship Workshop.*

BRUCE C. BIRCH is Professor of Old Testament at Wesley Theological Seminary in Washington, D.C. He is a minister of The United Methodist Church and a member of its Board of Church and Society. He chairs the section on Old Testament Theology of the Society of Biblical Literature, and is coauthor with Larry Rasmussen of books mentioned below.

ROBERT MCAFEE BROWN is Professor of Theology and Ethics at the Pacific School of Religion, Berkeley, California. Among his numerous books, three recent writings that deal with liberation themes are: *Theology in a New Key* (Westminster Press, 1978), *Gustavo Gutiérrez* (John Knox Press, 1980), and *Making Peace in the Global Village* (Westminster Press, 1981).

WALTER BRUEGGEMANN is Professor of Old Testament at Eden Theological Seminary, St. Louis, Missouri. He is a minister of the United Church of Christ. His recent publications include *The Land, The Prophetic Imagination,* and *The Creative Word* (Fortress Press).

RICHARD D. N. DICKINSON is Dean and Professor of Christian Ethics at Christian Theological Seminary in Indianapolis, and a minister of the United Church of Christ. He is a member of the World Council of Churches' Commission on the Churches' Participation in Development, for which he wrote *To Set at Liberty the Oppressed: Towards an Understanding of Christian Responsibilities for Development/ Liberation* (1975).

GABRIEL FACKRE is Abbot Professor of Christian Theology at Andover Newton Theological School, Newton Centre, Massachusetts. He is currently engaged in writing a systematic theology, the introductory volume of which is entitled *The Christian Story* (Wm. B. Eerdmans Publishing Co., 1978).

WILLIAM E. GIBSON is Coordinator of the Eco-Justice Project, a church-university network sponsored by the Center for Religions, Ethics and Social Policy, located at Cornell University, Ithaca, New York. His most widely read publications are a quarterly newsletter, *The Egg,* and an ecumenically sponsored adult curriculum, *A Covenant Group for Lifestyle Assessment* (United Presbyterian Church, Program Agency; Revised 1981).

CATHERINE GUNSALUS GONZÁLEZ, an ordained Presbyterian minister, is Professor of Church History at Columbia Theological Seminary in Decatur, Georgia. Together with her husband, Justo L. González, she has authored *Liberation Preaching* and a number of other books.

JUSTO L. GONZÁLEZ was a seminary teacher in the United States and Puerto Rico for sixteen years, prior to becoming a full-time writer. He is currently working on a history of Christianity to be published by Harper & Row.

NEILL Q. HAMILTON is Professor of New Testament at the School of Theology and Graduate School of Drew University, Madison, New Jersey. He is the author of *Recovery of the Protestant Adventure* (Seabury Press, 1981), and is developing an organic view of the Christian life to guide clergy and laity in spiritual maturing, in a book to be published soon.

FREDERICK HERZOG is Professor of Systematic Theology at Duke University Divinity School, Durham, North Carolina. His writings on liberation theology include a study of the Fourth Gospel (1972) and *Justice Church* (Orbis Books, 1980). Together with Letty Russell, he cochairs the Liberation Theology Group in the American Academy of Religion.

DIETER T. HESSEL is Associate for Social Education in the Program Agency of The United Presbyterian Church in the U.S.A., where he is responsible for developing leadership and educational resources. In addition to numerous articles on particular issues, he is author of *Social Ministry* (Westminster Press, 1982), a whole approach to parish life and mission.

EDWARD M. HUENEMANN is Associate for Theological Studies and Planning in the Program Agency of The United Presbyterian Church in the U.S.A., and a frequent contributor of papers to theological conferences involving the Reformed and Presbyterian Churches.

PAUL LEHMANN is Emeritus Professor of Systematic Theology at Union Theological Seminary, New York, and author of *The Transfiguration of Politics* (Harper & Row, 1975). A provocative lecturer and beloved teacher, he is best known for *Ethics in a Christian Context* (1963).

DONALD S. MARSH has been the Choirmaster and Director of Arts and Christian Education of the First Presbyterian Church of Port Jervis, New York, since 1961, and is also the president of Proclamation Productions, Inc., which publishes much of the music he has coauthored with Richard Avery.

CHRISTOPHER MORSE is Associate Professor of Systematic Theology at Union Theological Seminary, New York. He entered seminary teaching after several years of pastoral experience in The United Methodist Church. He is author of *The Logic of Promise in Moltmann's Theology* (Fortress Press, 1979).

WALTER L. OWENSBY is Director of Inter-American Designs for Economic Awareness, a program of the United Presbyterian Church, and editor of *Third World Sermon Notes,* a quarterly commentary on selected lectionary passages. He has extensive experience in ministry in Latin America.

SCOTT I. PARADISE is Episcopal Chaplain at Massachusetts Institute of Technology. He served with the Sheffield Industrial Mission and Detroit Industrial Mission before becoming Executive Director of Boston Industrial Mission. He is author of *Detroit Industrial Mission, A Personal Narrative.*

EUNICE BLANCHARD POETHIG is Associate Executive for Congregational Life in the Presbytery of Chicago, and editor of *150 Plus Tomorrow: Churches Plan for the Future* (Presbytery of Chicago, 1982). She was a fraternal worker in the Philippines and is completing a Ph.D. in biblical studies.

LARRY L. RASMUSSEN is Professor of Christian Ethics at Wesley Seminary, Washington, D.C., and author of *Economic Anxiety and Christian Faith* (Augsburg Publishing House, 1981). He is coauthor, with Bruce Birch, of *Bible and Ethics in the Christian Life* (Augsburg Publishing House, 1976) and *The Predicament of the Prosperous* (Westminster Press, 1978).

ROSEMARY RADFORD RUETHER is the Georgia Harkness Professor of Applied Theology at Garrett-Evangelical Theological Seminary, Evanston, Illinois. A Roman Catholic lay theologian, she has written and lectured widely on issues of feminism, liberation theology, and peace and justice themes. Her most recent book is *To Change the World: Christology and Cultural Criticism* (Crossroad Publishing Co., 1981).

JAMES A. SANDERS is Elizabeth Hay Bechtel Professor of Intertestamental and Biblical Studies at the School of Theology, Claremont, California, and Professor of Religion at Claremont Graduate School. A leader in research on ancient manuscripts, as well as a popular lecturer, he is the author of *Torah and Canon* (Fortress Press, 1972) and *God Has a Story Too* (Fortress Press, 1979).

ROY I. SANO is Associate Professor of Theology and Pacific and Asian American Ministries at Pacific School of Religion. He is the author of *From Every Nation, Without Number* (Abingdon Press, 1982) and *Theologies of Asian American and Pacific People* (PACTS, 1798 Scenic Ave., Berkeley, Calif. 94709).

DOROTHEE SOELLE resides in Hamburg, where she is a writer, lecturer, and leader of the German peace movement. Each spring term, she teaches systematic theology at Union Theological Seminary, New York. Recent books in English include: *Beyond Mere Obedience* (Pilgrim Press, 1982) and *Revolutionary Patience* (Orbis Books, 1977).

ESTHER C. STINE is Associate for Leadership Development in the Program Agency of The United Presbyterian Church in the U.S.A., and a frequent presenter of theological papers to gatherings of church leaders. Formerly she taught religion at Maryville College in Tennessee and at McCormick Theological Seminary, Chicago.

JOHN H. WESTERHOFF III is Professor of Religion and Education at Duke University, Durham, North Carolina, and editor of the journal *Religious Education*. Among his books which have achieved critical acclaim are: *Values for Tomorrow's Children, Will our Children Have Faith?, Tomorrow's Church,* and *Inner Growth/Outer Change.*

GAYRAUD S. WILMORE is Martin Luther King, Jr., Professor of Black Church Studies at Colgate Rochester/Bexley Hall/Crozer Theological Seminary in Rochester, New York. During the civil rights period, he was Executive Director of the Council on Church and Race of The United Presbyterian Church in the U.S.A. His books include *Black Theology: A Documentary History* (with James H. Cone, Orbis Books, 1979) and *Last Things First* (Westminster Press, 1982).

WALTER P. WINK is Professor of Biblical Interpretation at Auburn Theological Seminary, New York, and an influential teacher of Bible study methods for clergy and laity together. See his book *Transforming Bible Study* (Abingdon Press, 1980).

JOHN H. YODER teaches theology at the University of Notre Dame and at the Associated Mennonite Biblical Seminaries, Elkhart, Indiana. He has often represented the Mennonite denomination in ecumenical conversations regarding matters of war, peace, and violence. He is the author of *The Politics of Jesus* and *The Original Revolution.*

PREFACE

This volume shows the cooperative effort of many writers and advisers. Together they produced twenty-two expository essays that interpret clusters of texts within seasons across the three-year cycle of Scripture readings recommended in the ecumenical lectionary. In addition, there are five articles exploring whole seasonal approaches to worship-education-action, with leads for adult study, utilizing the above essays.

The writers have provided related guidance for social-ethical interpretation of Scripture, ways to cover more of the Old Testament, and ways to avoid noncontextual use or forced linkage of texts. (Except on feast days, all three Sunday lections are seldom supposed to relate thematically!)

The resulting volume is intended for use by parish pastors, educators, and committees who are planning for socially faithful life and mission within each season of the Christian year.

This book follows "A Consensus Lectionary of Readings," which was prepared by the North American Committee on Calendar and Lectionary and recommended, by the Consultation on Common Texts, for trial use in the churches that have been using variations of the ecumenical lectionary. The consensus lectionary smoothes out minor differences among denominations in lessons throughout the period of Advent to Pentecost and makes major changes in Old Testament readings for the Sundays of "Ordinary Time" after Pentecost. The Gospel readings remain unchanged. The three-year cycle remains the same: Year A begins Advent 1983, 1986; Year B begins Advent 1984, 1987; Year C begins Advent 1985, 1988.

Special thanks are due to the ecumenical group of authors who wrote so thoughtfully within severe space constraints; to John Westerhoff for his public encouragement and cogent advice about the development of a whole liturgy; to George M. Wilson, whose parish experience and liturgical creativity in lectionary use shaped my thinking about this project; to Richard Avery, Donald Marsh, James

15

and Margaret Adams, Scott Paradise, and Eunice Blanchard Poethig, who gave more time than originally expected to making the most of each season; to advisers James Kirk, Lewis Briner, John Purdy, Esther Stine, David McShane, Horace Allen, and Harold Daniels; and to my administrative and editorial assistant, Neena Mitchell. Financial support for the development of this book and authors' fees came from Major Mission Funds administered by the Discipleship and Worship Program, and from the budget of Church Education Services in the United Presbyterian Program Agency Unit on Ministries with Congregations. Authors and editor receive no royalties from sale of this volume. The entire effort is part of our service to the ecumenical church which witnesses to the Word in the world.

D. T. H.

FOREWORD

John H. Westerhoff III

SOCIAL THEMES OF THE CHRISTIAN YEAR emerged from a conference in Oregon attended by Presbyterian pastors and educators. Dieter Hessel was at that gathering. In a lecture on liturgy and education, I made the point that the lack of integration between worship, nurture, and witness in parish life worked against the church's call to mission and ministry. I gently but publicly encouraged Dr. Hessel to develop a resource for planning parish life around the church's year and its lectionary. He accepted that challenge and this unique book is a result.

We are entering a period of possible spiritual rebirth. A new interest in the religious affections, the transcendent, and the sacred has emerged from an era in which some believed that God was dead. The church needs to affirm this return of the sacred, but beware of any movements that deny the materialistic, worldly aspects of Christian faith. The central role of reason and the call to social, political, and economic responsibility are a challenge to the potential heresies of *pietism,* with its excessive concerns for right feeling and emotion, and *quietism,* with its excessive concern for spiritual unity with the transcendent God. A healthy spirituality is one that integrates piety and politics, the material and the spiritual, the sacred and the secular, the life of contemplation and that of action.

We live in a time of lost confidence in our social organizations and we have witnessed a breakdown of our primary institutions. We have lost hope in our visions and we are uncertain of our ability to reach them. Confronted by social evil, we experience powerlessness; confronted by social good, we experience apathy. Hedonistic individualism and privatized religion are tempting ways out of our frustrations. Conscious of the difficulties, problems, and personal sacrifices inherent in any form of democratic socialism and shared intentional power, we find ourselves being drawn once again toward obsessive militarism and more centralized capitalism, which promise to protect individual freedom and to deliver the goods—at steeper social cost. In just such a day, the world needs a faithful church to advocate, and

17

act on behalf of, a new social vision and to shape through sacrificial service and liturgical signs an alternative future. This book is committed to these ends; it is also founded upon certain *theological assumptions*.

First, it assumes that we are our community. Human beings can best be understood as members of a community. We know people by the groups to which they belong. We cannot be Christian or even human alone. It is through baptism that we are made Christians, that is, through a process of initiation into a community that shares a common memory, vision, mission, rituals, authority, and family-like life together. And it is through reflective action within this community that we become the Christians our baptism announces we are. This resource therefore presents a model for responsible, faithful life in worldly community.

Second, this volume assumes that God has acted in Jesus Christ to reclaim all human life, including the political, social, and economic. Christians are those who risk living as if God's reign of peace and justice, equality and freedom, unity and the well-being of all persons has already come, and thereby enhance its coming. This resource, therefore, understands salvation to be a social event and strives to overcome any disjunctures between personal fulfillment and a passion for social justice, between community worship and social involvement, between inner religious experience and political-social transformation.

Third, this resource assumes that our human vocation is to act with God on behalf of the humanization of all life. While acknowledging that we are all the product of our history, it affirms that we are also, and more importantly, the producers of our history and therefore capable of changing human life, including its social arrangements. In this process education plays a fundamental and essential role. Therefore this resource is also founded upon certain *educational or catechetical assumptions*.

1. When learning is separated from parish life, it is apt to be separated from both the community's life and its action in the world. The proper function of learning is to bridge them. In this process, some important learning takes place with children, youth, and adults together or intergenerationally. The benefits of such opportunities have become obvious and should be affirmed. At the heart of this volume are suggestions for parish activities that link worship, nurture, and witness.

But there is also some learning that older persons must do alone. This resource, therefore, also provides ideas for adult study in various settings. Indeed, adult learning is foundational to all nurture in the church, for without it we would lack the mature leaders necessary for healthy intergenerational learning. A method for reflective action among all ages remains central to the learning process that follows.

Liturgy describes the activity of a religious community. It has two interrelated dimensions, namely, cultic life or our ritual life of symbolic actions, and daily life or our worldly corporate and individual actions. Each directly affects the other and so a change in one necessitates a change in the other, experiences in one need to be related to experiences in the other.

The historic function of catechesis or nurture (Christian education) is to aid the integration of worship and witness, ritual life and daily life. It does so by helping the community to reflect on its daily life and prepare for its ritual life, and to reflect on its ritual life and prepare for its daily life.

2. This book assumes that Christian education is best understood as praxis, or reflective action. There are various ways of relating to life and learning. Typically the church has focused on the speculative life and the quest for truth through intellectual contemplation and reflection. In emphasizing this approach the church tended to neglect intuitive and affective ways of knowing and to ignore ethical living in a sociopolitical, economic context. A method of shared praxis, while affirming both intellectual and intuitive ways of knowing, moves in an interpretive circle between life experience and action/reflection on that experience. Through our critical reflection-in-community on present activity, both social and personal, in the light of the good news of God in Christ, we can discern the will of God and be empowered to act in cooperation with God's rule.

3. Last, this resource assumes a way of life and not a system of doctrine or a pattern of ritual. Jesus taught us the way of perceiving reality (faith), God's way of relating to us (revelation), and how to act personally and socially in the world (vocation). The aim of Christian education is to do likewise so that the church as the body of Christ might continue to transform culture. As such the church is judged by the degree to which it becomes a sign and witness in the world to the reign of God. The purpose of this volume is to be faithful to these theological and catechetical assumptions and, thereby stimulated, to encourage the church to reform its faith and life and thus fulfill its humble calling in the mystery of God's providence.

INTRODUCTION:
A LIBERATING APPROACH
TO THE LECTIONARY

Dieter T. Hessel

The ecumenical lectionary for the Christian year has gained increasing parish acceptance, and for the rest of this century it is likely to remain a common interdenominational resource. Given its increasing use by the church's pastors, educators, and officers, this lectionary deserves our disciplined examination and creative appropriation.

While it should *not* be our only guide for public worship, educational ministry, and mission planning, the consensus lectionary can:

a. Provide regular, orderly exposure to biblical covenant history and the church's original witness to Jesus Christ;

b. Push preachers and teachers to examine unfamiliar or difficult passages, and to develop a wider scriptural base for their preaching and teaching;

c. Enhance more coordinated planning of public worship, educational ministry, and missional action around seasonal texts and themes;

d. Encourage advance study of the Sunday lessons by preachers from several congregations, by laity with clergy in each congregation, and by committees and families of the parish;

e. Foster responsible freedom to explore the Scriptures in an orderly way through coverage of weekly Old Testament, Epistle, and Gospel lessons (and a Psalm) that are only sometimes thematically related;

f. Offer a framework for biblical-theological discourse among the laity.

SOCIAL THEMES OF THE CHRISTIAN YEAR is designed to complement —or to overcome some of the deficiencies of—available interpretive aids and liturgical guides to the lectionary. Several series of commentaries have appeared that offer exegesis and exposition of the weekly lessons.[1] There are also related guides, of varying quality, for parish pastors and educators.[2] These publications offer little explanation of the theological structure of the lectionary;[3] they tend to ignore the forest while focusing on three trees each week.

Nor do the available commentaries develop a liberating social interpretation of the lessons, and seldom do they suggest how to integrate exegesis and ethics in a whole approach to worship, nurture, and witness. To date, the published exegesis and exposition of the lections remains disturbingly indifferent to theological ethics and seldom probes adequately the *dual context of biblical interpretation* —both the canonical setting and the present situation in which we read Scripture.

To work within the framework of the consensus lectionary with a deeper appreciation of its overall strategy is to uncover startling Spirit within stereotyped seasons, to illumine faithful pilgrimage beyond familiar patterns, and to gain revolutionary perspective on a routine cycle. In so doing, we can give liberating dimension to frequently domesticating piety, develop new praxis in the midst of mundane existence, and discern solid theological truth that speaks to our experience of shaking events. If the Christian year is a revolutionary year, and if it is as continuously protestant as it is deeply catholic, then we must enter the tug-of-war over how congregations interpret and utilize the lectionary's Scripture lessons.

THE PURPOSE OF THIS BOOK

With these concerns in mind, Church Education Services and Discipleship and Worship, two sections of the United Presbyterian Program Agency Unit on Ministries with Congregations (where I work), welcomed the development of this resource. In the pages that follow:

1. We (the authors and editor) identify socially significant theological themes of the Christian year, overcoming the fragmenting effect of text-by-text commentaries. "Social" themes are broadly understood to encompass interpersonal relations and ethical vision, as well as sociological-historical-political dynamics.

2. We interpret clusters of texts for each season of the church year, spanning the three-year cycle of the lectionary. The resulting combination of essays is of continuing value in orienting parish leaders throughout Years A, B, and C, and should function as a companion to available commentaries and handbooks on weekly lessons.

3. We highlight a liberating social hermeneutic that features ethics and praxis in its discipline of biblical interpretation. This method of interpretation complements existing lectionary commentaries, few of which have developed this perspective. Our communal Bible study method is critically conscious, contextually shaped, canonically informed, and Christologically disciplined.

4. We illustrate a whole approach to worship, education, and action that recovers the full liturgy and enables the people's discipleship in the light of God's action in the world. In addition to interpreting clusters of texts for each season, the essays in this book offer help to congregations in planning holistic worship-nurture-witness for

each season consistent with the exposition of biblical social themes and relevant special days. The concluding article for each season shows how to coalesce congregational praxis around disciplined use of the lectionary.

5. We conclude with a critical analysis of the lectionary concept, and offer leads for reform that would include some crucial missing passages. Our lectionary criticism illustrates orderly freedom in disciplined use of an always-reformable lectionary.

Our most important objective is to develop a socially alert *congregational* life-style—a piety and praxis of worship-study-action that embodies the spirit of lectionary texts, enabling laity and clergy together to recover biblical memory and to participate in whole liturgy. This volume's concluding article for each season, written by an educator-liturgist, suggests how to pick up on the story line of the season and, building on the biblical exposition in the preceeding essays, proposes symbolic actions in worship, methods of learning, and occasions for action that seek to embody the season's biblical social themes.

THE LECTIONARY'S WHOLE LITURGICAL FUNCTION

In the context of study, worship, and action, the lections for each Sunday and feast day can evoke the Word rightly preached and heard, the sacraments rightly administered and received, and the people actively responding in disciplined faithfulness. Such is the whole liturgical function of the church. *Leitourgia,* biblically understood, is the people's work in the light of God's work. Liturgy is the summit of the church's activity and the source of sanctification. In the cycle of true liturgy, participants engage God's past, present, and future, and experience the interplay of doing and being, acting and reflecting, fasting and feasting, sacred and secular, worship and witness.

A biblical perspective on liturgy underscores the dangers of religious ritual and challenges the tendency to reduce its scope to occasions of worship. Paul disliked cultic cycles (Gal. 4:9–11; Col. 2:16f.); he viewed Christ as the end of the law of the cult. Jesus' early followers shared a kingdom life-style that superseded prevailing ritual requirements. They also grasped Jesus' prophetic disdain for prescribed sacrifice and solemn assemblies. In him they experienced liturgy that does loving justice, life-style that includes the outcast, witness that empowers the meek.

When lessons of Scripture are read with this dynamic liturgical function in mind, they become for us what they were originally— resources for worship, nurture, and witness written down and treasured by the community of faith. Liturgical shaping and use of Scripture coincided originally with the emergence of local congregations or synagogues instituted 2,500 years ago when the covenant people were dispersed in Babylonian exile. Bereft of Temple and king, the people together recovered, celebrated, and transmitted their faith tradition. Many of the books of the Hebrew Bible were composed during this period as a way of recording the key narratives and repeating them in the major liturgical moments of Judaism's yearly calendar. Ancient strands of story, song, poetry, confession, and prayer were preserved for worshipers to repeat, to mull over, and to teach to the next generation.

Portions of what became the Gospels and Epistles were sent around and read aloud in the early Christian congregations as the basis for prayer and proclamation. Together they contain the Jesus story and sayings, words of blessing, acclamations of praise, hymnic confessions, practical moral instruction, and advice on sacramental and ecclesiastical procedures. These messages from the church to the church in the world continue to give the believing community a faithful identity and to equip it for ministry. As the worshiping-teaching-acting church utilizes this material in a whole praxis, it recapitulates the dynamics that originally shaped the canon.

From Weekly to Yearly Cycle

The early church developed weekly Sunday worship which Justin Martyr, writing in A.D. 150, described as a sequence of lengthy readings from the Apostles and Prophets, followed by a leader's homily on one of the readings, prayers offered by the people, Communion at the Lord's Table, and a collection of money offerings for the diaconate.[4] Precisely because the Christian movement was not broadly established with a settled canon, the church did not yet have a yearly cycle to recall the Messiah's advent, baptism, ministry, passion, resurrection, and gift of the Spirit.

Gradually, the Christian year evolved from three primitive festivals: Epiphany (which transformed a pagan celebration) and Pascha and Pentecost (which arose out of the Jewish environment). These three "unitive" festivals commemorated respectively incarnation and baptism, passion and resurrection, ascension and the Spirit. Good Friday and Easter vigils evolved in response to Holy Land pilgrims of the Constantinian era. Christmas developed in Jerusalem and Asia Minor to sacralize the winter solstice. Later, the Roman rite introduced a four-Sunday Advent, Epiphany devoted to the Magi, a three-Sunday cycle before Lent, and Ash Wednesday. "Two distinctive marks of the earliest lectionary systems are a complete absence of festivals of the Virgin and a very limited list of saints' days."[5] While both healthy and dubious traditions of observance accumulated around each season, each has profound theological-ethical significance that the rest of this book explores.

OUR METHOD OF BIBLICAL INTERPRETATION

The authors and editor of this volume share a method of biblical interpretation that is critical, canonical, Christological, contextual, and communal. Our interpretive minds work not sequentially but dynamically in entertaining all five dimensions as we probe, and are questioned by, biblical texts.

1. *Critically conscious.* Liberating theological reflection begins with prophetic imagination or alternative consciousness (Brueggemann)—which questions the dominant world view and criticizes the status quo because it is hopeful for a better future. The active community of faith brings to its interpretation of biblical texts an expectation of God's transforming action and an "exegetical suspicion" that important human social realities have been overlooked in prevailing interpretations of the Bible. "Liberation hermeneutics is the decision to look at all Scripture first against the backdrop of despair, deprivation, and exploitation which characterizes the circumstances of most of humanity and to ask what God's word says about that reality" (Owensby).

When the oppressed share what they have experienced, they help us see the Bible with new eyes. Thus Walter Wink reports: "Quite against my previous inclinations and conclusions, I was forced to consider the hypothesis about the priority of women in the resurrection appearances as proposed by Prof. Elisabeth Fiorenza. . . . The critical method and my hermeneutical principles proved helpful, as I sorted through all the data. But, as is so often the case, we do not see new possibilities of interpretation by ourselves; we must be helped to see them by others whose own oppression or experience gives them a unique angle of vision. I still needed someone else—a woman who has experienced the whole gamut of male ploys *to deny her power*—to help me see how this had been done to women even in the resurrection narratives."

2. *Canonically informed.* A liberating hermeneutic presupposes that interpreters are using contemporary exegetical commentaries that deliver the results of historical-critical scholarship and show what is going on in whole biblical books. Scholars help us to discern the life-styles of communities that formed the books of the Bible, and how they handled traditional stories and sayings in relation to their situation. Scholars also explore the biblical authors' theological purpose for modifying and connecting familiar stories or sayings.

The Epistles and Gospels of the New Testament were written to interpret the new life of faith, building on its origins in and continuity with Israel's story. Canonical interpretation that highlights intrabiblical connections and Hebraic roots is evident in the essays of this volume: e.g., those by Fackre, Morse, Wilmore, Brown, Lehmann, González.

One of the hazards of Christian lectionary usage is a tendency to let calendar dominate canon, and thus to ignore large chunks of a biblical story that is historically normative for faith (Sanders, Ruether). Therefore, it behooves us to consider texts in the context of whole books and periods of biblical history, lest we draw mistaken analogies or miss corollary meanings for our time.

3. *Christologically based.* The Bible can be faithfully interpreted by Christian communities engaged in worldly ministry, trying to be faithful to the One whose life, death, resurrection, victory over the powers, and promised coming have set the pattern for the church's mission. The people of the church are called to join God in the liberation struggle, acting for justice in the light of God's praxis in the Messiah Jesus (Herzog).

A liberating hermeneutic finds in Messiah Jesus the concrete focus and human goal of God's movement to free and unite the world. Jesus is a different Liberator than his contemporaries expected, and therefore his methods of freeing people deserve attention in a social hermeneutic.

At the center of all biblical interpretation is the politics of God. In each passage under study, consider what is the direction of God's action, and how God responds to the power or powerlessness of various people mentioned in the passage (González).

4. *Contextually shaped.* Scripture is understood in a two-way flow between biblical text(s) seen in historical-critical perspective, and human experience, which includes personal and political events. In this dual context of interpretation, exegesis-exposition-ethical decision occur together; they are not sequential. The liberating significance of the historical-critical method is lost whenever we disregard the hermeneutical circle, and subject only past texts to historical-critical examination while ignoring the historical forces that shape our own problematic present (Soelle).

Precisely because the prevailing interpretation of the Bible has not taken important pieces of data into account, we must pay more attention to the historical context in which we read biblical texts, and particularly the voices of today's nonpersons. What we bring to Scripture conditions what we draw from it. What we bring becomes more faithful when we hear the oppressed telling us of their struggle for justice, and begin to share their view from below (Brown).

One of the ways to hear the text more faithfully is to reassign the cast of characters and our place in the cast. Imagine hearing and discussing the passage in a different cultural setting or situation of powerlessness in the face of power. Bring to the passage the experience of racial and/or ethnic groups and women, as well as less privileged classes and countries (González).

5. *Communally developed.* Biblical interpretation is best done by people in mission thinking and acting communally. The congregation in social ministry is the locus for a liberating hermeneutic as people encounter the text through action/reflection. Action that is concurrent with reflection leads to fresh inquiry that engages heart, hands, and head.

At the center of a hermeneutic that engenders and is informed by praxis is the discipline of looking for corporate, public, and political meanings of the passage(s), as well as individual, private, and personal content. The personal and the political are two sides of whole behavior within the believing community.

A liberating social hermeneutic is ecclesial, in that it arises within a present-day community that struggles with issues in faith and looks for illumination from other communities engaged in similar struggles. The biblical communities of faith hold a special place here, since theirs is the claim that God's reality, and the world's, is seen with compelling clarity in the story of Israel and Jesus (Rasmussen).

Theological reflection flows out of and into faithful ministry by members of the church. "In each time and place there are particular problems and crises through which God calls the church to act. The church, guided by the Spirit, humbled by its own complicity and instructed by all attainable knowledge, seeks to discern the will of God and learn how to obey in these concrete situations" (The Confession of 1967, adopted by The United Presbyterian Church in the U.S.A.).

PART ONE
INTERPRETATIONS

I. ADVENT–CHRISTMAS

Sunday or Festival	Year	First Lesson	Second Lesson	Gospel
1st Sunday in Advent	A	Isa. 2:1–5	Rom. 13:11–14	Matt. 24:36–44
	B	Isa. 63:16 to 64:8	I Cor. 1:3–9	Mark 13:32–37
	C	Jer. 33:14–16	I Thess. 3:9–13 or I Thess 5:1–6	Luke 21:25–36
2d Sunday in Advent	A	Isa. 11:1–10	Rom. 15:4–13	Matt. 3:1–12
	B	Isa. 40:1–5, 9–11	II Peter 3:8–14	Mark 1:1–8
	C	Mal. 3:1–4	Phil. 1:3–11	Luke 3:1–6
3d Sunday in Advent	A	Isa. 35:1–6, 10	James 5:7–10	Matt. 11:2–11
	B	Isa. 61:1–4, 8–11	I Thess. 5:16–24	John 1:6–8, 19–28
	C	Zeph. 3:14–20	Phil. 4:4–13	Luke 3:7–18
4th Sunday in Advent	A	Isa. 7:10–16	Rom. 1:1–7	Matt. 1:18–25
	B	II Sam. 7:8–16	Rom. 16:25–27	Luke 1:26–38
	C	Micah 5:1–4	Heb. 10:5–10	Luke 1:39–55
Christmas Eve or Day		Isa. 9:2–7	Titus 2:11–14	Luke 2:1–21
		Isa. 62:1–4, 6–12	Col. 1:15–20 or Titus 3:4–7	Matt. 1:18–25
		Isa. 52:7–10 or Zech. 2:10–13	Heb. 1:1–12	John 1:1–14
1st Sunday After Christmas	A	Isa. 63:7–9	Heb. 2:10–18	Matt. 2:13–15, 19–23
	B	Isa. 61:10 to 62:3	Gal. 4:4–7	Luke 2:22–40
	C	I Sam. 2:18–20, 26	Col. 3:12–17	Luke 2:41–52
2d Sunday After Christmas		Jer. 31:7–14	Eph. 1:3–6, 15–23	John 1:1–18
New Year's Eve or Day	A	Deut. 8:1–10	Rev. 21:1–6; 22:1–5	Matt. 25:31–46
	B	Eccl. 3:1–13	Col. 2:1–7	Matt. 9:14–17
	C	Isa. 49:1–10	Eph. 3:1–10	Luke 14:16–24

The time of Advent looks forward to the eschaton and back to the Nativity. It moves in a spiral from judgment to hope to watchfulness. Christmas celebrates the inbreaking of God's commonwealth and the historical significance of Jesus Christ.

A. THEMATIC ESSAYS

1

VISION OF SHALOM
AND HOPE OF GLORY

Gabriel Fackre

Vision of Shalom	Jer. 33:14–16; 31:10–13 Isa. 2:1–5 (Micah 4:1–4)		
and	Isa. 40:1–5, 9–11; 35:1–6, 10; 61:1–4, 8–11 Zeph. 3:14–18		
Hope of Glory	Isa. 63:16 to 64:8 Mal. 3:1–4 Isa. 11:1–10	I Thess. 3:9–13; 5:1–6, 16–24 II Peter 3:8–14	Mark 13:32–37 Matt. 24:36–44

Advent anticipations of the Great Day (the day of the Lord) have been understood in three ways. Lectionary readings at the season's inception in the sixth century fixed on *messianic longings* and thus preparation for the day of Christ's birth. The early Middle Ages widened the horizon to include the *Second Advent.* And whenever the prophetic texts have been studied in their ancient setting of exile and return, a third dimension of hope emerges: the *promise of glory* to come in our day-to-day history as well as what came at its Center and will come at its End. We shall view the seasonal lessons here through these trifocal lenses.

The overcast skies of the late twentieth century color all the future we see in Advent perspective. The doomsday clock of nuclear proliferation is four minutes to midnight. From the light that comes from that day there will be no hiding place. "When people say, 'There is peace and security,' then sudden destruction will come upon them" (I Thess. 5:3). "Two men will be in the field; one is taken and one is left. Two women will be grinding at the mill; one is taken and one is left" (Matt. 24:41). To modern ears there is power and terror in these texts. "Take heed, watch . . ." (Mark 13:33).

The apocalyptic messenger of the twentieth century exploits our fascination with doomsday visions. The television seer offers a guided tour of things to come, and safe passage through the tribulation. How easy it is to huckster the maps and calendars of the late great planet earth!

Paul dealt peremptorily with the diviners and chart makers of his own time who were diverting the church at Thessalonica. "As to the times and seasons, . . . you have no need to have anything written to you. For you yourselves know well that the day of the Lord will come like a thief in the night" (I Thess. 5:1–2). The apostle here echoes the risen Lord's own theme: "It is not for you to know times or seasons which the Father has fixed by his own authority" (Acts 1:7). And the lections twice take pains to underscore Jesus' counsel of mystery and modesty: "Of that day or hour *no one* knows" (Matt. 24:36; Mark 13:32). Our Advent texts, indeed, show a better way to face into the storms and see what God has in mind and on hand.[1]

I. WHAT IS EXPECTED?

Vision defines reality in the Advent lectionary. The prophet projects on the screen of the future what is ultimately so. We shall explore the shape of things to come in a cluster of festival texts that covers the three-year cycle: Isa. 2:1–5; 11:1–10; 35:1–6, 10; 40:1–5, 9–11; 61:1–4, 8–11; and I Thess. 5:1–6 with its "thief in the night" parallels in Mark 13:32–37 and Matt. 24:36–44.

Isaiah looked for a king of Davidic lineage who would right the wrongs which this poet-seer of the eighth century B.C. found all around him. "He shall not judge by what his eyes see" (Isa. 11:3). The haughtiness of "the mighty man and the soldier" (Isa. 3:2), the plunder of the helpless by the rich, the dishonesty of the judge, the exploitation of the fearful by "the diviner . . . and the skilful magician and the expert in charms" (Isa. 3:2, 3) are not the last word.[2] There is real historical hope for a ruler who "with righteousness . . . shall judge the poor, and decide with equity for the meek of the earth" (Isa. 11:4).[3]

This expectation that God will bring a more human tomorrow continues in "the Babylonian Isaiah" addressing a community in exile and looking for a new exodus. "Speak tenderly to Jerusalem, and cry to her that her warfare is ended. . . . Make straight in the desert a highway for our God. . . . He will feed his flock like a shepherd" (Isa. 40:2, 3, 11).[4] And the Isaianic heritage continues into the later period of a rebuilt Temple and the dream that Israel will fulfill the ancient priestly role of instructing the nations in the ways of God bringing "Good tidings to the poor, . . . liberty to the captives, . . . the opening of the prison to those who are bound" (Isa. 61:1).

The historical impetus in all these texts is summed up in the year of jubilee (Lev. 25:10), which lies behind the mandate to "proclaim liberty." The liberation of slaves in the hallowed fiftieth year is a paradigm for the right to hope that God shall bring bondage to an end. Faithfulness to this intrahistorical expectation in the Advent lessons means identifying and celebrating the human hopes in our own time that are in continuity with the prophetic pointings to justice for the poor, equity for the meek, and release for the enslaved.

Wound together with the green thread of penultimate historical hope is the yellow thread of ultimate eschatological promise. In this second kind of Advent passage a climatic sun rises to bring the Day of Shalom when final freedom is secured, full justice is done and a lasting peace made among God, nations, persons and nature. In the memorable second chapter of Isaiah this day shall find "all the nations" flowing to "the mountain of the house of the LORD." Universal fulfillment will mean that all peoples "shall beat their swords into plowshares and their spears into pruning hooks; nation shall not lift up sword against nation, neither shall they learn war any more" (Isa. 2:4). Shalom![5]

The final Shalom entails justice as well as peace, righteousness together with harmony, the liberation that underlies reconciliation. For the One who rules this new commonwealth says, "I the LORD love justice, I hate robbery and wrong" (Isa. 61:8).[6] And the New Testament apostle of the last things joins the expectant Old Testament prophet in the vision of the righting of every wrong and the mending of every flaw. The Matthew 25 norms fill out the Matthew 24 picture of One for whom we wait: "Come . . . , inherit the kingdom . . . ; for I was hungry and you gave me food, I was thirsty and you gave me drink, I was a stranger . . . , sick . . . , in prison and you came to me" (Matt. 25:34-36).

Shalom in consummation means the healing of nature as well as history. No more shall it be red in tooth and claw, for "the wolf shall dwell with the lamb, and the leopard shall lie down with the kid" (Isa. 11:6).[7] The ravaged and barren earth shall be reborn: "The wilderness and the dry land shall be glad, the desert shall rejoice and blossom" (Isa. 35:1). The enmity between humanity and nature shall cease: "The sucking child shall play over the hole of the asp" (Isa. 11:8). The tormented human body shall be made whole: "The eyes of the blind shall be opened, and the ears of the deaf unstopped" (Isa. 35:5).

The Christian encounter with these passages draws out yet another layer of future orientation. Following the precedent of Israel, which discovered ever-new meaning in earlier prophecy over two hundred and fifty years of the great scroll, the Advent lectionary finds beaten swords, the gentled wolf, and a blooming desert in an *incarnate* Shalom. Here is the longed-for shepherd who will "gather the lambs in his arms . . . [and] carry them in his bosom" (Isa. 40:11). Jesus himself provided the warrant for this kind of futuring as he rose to read from the sixty-first chapter of Isaiah: "Today this scripture has been fulfilled in your hearing" (Luke 4:21). *He* is the Lord spoken of in subsequent verses who loves justice and hates robbery and wrong (Isa. 61:8). *He* shall judge the poor with righteousness and "decide with equity for the meek of the earth" (Isa. 11:4), the church declared. *He* will open the eyes of the blind and unstop the ears of the deaf, and "sorrow and sighing shall flee away" (Isa. 35:10). As "truly human, truly God, and truly one" (Chalcedonian Definition), he brings together the two converging streams of historical and transhistorical expectation. He is the Vision made flesh, Glory among us.[8]

Interpreters of the three kinds of hope expressed in the Advent lessons have sometimes missed their underside. An astringent realism keeps company with the hope. Judgment as well as redemption resounds in these texts. "The burning sand shall become a pool," but at the same time "the haunt of jackals shall become a swamp" (Isa. 35:7). "Vengeance" is announced (Isa. 35:4; 61:2) and "recompense" is declared for robbery and wrong (Isa. 61:8). While biblical usage gives "recompense" a fuller significance than some modern renderings that stress the positive meaning of "setting right," the negative meaning of "settling accounts with evil" is also indicated. Advent knows of a light that shall come along the paths of history and at history's Center and End, with its "refiner's fire" (Mal. 3:2).

II. WHAT IS TO BE DONE?

What do visions do? A. H. Curtis has asked this question of the vision texts in the Old and New Testaments.[9] The recurring answer is that they impel to action. Vision evokes mission. The paradigm of visionary imperative is Isaiah's experience in the Temple. "In the year that King Uzziah died I saw the Lord. . . . Then I said, 'Here am I! Send me' " (Isa. 6:1, 8).

The indissolubility of vision and action is carried over in the Isaiah Advent passages. Thus we are taken up the mountain to see the nations flowing to the house of the Lord where the judgment is rendered that they shall learn war no more. *Therefore:* "Come . . . , that he may teach us his ways" (2:3), and "Come . . . , that we may walk in his paths" (2:3). There the great sun of Shalom makes the day: "Come, let us walk in the light of the LORD" (2:5). One can hear the cadences of Martin Luther King, Jr., who went up the mountain and saw the Promised Land, and whose dream hardened into deed. Hope mobilizes.

On the heels of the memorable Isaiah-Micah text comes a description of other kinds of future focus current in a culture under judgment: "Thou hast rejected thy people, the house of Jacob, because they are full of diviners from the east and of soothsayers like the Philistines" (Isa. 2:6). Decadent times produce seers of the future whose diverting scenarios paralyze action. Hope mobilizes but wishful thinking immobilizes. False prophets are these mystical cognoscenti of the East who invite us on a sojourn in and down and thus away from history! False prophets are the Philistine soothsayers who promise an effortless step into a benign future! These are visions that forecast an easy peace when there is none. Biblical dreams disturb; they leave us restless with the way things are, strangers and pilgrims in the land "filled with silver and gold, . . . horses, . . . chariots, . . . idols" (2:7, 8). Thus "the LORD of hosts has a day against all that is proud and lofty" (2:12), and the light of that day makes the true seer discontent with the chariots and spears that militate against it. Nation shall not lift up the nose cone of intercontinental missile against nation, neither shall they learn war anymore!

On all three levels of our Advent texts we see *the shape of mission that issues from vision.* In the hopes and mandates for history, "They shall not hurt or destroy [on that] holy mountain" (Isa. 11:9). There will be justice for the poor and equity for the meek (Isa. 11:4). The blind shall see and the deaf shall hear (Isa. 35:5). Nature will not be exploited but the deserts will bloom instead (Isa. 35:1). Warfare shall be ended (Isa. 40:2). The knowledge of the Lord shall be in the land (Isa. 11:9). Thus in preparation for the good things and the good one to come in history, the visionary is called to a righteousness that befits the Glory to be.

The Advent eye perceives that the Glory to come is Jesus Christ, the One who also calls for liberty to the captives and the binding up of the brokenhearted. "I the LORD love justice, I hate robbery and wrong" (Isa. 61:8) And that One who came shall come again at the end of time to right every wrong. He shall bring the final realm of God when "everlasting joy" enters and "sorrow and sighing shall flee away" (Isa. 35:10). History shall be redeemed and nature transformed. The fullness of Shalom shall come "and the glory of the LORD shall be revealed and all flesh shall see it together" (Isa. 40:5). A peculiar biblical psychology is at work in this envisioning process. Instead of resignation being induced by the prospect of ultimate victory ("pie in the sky by and by"), action is evoked. We have to do here with an explosive mix, eschatology cum ethics. The judgment and the lure of the future make us restless with the historical givens. Fixed upon the ultimate Vision and its penultimate possibilities, with warrants in incarnational Reality, the Advent seer is stirred to set up signposts to the City of God and make straight the historical highway that leads to it. And that seer does so with a firmness of intent born of the confidence that nothing can separate us from the final Goal.

Because the biblical vision is not the fantasy of the diviner and the soothsayer, hard facts as well as bright hopes are disclosed by its light. In history, in messianic expectation, and at the consummation, judgment awaits those who resist the vision. God shall "smite the earth [and] slay the wicked" (Isa. 11:4). The chapter from which Jesus read the messianic words goes on to say: "I hate robbery and wrong;

I will faithfully give them their recompense" (Isa. 61:8). The one who "will feed his flock like a shepherd" will also "come with might, ... his recompense before him" (Isa. 40:11, 10). Let there be no illusion that Shalom means an undisturbed peace for the unrighteous. "When people say, 'There is peace and security,' then sudden destruction will come upon them" (I Thess. 5:3). We have to do with a *holy* love to which we are accountable as well as a holy *love* which lures.[10]

III. WITH WHAT SPIRIT?

Things are to be done by us in response to things that will be done by God. But how shall we carry out the Advent imperatives that come from the Advent promises? What is the frame of mind appropriate to the visions and action?

In the Advent texts there are refrains about the spirit in which the vision is seen and done. A dominant one is clearly heard in the words, "Say to those who are of a fearful heart, 'Be strong, fear not!' " (Isa. 35:4). It is echoed in the call, "Put on . . . for a helmet the hope of salvation" (I Thess. 5:8). The noun births the verb. *Trust* in the future is commensurate with the promises of the God of the future.

Considering the state of affairs to which the Isaiah scroll is addressed—the agony of the Assyrian captivity of the Northern Kingdom and the parlous conditions in Jerusalem assumed in the earliest Isaiah material, the Babylonian exile of Isaiah 40–55, and the backsliding and fits and starts of the postexilic period—talk of hoping did not come easily. The same is true of the apostolic counsel given in times of great travail. The promises could not be established by appeal to the historical data. They were an assurance of things hoped for, based on evidence of things not seen. Indeed, hope does require signs. That is what distinguishes it from wishful thinking. But biblical hoping rises out of perceptions granted to the eye of faith. In spite of the world's contrary claims, it sees in events past and present portents of things to come. The prophet can speak of promise in the worst of times. Thus hope for history has its warrants in the mysterious workings of God in and through historical anguish; messianic hoping takes form in the man of sorrows acquainted with grief (Isa. 53:3); Christian envisioning of the consummation finds its evidence in the appearance and vindication of the Suffering Servant. On all three levels of Advent expectation the seed of power to maintain the vision and act toward it thrives in the most infertile of soil. Here is a hoping that refuses to be "servile before the factual" (Bonhoeffer).

A second undergirding of the spirit as it faces forward is *sobriety*. This kind of expectation is free of illusion. Yes, there will be victory for the purposes of God. That is why we have a right to hope. But "wail, for the day of the LORD is near; as destruction from the Almighty it will come!" (Isa. 13:6). As here, we sometimes have to go outside the conventional Advent texts in Isaiah to get the full force of the implication buried in them, "the day of vengeance of our God" (Isa. 61:2). But the New Testament readings in Advent eschatology leave no doubt about the sober watchfulness necessary, the warnings that go with the hopings. "Watch therefore, for you do not know on what day your Lord is coming. . . . If the householder had known in what part of the night the thief was coming, he would have watched" (Matt. 24:42, 43). "Watch therefore—for you do not know when the master of the house will come" (Mark 13:35). The partner of hope is sobriety. "Keep awake and be sober" (I Thess. 5:6).

In these reminders that the One who comes is a consuming fire as well as a shining light we meet again the profound biblical dialectic of holiness and love. The Advent texts do not let us forget that this means, among other things, that those who trample the poor, beat their plowshares into swords, love robbery and wrong, proclaim tyranny, and shut the doors of the prison will have their "reward" (Isa. 40:10). They—we—are the persons and nations who are the "adversaries" of God, and the prophet prays God that such might "tremble at thy presence!" (Isa. 64:2). There is *trembling* to be done in Advent. The historical mills of God grind slowly but exceeding fine; the high and mighty are brought from their seats by the Christ who comes not with an easy peace but with the sword of a righteous Shalom; and he shall come again to judge the quick and the dead: holy *love* is *holy* love.

The spirit of Advent vision and action is great expectation and a watchfulness without illusion. Holy love means sober hope.

CONCLUSION

Advent makes a place for seers on the saints' days of the Christian calendar. Visionaries are among the most valued members of the biblical communities. They save us from myopia. They are our "critics-in-residence" (Donald Michael). These faithful futurists have seen the Not Yet and want us to do something about it in the Now.

Advent, therefore, means preparation. It calls us to attention before what and who is to come. For the Just One there shall be justice. For the realm of Shalom hereafter there shall be peacemakers here. We make ready for the Liberator by acts of liberation Now, and we prepare for the Reconciler as agents of reconciliation Now. To those who work and pray toward these visions, and live by their grace, the benedictory Word is addressed: "May the God of peace sanctify you wholly; and may your spirit and soul and body be kept sound and blameless at the coming of our Lord Jesus Christ. He who calls you is faithful, and he will do it" (I Thess. 5:23–24).

BIBLIOGRAPHY

Brueggemann, Walter. *Living Toward a Vision: Biblical Reflections on Shalom.* United Church Press, 1976.
Fackre, Gabriel. *The Christian Story: A Narrative Interpretation of Basic Christian Doctrine.* Wm. B. Eerdmans Publishing Co., 1978.
Holladay, William L. *Isaiah: Scroll of a Prophetic Heritage.* Wm. B. Eerdmans Publishing Co., 1978.
The Interpreter's Bible. "Isaiah" and "I Thessalonians." Vols. 5 and 11. Abingdon Press, 1956, 1955.
The Interpreter's Dictionary of the Bible. "Isaiah" and "First Thessalonians." Vols. 2 and 4. Abingdon Press, 1962.
Kaiser, Otto. *Isaiah 1–12, A Commentary,* and *Isaiah 13–39, A Commentary.* Tr. by R. A. Wilson. Westminster Press, 1972, 1974.

2

ADVENT:
EXPECTANCY, BUT WITH COSTS

Richard D. N. Dickinson

Watchful Preparation and Creative Obedience	(Illustrated by the ministry of John the Baptist in 2d and 3d Sunday readings)	Matt. 3:1–12 Mark 1:1–8 Luke 3:1–6 Matt. 11:2–11 John 1:6–8, 19–28 Luke 3:10–18
	(Illustrated in the gracious behavior of Christians)	Rom. 13:11–14; 15:4–13 Phil. 1:3–11; 4:4–9 I Cor. 1:3–9 James 5:7–10 Titus 2:11–15 Col. 3:12–17

Watchful expectancy is the mood of Advent—a time when the deepening winter darkness turns, almost imperceptibly, toward the slowly lengthening light that nourishes the new life of spring. It is a time when, today, the Christian community longs for the reign of God to overcome the weariness, oppression, and sin that surround and suffuse its life. Advent is a time in the Christian year when the community watches, still expectantly, for the light of the star, the sign of new birth, and the new experience of God's presence and power in human affairs.

I

The lectionary directs our attention to John the Baptist's prominent role in preparing the way for Jesus' messianic ministry. Mark, the earliest Gospel, makes John's ministry the starting point of the account of Jesus' ministry, identifying John with Elijah, whose coming would precede the day of the Lord (Mal. 4:5–6). Luke takes pains to lift up John as the link between Jesus and both the prophetic tradition of Isaiah and the covenantal relationship between Yahweh and the people of Israel (Luke 1:72–74). For the multitudes flocking to hear his message there could be no mistaking John's connection with the long-interrupted prophetic tradition. Though born of a priestly family, John made his home in the wilderness of Judea, wore a coat of camel's hair and a leather belt (reminding the people of Elijah), and eating wild honey and locusts. He was self-effacing about his own role—that of the voice crying in the wilderness, the one who baptized only with water, the one who counted himself not worthy to unlace the Master's sandals.

The early Christians saw John as a bridge between the prophet Isaiah and the ministry of Jesus: he was "the voice of one crying in the wilderness: 'Prepare the way of the Lord, make his paths straight. Every valley shall be filled, and every mountain and hill shall be brought low, and the crooked shall be made straight, and the rough ways shall be made smooth; and all flesh shall see the salvation of God' " (Luke 3:4–6). He was a popular success: "the multitude came forth to be baptized"; he gathered about him loyal disciples, Jesus said of him that "among those born of women none is greater than John" (Luke 7:28); Herod had him imprisoned and beheaded almost certainly because he created public unrest. Yet John pointed beyond himself to the one who was to come, whose sandals he was unworthy to touch. He pointed beyond the current sinful society in which "even now the axe is laid to the root of the trees" (Luke 3:9). Judgment is now upon us, but John points beyond to the messianic age of healing, restoration, salvation.

How does John's announcement of judgment and woe fit with Advent expectancy and hope? Precisely because John's preaching, so stern and demanding, so full of imminent judgment, so full of the sense of the fire and wrath to come, pushes us back beyond ephemeral and superficial bases of expectancy and hope, and confronts us with the usually ignored fact that our *only* basis for expectancy and hope is both the judgment and merciful love of God. As an active member of the covenant community, steeped in the prophetic tradition, John could recall how the people demanded their own king, to be like their powerful neighbors; he could recall the prophets before him decrying Israel's faithlessness, idolatry, immorality, injustice, and attraction to false religious and cultural ways. From the people's side the covenant was constantly violated; many attributed the tribulations of the people under Babylonia, Egypt, Syria, and Rome to Israel's infidelity. What was supremely clear to John was that the people had broken the covenant, and continued to violate it. They deserved Yahweh's judgment.

In the midst of accommodation and faithlessness, how could the covenantal relationship be reestablished through the intervening rulership of God? How could Israel prepare for, and participate in, the reassertion of the reign of Yahweh? John was exposed to differing answers to that question in his own day—the Zealots, the Pharisees, the Sadducees, and particularly in his immediate environment, the Essenes and the Qumran community which stressed purity, ablutions, separation from the world, and the pending battle between the children of light and the children of darkness. Though differing from the Qumran community in several respects (one baptism as compared with frequent ablutions; an appeal to the whole nation for repentance as compared with an appeal to a righteous remnant cut off from affairs of the world), John's message was charged with a sense of urgency; the coming of Yahweh was to be an imminent inbreaking into history—a divine inbreaking which would bring woe and joy, judgment and hope, destruction and newness.

Thus the witness of John the Baptist is a compelling text in Advent, a text of hope in the midst of anxiety; a text of expectancy mixed with uncertainty. It is a timely text for those who, at our own juncture of history, live precariously on the razor's edge of universal disaster through nuclear or chemical warfare, who experience a shaking of cultural and religious foundations, and who are entwined in gross injustices. Among these are genocide; massive suppression of human rights; spreading hunger; increasing external control over our lives through scientific and technological "advances" that were meant to emancipate us; and increasing concentration of political, economic, and cultural power. Thus all but a few people are becoming more dependent, more vulnerable, and more powerless to direct their personal and corporate lives. In a time when people can talk about "triage" and "lifeboat ethics" as if these were morally defensible public policies, or about the "winnability" of nuclear wars even if two thirds of the population were annihilated and the remainder were threatened with slow and agonizing death, there are still those who look expectantly toward God's intervention with both judgment and restoration.

II

What can we learn from texts of the lectionary about the character of gospel expectancy, obedience, and hope? To answer this question it is important to remember that John the Baptist was deeply rooted in the Old Testament community of faith, with its distinctive ways of understanding God's work and will. He was of priestly lineage and prophetic manner; he was thought by some to be a reappearance of Elijah; he was extolled by Jesus as greatest of the prophets; he tied his message to Isaiah's prophecy; he was recognized by Josephus as a latter-day prophet; undoubtedly he was greatly influenced by the religious ferment of which the Zealots and Essenes were such visible symptoms. Steeped as he was in this community, what are we to learn from John about the character of our hope?

Preeminently we are reminded that expectancy and hope are

rooted not in human efforts, but in the acts of Yahweh. Even John's ministry was initiated by Yahweh: "There was a man sent from God, whose name was John" (John 1:6). This is, in part, symbolized in the birth narratives of both John and Jesus; God was taking the initiative to redeem Israel despite its infidelity. This same theme is carried further in the assertion by John, and in Paul, that beyond the baptism of water, the faithful will be baptized "with the Holy Spirit and with fire" (Luke 3:16). It is God's faithfulness to people which is the *sole* cause for expectancy and hope.

Yet expectancy is not without its ambiguities, its costs. John's message is not easy for an idolatrous and perverse generation; baptism with the Spirit and with fire is not the soothing comforting hand on the head of a frightened child; it is also the laying of the ax to the unproductive tree, the burning of the chaff with unquenchable fire (Matt. 3:10, 12). Judgment is revealed as an integral and inescapable part of the liberating process of the reign of Yahweh; it is a judgment which, while radically threatening, is the basis for hope. For Yahweh takes creation seriously enough to exercise judging and healing power over it. Thus in John's witness, judgment is an inextricable part of the message of hope and expectancy, for without judgment people are caught in the interminable morass of perversity, rebellion, alienation.

Yet John did not counsel passivity, sitting back and waiting for God to do what God will do. No word is more crucial to John's teaching than "repent." The reign of God is imminent; judgment is upon us. How shall we endure (not escape) God's judgment? The first and extremely difficult step, then as now, is repentance. In our day we have lost important aspects of the idea of repentance. In our thinking it is often reduced to a psychological state of mind and spirit, a sense of contrition or being sorry. It is often narrowed down to presumed one-to-one relationship with God, without social and societal implications. While baptism with water is, for John, a crucial aspect and sign of repentance, his call to repentance had a much deeper meaning and requirement.

Repentance, for John, has more than a private moral dimension to it; it is also ethical and social in the sense that people are being called to repentance as a way of relating positively to the inbreaking reign of God. We are admonished to "bear fruit that befits repentance"; unfruitful trees are cut down and burned (Matt. 3:8). When they ask John what they shall do as evidence of repentance, the people are told to share their coats and their meat; tax collectors are to exact no more than the law requires; soldiers are to be content with their wages and to do no violence (Luke 3:10–14). Is this simply an interim ethic for the short period of time between John's preaching and the Lord's appearance in judgment? That would be easier to accept were it not for other passages.

More difficult to escape is the graphic testimony in another section of the Gospel narrative (Matt. 11:2–19; Luke 7:18–35). From prison John sent two of his disciples to ask Jesus if he was the expected Messiah, or whether they should look for another. Jesus' response shows that the marks of his messiahship (not necessarily "proofs" for an unbelieving world) are his power to bring things to wholeness and justice: "Go and tell John what you hear and see: the blind receive their sight and the lame walk, lepers are cleansed and the deaf hear, and the dead are raised up, and [most compellingly, according to Hebrew prophetic tradition] the poor have good news preached to them" (Matt. 11:4–5). We do not know John's response—whether he thought these were sufficient proof of Jesus' messiahship or even if he ever got the message. But it is clear that Jesus assumed them to be compelling arguments needing no further explanation, and that they were arguments John would understand and accept. Like rhetorical questions, they imply their own answer. Thus repentance was not perceived as mere remorse, or verbal confession, or ritualistic ablution; repentance required a radical turning anew to God, a reaffirmation of the covenant which implied special attention to the ethical and religious demands of the covenant community. The reign of Yahweh is conditioned by the readiness of people, through active repentance, themselves to prepare the way of the Lord, to make the rough places plain.

Repentance is not passive waiting but active expectancy characterized by the alignment of one's whole being with what God is doing in the world. Recently a sign on a local church bulletin board posted the familiar aphorism: "Hope for the best; prepare for the worst." A teacher colleague, with a "third eye" that sees beyond the ordinary, detected a subtle danger. Does not that saying imply that hope is passive, and that all one's energies should be expended in preparing for the worst? If all our energies are expended in preparing for the worst, who will expend energies to give an account of the hope that is in us? Contemporary parallels are only too obvious. When we spend all our energies on our fears—to build bombs rather than human wholeness and communities; to treat diseases rather than to promote health; to guarantee "security" rather than to expand justice and enlarge love—we have betrayed the notion of repentance and of faithfulness. "Repent," John insists, for repentance is the *sine qua non* for expectant watchfulness and for being received into the imminent reign of Yahweh. Thus repentant obedience is absolutely indispensable for the hopeful expectancy of Advent.

John's call parallels the Advent expectation in another way; it is a call to the *whole* community. It is not a call to private righteousness only, but to communal righteousness and wholeness, despite the fact that in much of Christian history there has been a trivializing of the gospel by reducing it to a one-to-one relationship with God (which has its parallel in reducing the gospel for the whole *oikoumenē* to one that is merely centered on humanity without regard for nonhuman nature). It would have been natural for John to interpret his message exclusively. The Qumran community stressed the purity of a small remnant divorced from the polluting world; purity was a main theme of the Pharisees and Sadducees. Yet John's vision seems to have appropriated the larger prophetic vision, a vision of the sovereignty of Yahweh over the whole of creation, with the Hebrew people as covenanting participants in that larger cosmic history.

The Israelite community has no status independent of its fidelity to God. John is disdainful of those who presume to have merit simply because they are the descendants of Abraham: "God is able from these stones to raise up children to Abraham" (Matt. 3:9; Luke 3:8). Lineage is not enough. Nor is correct ritual. John calls for more than the Qumran preoccupation with ritual purity and avoidance of contamination with the world. Incipiently, if not overtly, John revives the prophetic tradition that the ethical/moral witness of the community of the faithful is a necessary preparation for themselves, and for the world, for the imminent kingdom of Yahweh. That call to the Hebrew community to witness in all the world to the power, sovereignty, judgment, and love of Yahweh is reiterated eloquently in yet another of the Advent lessons (see Rom. 15:8–9).

III

What is the relationship between judgment, repentance and watchful expectancy, and the lectionary passages from Philippians and Colossians, which often have been used to instill a virtuousness not dynamically linked with issues of social change and social justice? In the midst of waiting for an imminent Second Coming, the virtues of compassion, kindness, humility, gentleness, patience, forbearance, forgiving without complaint, love (Col. 3:12–14) could take precedence over justice, or the struggle to make the community and world whole.

But perhaps the scales of our eyes can be removed if we try to see the meaning of the gospel through the eyes of the poor today, as through the eyes of the poor—the lame, the sick, the fishermen, the peasants, a carpenter family—the gospel was first seen and heard. One of the most striking and promising movements of our day is the emergence and growth, seemingly spontaneously, of what are called "basic ecclesial communities," groups of Christians springing up almost outside the established churches, almost always from among the poor, frequently gathered around common struggles for justice or a better life, and often searching the Scriptures and their own experience for keys to understanding the meaning of the gospel for their lives. Ernesto Cardenal's *The Gospel in Solentiname* is a thrilling account of such communities of faith, nurturing one another through common reflection on faith.

Among many aspects of these communities that help to reveal the relationship between the Pauline passages and the earlier lectionary passages, three might be stressed as having special importance:

1. The gospel really is good news to the poor. Time and again it appears that, as the Latin-American bishops claimed, God makes a special option for the poor, that the biblical testimony reveals the poor as the special covenantal agents of God's revelation in history. The stories of Solentiname bear this out, as the poor find so much in their daily experience that illumines, and that is illumined by, the gospel message. Even the day of the Lord is not ultimately threatening, because the judgment of God is also part of the reign and love of God in which the faithful can only rejoice.

2. The life of ecclesial communities, which have much in common with scattered Christian enclaves across the Roman Empire, also demonstrate the rich quality of community not based on striving after inordinate expectations, not consumed by consumerism, not possessed by possessions, not obsessed by the need to have and control things and people. The virtues lifted up in the Pauline passages are the virtues of human relationships, of temperate hope, of maturity of faith. They are virtues of organic human life, mutually enriching and supporting. While such organic connections were not always actually achieved (Paul had contentions to cope with), the values held before the community were highly relational values, as H. Richard Niebuhr pointed out, the typical values of the lower economic and social classes.

3. Equally important, today's ecclesial communities reveal another aspect of the relationship between expectancy and obedience. Among many of them the struggle is hard—the struggle to survive, to care for their families, to achieve justice and a better life. Weariness and despair often set in, wearing down the fringes of one's center. The struggle is costly, especially when it is for justice in an oppressive society. Even when it is no more than a refusal to pay homage to political authorities, it is often costly. Where does strength come from in the midst of such struggle? Very often the only sustaining strength comes from the power and faith mediated through an ecclesial community. It is crucial to keep that community nurtured by the virtues of which Paul speaks. That community can be a source of strength for survival and for continuing combat. Thus the quality of human relationships within that community are critical to the struggle itself.

Early Christian communities, like ecclesial communities today, were embattled; faith was costly, even sometimes deadly. The virtues of mutual support, mutual forgiveness, mutual encouragement must be seen in that context—not in the context of a polite society's formal etiquette.

In short, we must try to read these passages with fresh imagination, as through the eyes of those who are in the midst of active struggle for righteousness, justice. Base ecclesial communities help break open that new consciousness.

For the faithful, then, Advent is a time of watchful expectancy when the watchman awaits the reassuring, fear-dispelling pre-sun-rise glow. But for those who are not prepared—through the acceptance of God's judgment and active repentance (a living realignment with the purposes of God for justice and wholeness on earth)—it is a period of anxiety and desperation, a period when the promise of the reign of God is either hollow or threatening. For them Advent becomes mere ritual.

Living among the richest, most powerful, and perhaps most self-satisfied people of the world, it is profoundly unsettling and challenging to take this lectionary truly to heart and mind. It is speaking to us, "Come now, you rich, weep and howl for the miseries that are coming upon you. Your riches have rotted and your garments are moth-eaten. Your gold and silver have rusted, and their rust will . . . eat your flesh. . . . You have lived on the earth in luxury and in pleasure; . . . you have condemned, you have killed the righteous man" (James 5:1–3, 5–6). Yet it speaks to us not only as rich Americans but also as Christians. "Be patient [not inactive], for the coming of the Lord is at hand" (James 5:7–8).

3

CELEBRATING THE INCARNATION

Christopher Morse

Celebrating	Isa. 7:10–16;	Rom. 1:1–7;	Matt. 1:18–25;
the Incarnation	9:2–7; 62:1–4,	16:25–27	2:13–23
(4th Sunday in Advent,	6–12; 52:7–10	Heb. 1:1–9;	Luke 1:26–55;
Christmas Eve and Day)	II Sam. 7:8–16	2:10–18;	2:1–52
	Micah 5:1–4	10:5–10	John 1:1–14
	Zech. 2:10–13	Col. 1:15–20	
		Eph. 1:3–10,	
		15–23	

Preaching a scriptural passage is rather like trying to ride a bucking horse. The subject refuses to be harnessed despite our most determined efforts at domestication. We know, but always have to learn anew as if for the first time, that what sustains us in preaching, as in all the life of faith, is a miracle of grace that we have no power to produce or to control. In the providence of God, dry bones on occasion are made to live. Through such as Balaam's ass, and ostensibly its posterity, the gospel at times is heard. It is this miracle on which we all depend. The manger comes with the manure. The treasure, as Paul puts it, comes encased in garbage (surely the "earthen vessels" of II Cor. 4:7 plus the "refuse" and "offscouring" of I Cor. 4:13 must be said to equal garbage!). Without this hope we would not long dare to preach, nor would we wait upon the Scriptures with all our powers of active engagement to receive fresh manna from God. This miracle of grace that is promised but never subject to our conjuring or contrivance the church celebrates as the incarnation.

The lectionary readings for the 4th Sunday in Advent, Christmas Eve, and Christmas Day contain some of the most familiar passages in the Bible. The homiletical temptation to beat a dead horse rather than ride a bucking one is most acute when the text is one that is often read and heard. Familiarity may deaden us to its import. Only the grace of God can thwart the domesticating tendency in explicating the Scripture, but that grace enlists us to ask several questions continuously whenever we undertake to be faithful in textual interpretation and preaching.

1. To what extent have we imposed our mind-sets upon the text? No exegesis, to be sure, is without presuppositions. One may argue that a doctrine of the various gifts of the Spirit suggests that different peoples in different cultural contexts will have antennas for picking up certain signals of the gospel that others in other situations do not hear. Whenever exegesis becomes patent and predictable, however, an ideological taming of the text has occurred. This first question must be kept in view especially when we have a predetermined goal in approaching the texts, such as to highlight the "social" themes of the Christian year. Beware of using the text merely as a pretext.

2. To what extent have we bypassed the specific character of the text in moving toward some abstracted generalization? Rather than expounding maxims of moral or religious truth, the Scriptures of Advent and Christmas, and indeed of most of the Bible, narrate a story of the most implausible sequence. To engage a text in worship is to allow the alien peculiarity and the apparent irrelevance of the particular pericope to question the hearers as the hearers question it. Subsuming the particular under the general, no matter how popular or edifying the preacher's general opinions may be, is a common form of domestication.

3. To what extent is the sermon saying to the world what the world is already capable of saying to itself? The incarnation makes this question inescapable. Whatever sense is contained in the gospel, it is most uncommon sense indeed. Every attempt to force the gospel to conform to what is religiously or morally acceptable to a culture or community meets with the gospel's own resistance.

4. To what extent have we given primary regard to the disregarded in our exposition of the text? The disregarded are not the same in every time and place. That the gospel directs attention to "the least" of the brothers and sisters (Matt. 25:40, 45) is beyond dispute. Who are effectively "the least," or the most disregarded, in the situation addressed by the preaching? The incarnation is a message of embodied regard for those of "low estate" (Luke 1:48). Apart from these, we are told, the flesh and blood of Jesus Christ cannot be known.

From the limitless significance of the lectionary readings, four accents may be noted as one way of grouping an array of content. Detailed exegetical commentaries treating each of these passages are essential resources for the preacher and will be presupposed, though not explicitly referred to, in these necessarily brief comments.

I. THE PROMISE OF GOD'S ADVENT

However else the God of biblical faith is to be characterized, the message of Advent is that this God is a promiser. Paul speaks of the gospel for which he has been set apart as "promised" by God beforehand through the prophets in the Holy Scriptures (Rom. 1:2). Zechariah 2:10 conveys the promise of God's own coming. "Sing and rejoice, O daughter of Zion; for lo, I come and I will dwell in the midst of you, says the LORD." Ultimate reality, the inescapable fact of all life and death, is identified as One who enters into commitment and promise.

As the church confesses the life and death and destiny of Jesus as the Messiah of God it reads the writings of the Hebrew prophets in his light. "But you, O Bethlehem Ephrathah, who are little to be among the clans of Judah, from you shall come forth for me one who is to be ruler in Israel, whose origin is from of old, from ancient days" (Micah 5:2). God's coming is not an indefinite and abstract emergence. The advent occurs only in the context of this earth's governance. Identified with the little clan of Judah, the promised one whom Isaiah heralds as a child who is born and a son who is given bears the government upon his shoulder and brings peace (Isa. 9:6–7). Against all attempts to spiritualize God's promised advent in some disembodied sense, or to treat it as a general principle of metaphysical speculation, these Scriptures direct us to public matters. In the words of II Sam. 7:13, the Lord declares of this promised offspring, "I will establish the throne of his kingdom for ever."

The messianic hope conveyed in these Old Testament readings is not based upon any alleged human potential for creating the future. Quite to the contrary, the only hope for the new age of justice and peace resides in the commitment of God to the One in whom God's own righteous governance will be in our midst. From this One, says the Lord, "I will not take my steadfast love" (II Sam. 7:15). The promise is unconditional with regard to God's coming.

II. THE UNLIKELINESS OF THE INCARNATION

As the New Testament sees it, God's promise is not only given; it is kept. What is remarkable about the Christmas texts is how unlikely God's keeping of the promise seems to its recipients to be. In a sentimentalized celebration of a merry fa-la-la Christmas it is instructive to recognize the preponderance of references to *fear* in the Gospel narratives. At the angel's word to Mary she is "greatly troubled" (Luke 1:29). Because Archelaus reigns in Judea, Joseph is "afraid to go there" (Matt. 2:22). The head of government himself, Herod, is "troubled" at hearing rumors of the birth, and indeed, as Matthew records it, not only Herod, but "all Jerusalem with him" (Matt. 2:3).

The Lucan account of the shepherds is particularly significant in this regard. When the angel speaks, and the glory of the Lord shines around them, they are depicted as "filled with fear" (Luke 2:9). Of all the emotions that Christendom has come to associate with the Christmas season, fear would seem, at least officially, to have been granted the least recognition. Yet the undeniable anxiety that can attend a season in which one is obliged by custom to feel merry and warm-hearted may well be addressed by this persistent note in the Nativity accounts. In the case of the shepherds the announcement of a Savior's birth interrupted the existing darkness, disturbed the peace, and occasioned a journey. In view of this depiction of what is entailed in the incarnation an initial fearfulness is clearly not an inappropriate reaction. To what extent are our own fears reactions to the faithfulness of God?

A second example of the unlikeliness of the messianic birth is the unsuppressed suspicion of *shame* alluded to in Matthew's rendering of Joseph (Matt. 1:18–25). It is no trivialization of the profound mystery of the incarnate life of God in Jesus Christ, or of the virginity of that life's conception by Mary, which both Matthew and Luke narrate, to point out the violation of accepted mores that Matthew's account makes no effort to hide. Joseph, "being a just man," is unwilling to put his betrothed to shame. Any suggestion that Joseph is concerned to safeguard his own reputation, rather than Mary's, finds no warrant in this passage. It is her shame, not his, that he seeks to avoid. The resolve to "divorce her quietly" suggests not a callous rejection but a sensitivity to the inevitable censure by a community which perceives that its acceptable practices, in this case sexual, have been transgressed.

To view Joseph as other than "just" is to miss a radical point. It is God's incarnation in the coming of Jesus Christ which in this instance may be said to violate even the most sacrosanct community mores. The messianic birth is construed in this Matthean pericope as rather drastically reordering the demands of justice. The avoidance of shame by a quiet divorce from reality is overruled by the incarnational risk of shame that commands Joseph to take Mary as his wife. "When Joseph woke from sleep, he did as the angel of the Lord commanded him" (Matt. 1:24).

The unlikeliness to human eyes of the ways in which God in Jesus Christ keeps the promise to be present in the earth is perhaps most succinctly summed up in the words of the Fourth Gospel: "He came to his own home, and his own people received him not" (John 1:11).

III. THE POLITICAL CHARACTER OF THE INCARNATION

The life, death, and destiny of the incarnate Christ involve a locatable and datable social history (Luke 2:1–2). Very complex issues confront theology in attempting to understand the extent to which the significance of the incarnation may properly be said to be a matter of history, but that his story involves this earth's story in its sequence cannot be denied. Again, as in the messianic prophecies of the Old

Testament, government is what is at stake. The incarnation is no timeless myth occurring in some ideal world detached from the ruling authorities of this earth.

The texts from Hebrews in their own unique fashion emphasize this point. "For surely it is not with angels that he is concerned but with the descendants of Abraham" (Heb. 2:16). The coming of Jesus reveals the character of this present age. It is an age in which Jesus suffers. No more *subversive judgment* can be pronounced upon rulers of the present order than the judgment of Jesus' suffering and death. No greater hope can come to those in lifelong bondage than the hope that suffering and death are unable to destroy this Jesus. All that Christ undergoes is seen by the writer of Hebrews as overcome. That is why no attempt must be made to portray Jesus as an angelic being somehow apart from the human condition. "For because he himself has suffered and been tempted, he is able to help those who are tempted" (Heb. 2:18).

No one figure is given more mention in the Matthean story of the birth of Jesus than is Herod (Matthew 2). How surprising it is, therefore, that his prominence is so largely ignored by our traditional Christmas customs. With unmistakable irony Matthew's account unmasks the self-legitimating uses of public piety by the ruling authorities: "When you have found him bring me word, that I too may come and worship him" (Matt. 2:8). Only the angel's warning prevents the Wise Men from taking the course commanded by Herod. Worship itself in this incident is depicted as a political act. As if to make this fact irrefutable, Matthew does not shy away from relating the darkest scene of the entire Nativity. The coming of the Christ occasions violence, so great is the opposition of the ruler who can command death but not life (Matt. 2:16).

IV. The Good News Only God Can Make Significant

On two points all of the lectionary readings may be said to agree, despite the various ways in which this agreement is expressed. The news of Christ's coming is good beyond all other. And only God can vindicate this news and make it significant.

Zechariah's silent nights when confronted by the good news brought by the angel exemplify in the Lucan texts the utter inability of human power to signify this Gospel in one's own strength: "He made signs to them and remained dumb" (Luke 1:22). According to the readings from the Epistles, what is disclosed in Jesus Christ is "the mystery which was kept secret for long ages" (Rom. 16:25), "the mystery" of God's will, "according to his purpose which he set forth in Christ as a plan for the fulness of time, to unite all things in him, things in heaven and things on earth" (Eph. 1:9–10).

What is good beyond all telling is that no dominion has legitimacy except as it exists through Jesus Christ and for him. As the Colossian letter puts it, "In him all things were created, in heaven and on earth, visible and invisible, whether thrones or dominions or principalities or authorities—all things were created through him and for him" (Col. 1:16). John 1:3 stresses a similar claim; without him nothing has the status of God's created order. This is not an assertion of the hegemony of Christianity as a religion; it is the Johannine confession of the Christological reality as the true foundation of all creation, whether recognized and acknowledged by the creation or not. In Hebrews the Son is the one through whom God created the world (Heb. 1:2). What is at issue in these and other like passages is certainly at one level the understanding of what constitutes a Christian *realism*. Reality, not religion, is the primary concern. If this is correct, a truly Christian realism will define what is realistic by what happens in and to Jesus Christ, and not by so-called pragmatic considerations to which reference to Jesus becomes finally a mere appendix.

The good news which only God can make significant is seen in these readings of Advent and Christmas as the *hope* which only God can give. It is the hope to which the God of our Lord Jesus Christ calls us in giving us knowledge of him (Eph. 1:17–18). This hope is vastly different from conventional optimism and it unmasks all false hopes.

Nowhere is this clearer in the readings than in the perplexing introduction of Rachel's refusal in the very midst of the birth account, as given in Matthew. After King Herod's slaughter of the innocents we read: "Then was fulfilled what was spoken by the prophet Jeremiah: 'A voice was heard in Ramah, wailing and loud lamentation, Rachel weeping for her children; she refused to be consoled, because they were no more' " (Matt. 2:17–18). The dissonant note of Rachel's grief is the acknowledgment on the part of the Matthean text itself that there is grief in human life which refuses to be consoled.

Moreover, there is no hope for the world associated with Jesus of Nazareth which does not include with it the hopelessness of Rachel. Why is she here with a note so out of pitch and out of season with what in other reports are heavenly hosts praising God and singing at Christ's birth? Matthew in this instance is quoting words from the prophet Jeremiah. It is Jeremiah who first speaks of Rachel weeping some five hundred years before the birth of Jesus, at a time when the people of Israel were being taken into exile. And the Rachel to whom Jeremiah refers first appears in the pages of Genesis, a setting some one thousand years and more before the time of Jeremiah. Rachel was the mother of Joseph and Benjamin; from whom several of the northern tribes of Israel were descended. We are dealing here with ancient Hebrew tradition well known to those to whom Matthew's Gospel was first directed.

In the earliest references, as we have them in the book of Genesis, Rachel is a woman who dies in childbirth. She is remembered in the blunt way Genesis puts it (Gen. 35:16) as a woman in great pain, in "travail and hard labor." As her son Benjamin is being born, Rachel with her dying breath calls the child "Son of my sorrow" (Gen. 35:18). In this earliest tradition the name of Rachel calls to mind physical pain, the uncertainty of life, the loss of loved ones, and death: the suffering that occurs in the course of *nature*. When she died she was buried near Ramah, a place at Bethlehem, so it later came to be believed in some traditions. Her husband Jacob, we read in the words of Genesis, "set up a pillar upon her grave; it is the pillar of Rachel's tomb, which is there to this day" (Gen. 35:20).

In the prophecy of Jeremiah the figure of Rachel represents the suffering of those in Israel who are deprived of their freedom by an oppressive power in *history*. When Israel was conquered and many of her people were carried off into exile, the long march of prisoners passed down the road by Rachel's tomb. It was a road of bitter grief. Jeremiah is the one who hears the Lord saying, as the children of Israel are driven away into captivity, "A voice is heard in Ramah. . . . Rachel is weeping for her children; she refuses to be comforted" (Jer. 31:15). In this context Jeremiah speaks of Rachel in reference to the painful sorrow of victimization by a political enemy: the suffering that occurs in the course of history. What is different in this second reference is that Jeremiah hears a word of the Lord coming to Rachel and to those who suffer such oppression and exile. "Thus says the LORD: 'Keep your voice from weeping, and your eyes from tears. . . . There is hope for your future,' says the Lord" (Jer. 31:16–17).

In Bethlehem in the dark of night, Rachel's tomb and the Christ-child's birthplace come together. With this birth the Herods of this world are yet provoked to their destruction of the innocent. Rachel in Genesis is depicted as one who suffers physical pain in childbirth and sorrow in the natural course of life and death. Rachel in Jeremiah is referred to in connection with the loss of homeland and freedom as the victim of a history of exile and oppression. Rachel in Matthew, no doubt with these ancient Hebrew traditions in the background, in certain respects combines both of them in calling to mind Herod's slaughter of the children on the occasion of Jesus' birth. In both respects Rachel may be seen as exemplifying those things which most threaten to destroy human hope in this world.

The truth of the matter is that there is finally no cause for rejoicing if there is no consolation for the grief of Rachel. Yet we cannot in the last analysis give ourselves or our loved ones hope. All this the gospel knows and represents by the inclusion of Rachel. The call of faith is to join with her in the unmasking of all false hopes.

The unspeakably good news of the incarnation which the church is called to signify is that the hope we cannot give to ourselves and to those loved ones in the shadow of Rachel's tomb is promised to us. All who make their wilderness way from Bethlehem to Good

Friday in the company of Rachel may take heart: "There is hope for your future," says the Lord.

BIBLIOGRAPHY

Especially important for a thorough textual analysis of the most familiar "Christmas stories" is Raymond E. Brown, S.S., *The Birth of the Messiah: A Commentary on the Infancy Narratives in Matthew and Luke* (Doubleday & Co., 1977).

4

THE NEW YEAR—
A TIME FOR RENEWAL

Rosemary Radford Ruether

The New Year	Deut. 8:1–10	Col. 2:1–7	Matt. 25:31–46
(Eve and Day, plus	Eccl. 3:1–13	Eph. 3:1–10	Matt. 9:14–17
additional readings)	Prov. 8:22–31	Rev. 21	Luke 14:16–24
	Job 28:20–28		
	Isa. 45:18–22		

New Year's Day in the Christian calendar appears in a somewhat odd way. Coming at the end of the Christmas season, it appears to be a purely secular festival of drinking, noisemaking, and somewhat superficial making of new-year resolutions. This is perhaps where the saturnalia of the winter solstice celebration of the old Roman calendar remains without its Christian reinterpretation as the birth of Christ.[11] Many in the church would doubt that the New Year has any specifically biblical or Christian significance.

In fact, however, New Year is not so much an idea without biblical roots as an idea whose biblical roots have been somewhat lost or forgotten in the Christian calendar. In its ancient Near Eastern roots, New Year was a key point in the annual cycle of religious festivals. It was the origin of some of the central ideas of Judaism and Christianity. In the ancient Near East, the New Year festival was held, not at the winter solstice of the Roman calendar, but in the fall, at the end of the vintage harvest. This is still the time of the Jewish New Year of Rosh Hashanah. New Year in the Jewish calendar begins a ten-day period of intense self-scrutiny, penitence, and renewal of fidelity to God's commandments, culminating in Yom Kippur. The Christian calendar actually begins in the fall as well. The liturgical year starts with Advent, the season of preparation for Christmas.

I

In the ancient Near East, New Year was the pivot of the religious and cultic self-expression of society,[12] based on the agricultural cycle of planting and harvesting, of wet season and dry season. In this annual cycle of seasons, humanity saw the mirror of the whole drama of life, death, and renewal of life, both in nature and in society. Each year's cycle was a miracle that required the intense participation of the divine and human communities to make it happen.

Each year the miracle of new life, of the new grain and the new rains, ran its course. At the end of the cycle, the earth turned parched and dry. The vintage was gathered in with much rejoicing. Then the human community waited anxiously for the new rains that would make possible the new planting. In Canaanite and Babylonian mythology apparently this was understood to mean that the god who embodied the rains and the green growth died in his struggle against his brother and antagonist, the god of drought and death. The human community, the gods, the whole earth went into intense mourning for the death of the god of life.

We can catch the echoes of this intense mourning in many passages in the Psalms and the Prophets. One particularly dramatic expression of this is found in Isa. 24:4–13, which has adapted the Near Eastern festival of mourning at the end of the vintage season to the Hebrew vision of divine judgment. The prophet speaks of this as a time of desolation, outcry, and feeling of abandonment. The systems of order that hold together nature and society have collapsed. People feel that the whole world is slipping back into primordial chaos. Human infidelity to God's commandments, the violation of the divine statutes, have introduced the forces of death and destruction into the world. This affects not only human relationships with each other in society, but human relationships with nature as well. "The earth mourns and withers. . . . The earth lies polluted under its inhabitants. . . . All joy has reached its eventide; the gladness of the earth is banished. Desolation is left in the city."

But death and desolation are not the end of the story. In Near Eastern mythology the Goddess who represented not only love and war, but wisdom as well, went into intense activity. She was not about to let her beloved die. She went searching for the god of drought and death and defeated him. She winnowed the body of the dead god, the grain. She gathered up the pieces of his body and buried them. The new spring rains came down like a miracle after the long drought. The new spring green from the planted seeds began to push their way through the moistened earth.

The young Lord of creation had risen from the dead! The people were jubilant, dancing in the street and casting up their heads to catch the sweet water in their mouths. The previous mourning now turned to rejoicing. The king who had been dethroned during the time of penitence processed jubilantly back into the city, enthroned as a victor over the forces of chaos. In the palace a great banquet was held in which the whole community participated. The nuptial feast of the king and the Goddess was celebrated, and assured a fruitful harvest.[13]

II

The Hebrews criticized many aspects of this cultic and mythic pattern. For them, God transcended the drama of nature and history as its Lord, not within it as the expression of the death and rebirth of the life forces. Yet when we examine the actual ritual and symbolic patterns of the Hebrew Bible we discover that they have not totally denied this pattern, but creatively adapted and transformed it. Instead of the drama of the death and resurrection of the god (which was to return in a new way in Christianity), there is the drama of sin and repentance, of divine judgment and promise. Many of the old patterns of myth and cult are adapted to this new framework.

One key idea of New Year is divine judgment. At the end of the year the books of life are opened. People settle their accounts with each other. Debts are liquidated as a dispensation of grace from the more powerful to the less fortunate. It becomes possible to start over again without the burden of the past. The ancient Hebrews did not split the social from the moral. "Debts" included the whole structure of burdens that people had incurred in relation to each other. New Year is a time of forgiveness of debts, of ransoming of captives, of returning of land expropriated in payment of debts.

From this flowed the idea of a Great New Year, a sabbatical year at the end of a cycle of seven times seven years. Every fifty years there should be a jubilee, when accounts are settled, injustices undone, and society and the land renewed. The account of the jubilee in Leviticus 25 speaks of the restoration of land to those from whom it has been alienated. Slaves are freed. The land and the animals are allowed to rest. Ecological and social justice intertwine in this jubilee vision.[14]

Repentance, forgiveness, restitution allows society to be renewed. The Hebrews connected this with the ideas of rededication to the divine commandments and the reenthronement of Yahweh as King and Lord of creation. In the ancient celebration of New Year in the period of the First Temple (as some scholars reconstruct it), the king processed out of the city of Jerusalem in search of the Ark of the Covenant, which had been lost or stolen by enemies. He performed ceremonies of repentance and purification. The triumphal reentry of the king, bearing the restored Ark of the Covenant to the Temple, symbolized God's renewed favor upon the people and their representative, the Davidic king. The people waved lulabs and shouted their hosannas in the streets as the Davidic king journeyed triumphantly to the Temple and the palace on the white mule of royalty.[15]

The reenthronement of the king represented the reestablishment of God's sovereignty over the earth. God's judgments upon the earth were made secure. The enemies of Israel were vanquished. The forces of death and chaos were put down. The orderly fabric of the universe was shored up once again, just as God first defeated the winding Monster of Chaos in the original creation.[16] Every New Year, then, becomes a restoration of creation, recalling the first creation.

New Year not only looks back to the first creation, God's first defeat of the forces of chaos, the first act of salvation, but it also looks forward to the final act of salvation, the ultimate securing of the world against the enemies of God, the final enthronement of God as Lord of creation. The enthronement psalms hymn this yearly celebration of the reestablishment of God's reign (i.e., Psalms 93; 95; 98–100). In the prophets and in Christianity, this hope for the New Year of God's reign is read as messianic. Each New Year generated hopes that failed to be fulfilled. These hopes were then projected onto the future.[17] In the present the people have failed to fulfill God's commandments. They have fallen victim to their foes. Society and the world labor under alienating conditions. But someday will come the ultimate defeat of these alienating conditions, the ultimate establishment of God's reign, when all things will be made new and death and sorrow will be no more. In the cycle of the church's readings for New Year we find these ancient Hebraic and Near Eastern themes preserved. But they are also transformed and reinterpreted in the light of Christian faith in Jesus as God's Wisdom and God's Messiah, through whom God created the world in the beginning and will bring the world to judgment and final salvation in the End.

For the Hebrews, the incarnation of divine Wisdom is Torah, God's commandments. The call to return to fidelity to God's commandments is not merely a call to what we might think of as fidelity to a legal or moral code. It is the call to be in harmony with what the Chinese might call the Tao. Wisdom is the divine Will, which upholds the universe, gives the decrees to the winds and the waters, and sets the stars in their orderly courses, as much as it gives the commands of right ordering of human relations. Several of the New Year texts (Deut. 8:1–10; Job 28:20–28; and Prov. 8:22–31) speak of God's commandments, not only as the laws given in the desert, through which Israel is to live, but as pointing to the deeper mystery of God's Wisdom. Wisdom underlies the order of the world. It is the power through which God created the world in the beginning.[18]

Wisdom was there as the first of God's works. She was there when God established the heavens; when God made firm the skies above and assigned to the seas their limit, so that the waters should not transgress his command; when he marked out the foundations of the earth. The figure of divine Wisdom is spoken of as a female persona because the words for these powers of God active in creation are linguistically feminine. But also we have here an echo, in Hebraic thought, of the ancient Goddess, whose essential attribute was that of Wisdom.[19] The Hebraic God is androgynous, both He and She.

Although the nomadic Hebrews imaged the sovereign God in patriarchal terms, the immanences of God, God's Wisdom, Spirit, and Presence, were imaged as female.

III

For Christianity Jesus becomes the incarnation of God's Wisdom,
the "offspring" of God through whom God created the world in the
beginning, the mystery that upholds creation and reveals God's will
anew in the last days through Jesus the Christ (Eph. 3:1–10; Col. 2:1–7).
Through this fullness of God's Wisdom made present in the last days,
our lives are renewed. We are rescued from the old creation of sin
and made partakers of the new creation of salvation.

The revelation of God's Wisdom in Jesus points back to the first
creation, the dispensation of God's Wisdom as the original sustaining
power of all things. It also looks forward to the new creation, the final
judgment, the new heaven and earth, the new Jerusalem, the messianic banquet and the nuptials of God with the church in the world
to come.

In several of the New Testament texts for New Year, these themes
of the messianic future are spelled out. We have the ancient vision
of judgment reinterpreted in Christian terms. In Matt. 25:31–46 the
great assize of God is described. When the nations are gathered
before God's Envoy and God enters into judgment upon all the deeds
of humanity in history, the mystery of true fidelity to God will be
revealed. Then we will discover the key to the riddle of history,
namely, that our relationship with God or our alienation from God is
made concrete in our relationship to our neighbor. When we fed the
hungry, gave drink to the thirsty, welcomed the stranger, clothed the
naked, visited the sick and the imprisoned; or when we rejected these
basic offices of humanity, we were expressing our relationship or lack
of relationship with God. Relationship to God is not expressed
through "religious" laws and cultic acts unrelated to the real social
fabric of our lives. But it is expressed only through our relationship
to our neighbor. It is through this that our relationship to God will be
judged in the End.

In Luke 14:16–24 and Matt. 9:14–17, the ancient themes of the messianic banquet and wedding feast are reinterpreted. This banquet of
God with the chosen people will not be just for an ethnic and religious
elite. Indeed, when the call comes they may reject it, being too busy
with their worldly affairs. So God will send out the call to the poor,
the marginated, the despised of society, to those who are cultically
impure and who fall outside the institutionalized definition of the
righteous. These will be gathered by God into the great banquet of
the kingdom of God. Those who were too busy to hear the call will
remain outside.

This time of rejoicing, of celebrating the nuptials of God with God's people, is not only future, it is also present. The time of fasting and repentance is over. The disciples of John the Baptist mourned and fasted. The disciples of Jesus taste the presence of the Bridegroom already in their midst. It is not possible to put this new vision of God's presence in Jesus in the old wineskins of the laws and people of Israel. It has burst the bounds of this system of religion. It demands a new wineskin, a new vision, a new practice, even a new definition of God's people, to contain the new wine of God's presence.

But for the Christians, too, this messianic presence of God in Christ was a foretaste of things still incomplete. They experienced the vanquishing of the forces of evil; the renewal of life; a new relationship with God and each other in their new community. Yet the forces of death were still around and among them. These forces of death crucified God's Envoy. It was not only the Romans and the priests who expressed this denial of God's commands, but they themselves who lost faith and denied him. Thus, even in tasting renewal of life through him, they must continue to look forward to the Great Victory of God, the final New Year, when the new heaven and earth are finally established upon the earth (Revelation 21).

IV

Thus in the cycle of readings for New Year, Christians inherit a profound legacy of religious reflection built upon several layers of historical experiences: Canaanite, Hebraic, and Christian. These themes offer rich possibilities for interpreting our present lives and social situations. But these become meaningful only when they are incarnated today, as they were in biblical times, in the concrete contexts of people's real lives. The theme of New Year is that of crisis, but also new hope; of acknowledgment of sin, but also celebration of grace. New Year allows the church to tie together, in a particularly inclusive way, the themes of the old and the new, the Beginning and the End. But it also demands that these themes not be abstracted into a theoretical past and future. We should root this drama of the Alpha and the Omega in the present realities and possibilities of a particular situation and group of people.

New Year calls us to judgment, exposing our failure to love God by rejecting love for our neighbor. But New Year also calls us to new hope. Death is not the end of the story. Grace is possible. It is already present among us. God's coming reign is already in our midst. New Year demands a rejection of that "realism" which insists that evil is stronger than good and that nothing really can be changed. This is the "realism" of the comfortable status quo, which wishes to snuff out the hopes of the poor because these hopes entail an overthrow of their own systems of privilege. In our own times, as in the times of Jesus and the prophets, the establishment has always known how to use religion to justify itself. In this sense, the gospel, the hope of the Bible, the hope of New Year, is "unrealistic." It dares to continue to hope for a coming reign of God against the realities of human sinfulness.

The New Year vision also calls us to understand this hope for the new inclusively. The vision of the New Year is personal, social, and ecological. It calls for a regeneration of our relations with each other and with the earth. It calls us to undo the wrong of the past, the social relations that cast women, minority races, impoverished classes and nations, into servitude to the social and economic privilege of the few. It calls us to remake our exploitative relations to the animals and to the earth. It calls us to ransom the captives of past wars, to forgive the debtors of past mistakes, to proclaim liberty in the land.

The Prophets and the Gospels make clear that this "New Deal" of God's reign can only come about by overthrowing the present system of religious and social privilege. God's messianic Envoy finds these privileged groups too busy to hear the message. So it is the destitute, the unclean, and those without hope in the present systems of privilege that the Messiah gathers together for the banquet. How we will be finally judged depends ultimately on how we have related to these, God's people, the marginated of our religious and social structures. But we are not just stuck in our past. We can change. God's victory over sin and death makes new life possible. This is the awesome but also hope-filled message of New Year.

B. A Whole Approach

ADVENT–CHRISTMAS

Richard K. Avery and Donald S. Marsh

There is no better place to begin our special task than with the opening weeks of the Christian year. First of all, the Advent and Christmas readings cry out persistently and powerfully with news of God's loving will and purpose for the whole social order, the world and all who dwell therein. In fact, as one reads through these scheduled Scriptures for what they actually say, one can only be amazed and dismayed that the conventional interpretation of these passages in our churches is consistently individualistic, exclusively personal, and often sentimental. How unfaithful to these writings we have been!

Second, the seasons of Advent and Christmas offer a unique opportunity in the life of ordinary congregations for "social themes" to be taken up with popular enthusiasm and with important results. It is our own recent experience, as we work in a small church in a small city, that in the month of December with its Christmas preparations and celebrations people are ready to be moved, to have their sympathies expanded, and to respond to human needs and even global problems as at no other time of the year. They are eager for new meanings to emerge from the old stories, uneasy and even feeling guilty about frivolous and materialistic ways of celebrating Jesus' birth, and ready to have their celebrations transformed, deepened, opened up to embrace the world. Thus, at a Christmas Eve candlelight service several years ago in our own church (which is hardly a gathering of "radicals") many members of the congregation were immediately ready to sign a petition protesting a particular U.S. military offensive that had been mounted just before Christmas—and they did so with considerable feeling, by the glow of candlelight.

Third, in many churches the experiences of worship and nurture are already carried out imaginatively and with the active involvement of all generations. It is a time of ceremonials and symbols and special occasions, full of drama and music and pageantry and traveling about. The challenge we share in this chapter is for the transformation of these activities, rather than their elimination. Therefore, as

63

we take up representative themes below we shall in each case suggest ways for the reshaping of these traditional experiences of the seasons.

There is no simple "story line" or plot in the readings for these seasons. But there is a most interesting series of ambiguities. Several of the Old Testament readings proclaim the deliverance of a captive Israel, and these proclamations are inseparable from anticipations of a future Messiah; these messianic hopes often appear in the lectionary in obvious relation to the coming of Christmas and also in combination with Epistle readings expressing confidence in Jesus' imminent return; and in the midst of these weeks appears John the Baptizer preparing us for the presence of the adult Messiah. So we have a montage of challenges and words of encouragement, saying: Have faith! . . . Get ready! . . . Beware God's judgment! . . . Christ will come soon! . . . One has come who saves the world and us! . . . Don't give up! . . . Christ will come again!

Perhaps the most startling innovations for church leaders planning Advent and Christmas would be an emphasis on the prophetic promises of justice, liberation, and peace on the one hand and, on the other, proper attention to Advent's chief character, John the Baptizer. It is with the rediscovery of John, with his loud call to repentance, his eccentricities and vigor, that the local church can readily plan a different kind of Advent than we normally see.

Another motif of Advent readings, especially those for the latter Sundays from Hebrews, Colossians, and Ephesians, is the role of Christ as revealer of God, key to the meaning of history and source of true life for all people. With knowledge of this revelation Christians can face earthly powers with confidence and challenge evil systems without fear.

Emerging throughout the Advent season and also in the Christmas pericopes is God's concern for the *poor* and *oppressed,* the suffering and disregarded. We are clearly inspired by the prophetic texts and by the familiar Christmas narratives to think past the impulses of charity that are common in this season to *justice.* Justice for the suffering and rejected is a standard of judgment at "the day of the Lord," a promise to be fulfilled when God "makes things right" and a part of the Messiah's program as set forth exultantly by Mary the mother of Jesus.

Note also the Bible's emphasis on the role of *the common people* and common places. While Christmas sermons through the centuries have turned a loving light on these figures and scenes, they have often missed the revolutionary nature of this aspect of the story. Even more remarkable is the outrageous appearance in Christmas season pericopes of the element of *threat* to, and reaction from, established power, as in the story of Herod and the "slaughter of the innocents."

It is sad that of the two major "canticles" contained in Luke's

Gospel—the Benedictus of old Zechariah and the Magnificat of Mary —only one has a place in the lectionary. Many parish leaders will want to correct this oversight and may even wish to base a whole season of services on the four Lucan songs—the angels' Gloria and Simeon's Nunc Dimittis being the others. These four passages are almost overwhelming in their proclamations of liberation, reconciliation, and peace, presenting a God who dramatically turns things upside down in the social order. (See Hughes Old, *Praying with the Bible* [Geneva Press, 1980], Ch. 3, and pp. 42–45 for canticle music.)

While many preachers and planners of worship, education, and mission will choose to focus on readings for Christmastide in the regular lectionary pattern, others will wish to give attention to special readings for the New Year. Professor Ruether's essay in this volume is based on those special readings. Most notable for our present purpose among the regular Christmastide lections for the two Sundays after Christmas are the continuing emphasis on Jesus as a refugee from Herod, the incarnation of the divine Word-in-human-flesh, in full identification with human need and weakness, and Simeon's perception of the Messiah as both judge and threat.

Now we turn to specific themes emerging from the Advent and Christmas and New Year Scriptures as set forth in the essays preceding this article, illustrating possibilities for one theme from each essay. As we go through this exercise of imagination for planning in a local church, the writers of this article do so with certain assumptions: chiefly, that the Sunday service, classes, and gatherings, and any action undertaken by the church should all be participatory events, with all kinds of people of all ages eligible for involvement and leadership, meeting in environments that capture attention; also, that all the arts, drama, conversation, pantomime, ceremonies, physical movement, and music in a wide variety of styles may be used and experienced with the same validity as the spoken sermon, lecture, or printed materials—and that people learn more by *doing* than simply by *hearing*. With each of the four themes, we suggest, as noted above, "the transformation of a tradition" of the seasons.

1. THE VISION AND THE EXPECTATION

What are we waiting for? Gabriel Fackre, in the opening essay for these first seasons, has said: "Vision defines reality in the Advent lectionary. The prophet projects on the screen of the future what is ultimately so." How can such an idea come alive for the congregation and through the congregation? How can biblical hope for a new, God-given order shape our lives?

Worship. Consider the possibility of a theme for the whole Advent season: "The Hope of the World." With this theme, try to set forth what God wills for society and the world of nations as "projected on the screen" by the prophets. Begin the first service of the season with several people of various ages pacing silently about in front of the congregation: One moving about holding an empty plate, as if hungry and bereft; another in rags, trying to keep warm; a third dragging chains or in handcuffs; and several others impatiently looking at watches and big wall calendars. After a few moments, with the striking of a musical chord, let all the victims and time watchers freeze in position, as a reader declares the prophetic hope: "Be strong! Don't be afraid! Behold, your God will come with vengeance . . . and save you" (Isa. 35:4). Or have a soloist begin "O Come, O Come, Emmanuel."

Transform a tradition: Include in your services the lighting of the Advent wreath, with its four purple candles, but now identify it as "the wheel of hope." And clearly label the four candles according to the prophets' expectations: The first candle for JUSTICE, the second either for RIGHTEOUSNESS (or for REPENTANCE), the third for HEALING of nations and communities (and not just of personal ailments), the fourth for PEACE (or SHALOM). Have a wreath-making night for members or encourage families and all members to make their own wreaths for their dining tables, to light the appropriate candles each day at dinner or breakfast, and to offer a prayer—for victims of injustice the first week, for goodness in the world the second week, etc. Combine the Advent wreath ceremonies with such strong hymns as "O Come, O Come, Emmanuel" and "Come, Thou Long-expected Jesus."

Education. Besides carrying through the new meanings of the Advent wreath in Sunday church school classes and in homes, take up the theme of waiting and expectation with groups of the church: What are we waiting for? What do we want to happen? Explore two possibilities: (1) After studying the prophets' words in the various Old Testament pericopes of the season, prepare banners that, in word and symbol, announce what God will do, quoting the prophets: "God will comfort the brokenhearted!" "God will decide between the nations!" "(S)he will feed the flock!" (2) Prepare a graffiti board on which members young and old may answer the question, "What do you hope for?"

Witness. Create four pre-Advent task forces, allowing church members to volunteer or assigning active members to them, teams consisting of all ages, one team for each candle on the wreath. The job of each group will be to share concerns on the appropriate Sunday in relation to that theme, and to take one form of action in which other members are invited to join. The "Justice" task force, for example, may visit the local court or county jail, interview judges and attorneys, and report about the state of legal justice in the area. The "Healing" task force may investigate one scene of suffering in the world, one example of oppression, and address government officials about that situation, reporting that action to the congregation and inviting participation.

Bible study. For many contemporary church members a study of Old Testament prophets will be a new experience. In keeping with the suggestions above, share a word study related to the Old Testament lections, exploring the original meanings of justice, righteousness, repentance, healing (and mercy), and peace (shalom).

2. John's Call to Repentance

Worship. Let this most colorful and demanding biblical hero come alive for the people. For the reading of the Gospel lessons about John on Advent's 2d and 3d Sundays, have an actor assume the role, simply pantomiming the acts of baptizing and shouting the words of John to the congregation as he moves about them. (No need to dress him in camel's hair or skins; the people can use their imaginations.) An ax, symbolic of God's judgment, may be carried by the actor and then be left leaning against the pulpit during the sermon.

Two contemporary anthems are especially appropriate to this theme: Ron Nelson's stirring setting of Samuel Miller's words about God's judgment of religion, "God, Bring Thy Sword" (published by Boosey & Hawkes, Inc.); and, for children's and youth choirs, our own "Better Do Better," which we presume to recommend as a rather ironic setting of John's actual words (Proclamation Productions, Inc., Orange Square, Port Jervis, N.Y. 12771).

Education. Who are today's "voices in the wilderness"? Who are the people who call us to change and to "straighten out our lives" according to God's will? Children, youth, and adults alike can discuss this issue. In an Advent gathering, read about John and put his message in contemporary terms. Then cut from newspapers and magazines the pictures of modern "wilderness voices." Mount them nicely and put them up in the place of worship for all to see, taking time in a service to identify them, to give thanks for them, and to pray for help to change in response to their messages.

Witness. First, "transform a tradition" by distributing "alternatives" for Christmas gift-giving. Second, in honor of John, sponsor an early Advent "Day of Repentance" in your parish. Prepare a list, complete with biblical texts; call people of your community to repent of our nation's involvement in creating poverty in the world, of constant preparations for war, of prejudice and discrimination, of greed and smugness about our own economic situation.

Bible study. Certain questions from Isaiah's writings as taken up by John the Baptizer are most challenging: What does it mean to "prepare the way"? Repentance means turning, changing direction; is change possible for Christians today as we participate so inextricably in the actions of government, industry, unions, and other institutions, and as we are shaped by popular media? John turned aside any boasts of Jewish ancestry as resistance to his criticism (Matt. 3:9); what boasts do we make in the world today? (Note the sexist implications of "sons of Abraham.") As we look at John's dire predictions of judgment regarding Israel, can we see how they come true for the church? for a "believing" nation? On a more positive note, in answer to the inquiry John sent to Jesus from prison (Matt. 11:2–3), what would we write back to him in a letter: What do we hear and see as signs of the coming of the Messiah?

3. CHRISTMAS AND THE POWERS THAT BE

As the story of how God often confronts the powers of earth with the power of love in forms of lowliness, weakness, and servitude, the Bible comes to a climax in the stories of the one who came to die as a suffering servant. Especially in the canticles attributed to Zechariah and Mary, in the historical references that begin Luke 2 and in the descriptions of Herod's jealousy and cruelty, aspiring modern peacemakers can learn of God's strange war with mighty principalities and powers.

Worship. Christmas is a time for Holy Communion, the supreme dramatization of the confrontation of God's love with earthly powers. The large crowds who gather for Christmas services need to see and hear the *whole* gospel of the Word made human to save humans. Plan to bring our Advent theme to the Lord's Table, using symbols and prayers offered by the people.

A second suggestion is about Christmas decorations and music: Let them reveal the universality of God's love, and the engagement of God with the world of nations: Have a large map behind the crèche; put a globe on the Communion table; let the choir's offerings include carols of many nations; let Christmas prayers of intercession have their point of departure in the reading of headlines from visible newspapers.

Third, transform the traditional Christmas Eve Candlelight Service by interpreting the nature of the *darkness*—the darkness of individual sinfulness, and the darkness profoundly representing the corruptibility of powers on the earth, the evils inherent in mighty and long-lasting institutions, self-deceptions within the most noble human movements. In your Christmas Eve service, identify by name the various powers that most effectively shape our lives, mark the headquarters of international and national power blocs on a big map before the congregation, and have specific prayers by representative members about those powers. Analyze the words of that provocative hymn "Joy to the World" and of that revolutionary text contained in the Hallelujah Chorus of Handel. Then light candles and spread the candlelight as signs of salvation in the midst.

Other ideas for appropriate Christmas music are: Sydney Carter's haunting "No Use Knocking" and Alec Wyton's anthem setting of Christopher Smart's poem "Where Is This Stupendous Stranger," both in *Choirbook for Saints and Singers* (Agape Press, Carol Stream, Ill. 60187); the unusual musical cantata "Carols for Today," by Herbert Chappell (available from Belwin Mills Corp., Melville, N.Y. 11746); and our own song written for World Food Day, "Madonna and Child in a Starving World" (Proclamation Productions).

Education. Perhaps on the Sunday after Christmas, let an intergenerational gathering do a most unusual thing. Somehow, somewhere, hold a secret meeting—perhaps in an old, unused basement area of the church, perhaps in a vacated building or a nearby home. Meet quietly, surreptitiously by candlelight or a *few* flashlights. Identify then with families with small boys being sought by Herod's soldiers, "the children of Rachel" discussed in Christopher Morse's essay, "Celebrating the Incarnation," above. Then let it be explained that many Christians are still having to meet like this because of their faith or political beliefs. Identify those places—and incidentally identify the support which our own government is giving to many of the oppressing regimes of those lands and what the churches are doing to bring hope. Sing "Joy to the World" and other carols—but quietly! Pray for peace and freedom for those who are oppressed and who can only meet in hiding.

Witness. Mentioned above, at the beginning of this article, was the petition of protest about a Christmas bombing sent to the President of the United States by our church on a Christmas Eve. As an effort to "spread the light" of God's love and our hope for peace, such actions are uniquely possible on that holy night, and uniquely appropriate. Nonpartisan statements of concern and also of encouragement for peacemaking efforts by members of Congress and officials in the Administration should be first endorsed by church officers (not just by the clergy) and made available for the congregation.

Messages on behalf of refugees of the earth are appropriately sent at the time when we are honoring the family that became refugees in Egypt when fleeing from Herod's wrath! Demands of governmental attention to those whose human rights are violated may be properly addressed in the name of one who came to set all people free and then was constantly threatened by nervous governments.

Bible study. Let students of the Christmas texts learn carefully the precise shape of the governments at the time of Jesus' birth. Who was this Herod? Why was he insecure? Was Jesus actually a threat to governments during his later career? In what way is the Christian faith a threat to governments now? Is the United States Government nervous and jealous as Herod was?

Study the identity of "Rachel and her children" as set forth in Christopher Morse's essay. What consolation is there today for the suffering mothers of our own world? What message does the church have for the victims of such oppression? What does God will for us in response to such human grief? Who are the Rachels of the earth right now—the suffering mothers whose children are victims of earthly powers?

4. PEACE ON EARTH, GOODWILL TO ALL—A NEW BEGINNING

In the afterglow of Christmas, on the two Sundays during the twelve days of the season of Christmas, church leaders may, as noted previously, take up the special readings for the New Year or continue with regular readings for the season (which vary annoyingly among denominational versions of the "common" lectionary). In either case, taking our cue from Professor Ruether's essay, there may be a celebration of the passing of the old and the opening of new possibilities according to the biblical message of *salvation,* a state of health and unity for all people, and the *inclusive love* of the Messiah, at whose wedding feast all kinds of strange people are welcome for a "summit sacrament." Celebrate new possibilities in Christ and repent of what must be left behind with the old year.

Worship. Two possible approaches, transforming traditions. If a church ordinarily celebrates Holy Communion on New Year's Eve or Day or on the first Sunday of the New Year, let it become a simulation or dramatization of the messianic banquet described in Luke 14:15–24 and elsewhere, as an interpretation of the "Peace on Earth" theme. With loaves of bread made by recipes from different lands representing the longing of the hungry in those places, with the reading of sacramental words in different languages, and, especially, with the clear announcement (even by reading a list of people often excluded and oppressed) that female and male, rich and poor, well-clothed and ragged people of all colors and political persuasions are now welcome, let the sacrament be celebrated.

Or let a similar thing happen at a Christmas-New Year's church dinner, transformed into a liturgical event with prayers for all the kinds of people represented in the parable of the great feast and in our burgeoning world: A "Peace on Earth" banquet with the various kinds of bread and other foods. Decorate the tables in an unusual way—with *broken swords.* Prepare swords of wood to be symbolically broken in half. Alternatively, have broken military toys and guns scattered about the table or placed ceremoniously around the foot of the manger amid its poinsettias on the chancel of the place of worship.

Education and witness. Read, study, and prepare dramatic presentations (simple staging, complete with humor) of two related biblical events: The year of jubilee as presented in Leviticus 25 and the messianic feast in Luke 14. Children, youth, and adults can sit together and determine who in our own world and nation would benefit by the jubilee blessings. Prepare such a jubilee proclamation, in contemporary terms, to be read at a New Year service. Let groups and classes list the people whom the king would invite to the feast now, replacing those unwilling to come. What kinds of people are actually excluded from our churches now—because of our liturgical styles, or our implied prejudice against them—whom the king would have at the feast? Share this jubilee proclamation ecumenically with other churches in your community.

How can church boards and church organizations in our mainline denominations change the image of exclusive communities of religion? What kind of public presentations (through the media? through outdoor events? through involvement by members in social events of those often excluded?) can communicate the *inclusive* love of Jesus in the New Year? How can "enemies" become "friends" in our cities and towns through the witness of the churches? Such questions have a crucial place in the deliberations related to "peacemaking" efforts of officers and congregations.

II. EPIPHANY

Sunday or Festival	Year	First Lesson	Second Lesson	Gospel
Epiphany		Isa. 60:1–6	Eph. 3:1–6	Matt. 2:1–12
1st Sunday After Epiphany	A	Isa. 42:1–9	Acts 10:34–43	Matt. 3:13–17
	B	Gen. 1:1–5	Acts 11:4–18 or Acts 19:1–7	Mark 1:4–11
	C	Isa. 61:1–4	Eph. 2:11–18 or Acts 8:14–17	Luke 3:15–17, 21–22
		(or the readings for Epiphany)		
2d Sunday After Epiphany	A	Isa. 49:1–7	I Cor. 1:1–9	John 1:29–34
	B	I Sam. 3:1–10	I Cor. 6:12–20	John 1:35–42
	C	Isa. 62:1–5	I Cor. 12:1–11	John 2:1–11
3d Sunday After Epiphany	A	Isa. 9:1–4	I Cor. 1:10–17	Matt. 4:12–23
	B	Jonah 3:1–5, 10	I Cor. 7:29–35	Mark 1:14–20
	C	Neh. 8:1–4a, 5–6, 8–10	I Cor. 12:12–30	Luke 4:14–21
4th Sunday After Epiphany	A	Micah 6:1–8	I Cor. 1:18–31	Matt. 5:1–12
	B	Deut. 18:15–22	I Cor. 8:1–13	Mark 1:21–28
	C	Jer. 1:4–10	I Cor. 13:1–13	Luke 4:21–30
5th Sunday After Epiphany	A	Isa. 58:3–10	I Cor. 2:1–11	Matt. 5:13–16
	B	Job 7:1–7	I Cor. 9:16–23	Mark 1:29–39
	C	Isa. 6:1–8	I Cor. 15:1–11	Luke 5:1–11
6th Sunday After Epiphany	A	Deut. 30:15–20	I Cor. 3:1–9	Matt. 5:17–26
	B	Lev. 13:1–2, 44–46 or II Kings 5:1–14	I Cor. 10:31 to 11:1 or I Cor. 9:24–27	Mark 1:40–45
	C	Jer. 17:5–10	I Cor. 15:12–20	Luke 6:17–26
7th Sunday After Epiphany	A	Isa. 49:8–13	I Cor. 3:10–11, 16–23	Matt. 5:27–37
	B	Isa. 43:18–25	II Cor 1:18–22	Mark 2:1–12
	C	I Sam. 26:6–25 or Gen. 45:3–11, 15	I Cor. 15:35–38, 42–50	Luke 6:27–38
8th Sunday After Epiphany	A	Lev. 19:1–2, 17–18	I Cor. 4:1–5	Matt. 6:24–34 or Matt. 5:38–48
	B	Hos. 2:14–20	II Cor. 3:1–6	Mark 2:18–22
	C	Job 23:1–7 or Isa. 55:10–13	I Cor. 15:51–58	Luke 6:39–49
Last Sunday After Epiphany (Transfiguration)	A	Ex. 24:12–18	II Peter 1:16–21	Matt. 17:1–9
	B	II Kings 2:1–12a	II Cor. 4:3–6	Mark 9:2–9
	C	Ex. 34:29–35	II Cor. 3:12 to 4:2	Luke 9:28–36

Sunday or Festival	*Year*	*First Lesson*	*Second Lesson*	*Gospel*
Readings for Special Day on Christian Unity		Isa. 11:1–9 Isa. 35:3–10 Isa. 55:1–5		

Epiphany—God's revelation or manifestation to the Gentiles *(Apparitio Domini)* illumining the world's darkness; God's power to bring forth new life from the waters of the earth. An ancient Byzantine hymn rejoices, "When you, O Lord, were baptized in the Jordan, the worship of the Trinity was made manifest." In the Sundays after Epiphany, it is appropriate to explore the life-style of the baptized; the nature of the Messiah we encounter and follow; the life of martyrs such as Martin Luther King, Jr.; the unity of the church in mission.

A. THEMATIC ESSAYS

1

JESUS' BAPTISM AND THE CALL OF DISCIPLES AND PROPHETS

Walter L. Owensby

Jesus' Baptism		Matt. 3:13–17
		Mark 1:4–11
		Luke 3:15–22
Call of Disciples	Deut. 18:15–22	John 1:29–42
and Prophets	Isa. 9:1–4; Jer. 1:4–10	Matt. 4:12–23
	Isa. 6:1–8	Mark 1:14–20
	I Sam. 3:1–10	

Jesus' baptism by John is crucial to the understanding of Jesus' self-image and what it means to be his disciples.

If he had not baptized Jesus, John might well have been forgotten in Christian tradition. On the other hand, if he had lived a hundred years earlier, we would probably know a great deal more about him. That paradox is explained by the fact that John lived in the shadow —or better, in the corona—of Jesus. Because the New Testament focuses on the Christ event, the importance of John tends to be over-looked. Yet what we see in his ministry is nothing less than the revival of the spirit of the biblical prophets.

His influence was not as ephemeral as a quick reading of the Gospels might make it seem. There is no evidence of when he began his prophetic career, but his wilderness preaching attracted multi-tudes. From north and south they came, from Galilee and from Judea. The crowds became a movement and predictably the religious estab-lishment became concerned. As with Jesus, priests were sent to test and entrap John (John 1:19, 24). Not only did he address the multi-tudes, he had his close disciples as well. Some were among the first followers of Jesus (John 1:37). Not all, however, were merely passed along, nor did the movement end with John's death. Fully thirty years later, groups of his disciples were still carrying on John's ministry and baptizing (Acts 18:25).

In a sense, Jesus was John's successor. He did not begin to preach until after John's imprisonment, and then did so with the same tones as the Baptizer. After Herod beheaded John, the superstitious even wondered if the Galilean might really be the reincarnation of John!

This was not due to slavish imitation. Jesus had no need to mimic. What we see in his baptism by John is Jesus' decision to take upon himself the prophetic spirit as his model of ministry. More than a prophet he surely was, but not less.

Soon after his baptism Jesus began to gather around himself a band of followers, a committed community to whom he could reveal himself and his vision for the world. The call to discipleship was a call to share Christ's commitment to the prophetic vision. There are many facets to that prophetic spirit, but two seem crucial.

I. A COMMITMENT TO JUSTICE

Justice was not merely a theme in the preaching of the prophets; it was the organizing principle of their message—their very reason for being. Above all else, a prophet was called to proclaim God's justice —to demand it as the people's response to the covenant relationship.

The covenant was established when the Israelites were a landless desert people living a tenuous nomadic existence where the life of any one person depended upon the cohesiveness of the community as a whole. A shared life was the symbol of a shared faith in the God they were coming to know. All partook together of the plenty or poverty that God and circumstance supplied. But when the Israelites settled in the Land of Canaan, things began to change. Wealth in land was more sure and enduring than the wealth of flocks and herds, so property became increasingly private. An economic elite developed despite laws that in theory canceled debts and restored lost lands in the year of jubilee. Temple worship replaced that of the Tabernacle, and priests assumed a privileged position. Merchants in the new cities soon lived in a kind of luxury that made them a different class from others with whom, only a few generations before, they had shared nomadic life.

In the face of such growing inequalities, the prophets called the people again to the covenant faith which stood for a certain relationship with God and with one another in community. This is basic to Epiphany enlightenment. Yahweh sides with the poor and the distressed (Isa. 9:4).

The prophets did not just announce a general truth, however. They engaged in condemnation of specific acts by people, groups, classes, and trades. We need only remember such verses as these: "Shall I acquit the *man with wicked scales? . . .* Your *rich men* are full of violence" (Micah 6:11–12); "The Lord enters into judgment with the *elders and princes"* (Isa. 3:14); "Hear this word, you *cows of Bashan, . . . who oppress* the poor" (Amos 4:1); "Woe to those who are at ease in Zion, . . . the *notable men"* (Amos 6:1); "Woe to *those who decree* iniquitous decrees, and the *writers* who keep writing oppression"

(Isa. 10:1); "Woe to *the proud crown*" (Isa. 28:1); "Nathan said to *David,* 'You are the man' " (II Sam. 12:7).

Everyone favors justice for the poor and oppressed in a generalized, abstract way. But prophetic truth is seldom general. A word of hope for the poor is a word of challenge to the rich; justice for the oppressed means judgment of the oppressor.

Israel, of course, is not the only people that has forgotten, overlooked, or tried to circumvent that message. In today's church we have quite subtle ways of avoiding it. A case in point is how the words of John the Baptist are often dealt with. In his popular Bible commentary series, William Barclay notes in regard to Luke 3:7–18 that there are three characteristics of John's message.[1] First, it demanded that people share with one another. Barclay devotes four lines to developing this concept. Second, it ordered that people not leave their jobs but "work out [their] own salvation by doing that job as it should be done." Barclay devotes twenty-three lines to this, including two verses of a Negro spiritual which seems to endorse the idea that the person hoeing cotton should merely accept the position of slavery. Finally, John's message points to judgment. Here Barclay devotes seven lines and closes out with an additional four in conclusion: "So John painted a picture of judgment, but it was a judgment which a man could meet with confidence if he had discharged his duty to his neighbor and *if he had faithfully done his day's work.*" Thus a total of thirty-four lines of commentary are given to the role of faithful work as a response to the gospel and only four to the concept of sharing with equity.

Here we see the way in which the gospel has been used to bolster the economic status quo by fostering dutiful labor without questioning the justice of the system in which it occurs or the fairness of the sharing of benefits. Quite a different message might have been communicated had Barclay placed equal emphasis on the concept of equitable sharing or that of the justice involved in not exploiting positions of power.

For Jesus, work was not an absolute good. His disciples were not told to adjust to the demands of their trades as a religious duty. They were called from their trades. The point, of course, is not that he was opposed to labor—after all, Jesus was a carpenter. Nor was he careless about family or financial responsibilities—these may well explain why his ministry did not begin until age thirty. But he clearly declined to endorse the concept of life being defined by employment. God may indeed call us to discipleship in our job, but we may also be called away from that to which family or society has assigned us. The doctrine of the Christian calling can never be construed as complicity in an unjust economic relationship—whether for ourselves or for others.

John's counsel to the soldiers and tax collectors to be content with their wages was a specific word to those who had an adequate income (Luke 3:12–14). Its main thrust was that they should not use positions of power to take advantage of others. It was not a dictum calling for passivity in the face of labor exploitation.

In Guatemala, there are 600,000 Indians who migrate for sixty to ninety days to work twelve-hour shifts in the cotton harvest for $1.25 per *day.*[2] One cannot imagine Jesus accepting baptism from a prophet who would tell people to be content with such a wage.

Castle & Cooke (better known as Dole) has for years been moving its pineapple production from Hawaii to the Philippines, where the going rate for field labor is 25 cents an hour.[3] Who could believe that people baptized in the tradition of John would favor quietism over union organization in such a circumstance?

Faithful submission to human institutions is not the theme of the prophets—righteousness that leads to justice is. When Jesus calls us to be disciples with a vision of the prophets, it is a call to challenge and change such structures of injustice.

II. A FAITH BEYOND NATIONALISM

Jesus was baptized. For two thousand years that has been a theological problem for Christians, since John's baptism was one of repentance and the forgiveness of sins. But there is a theological issue here quite apart from the question of our Lord's purity. Baptism had been practiced by the Jews long before John, but only as a requirement for Gentiles who wished to convert to Judaism. It was a symbol of their need for special cleansing because they were thought to be shut off from God in a way that Jews were not. *Thus when John required baptism of all, it took on political significance.* It represented the repudiation of exclusive particularism and religious nationalism in favor of a spirit of universalism under the Lordship of Yahweh. Not given to subtlety, John made the point inescapably clear: "Do not presume to say to yourselves, 'We have Abraham as our father'; for I tell you, God is able from these stones to raise up children to Abraham" (Matt. 3:9).

John would not allow God to be boxed in by nationalism or elitism. It was into this denationalized kingdom perspective that Jesus received baptism. By that act he associated himself with the total rejection of any absolute claims by the state or any absolute commitments to it.

That, of course, was a prophetic message. When Jeremiah was called, God said, "I have set you this day over nations and over kingdoms, to pluck up and to break down, to destroy and to overthrow, to build and to plant" (Jer. 1:10). Jonah went to Nineveh and was angered by God's grace. Micah prophesied to both Samaria and Jerusalem. Amos crossed the boundaries of both class and nation as this shepherd from Judah dared to address the elite and the court of Israel. He shocked his hearers by insisting that God was at work among all the nations. Ezekiel as well as Jeremiah echoed the same theme in their conviction that Jerusalem would fall to Nebuchadnezzar. Second Isaiah also pointed to Cyrus and the Persian Empire as instruments of God's will.

In a day of so-called religious revival that has a dangerous affinity for political power and superpatriotism, nationalism is a crucial issue for us. The present American version of the kind of nationalism rejected by Jesus and John as well as by the prophets comes dressed as a moral crusade and with the voice of a bevy of radio and television preachers.

The main danger of the religious right is not its ability to influence legislation on behalf of its "moral" agenda. (A strange selection of issues it is: opposition to abortion, homosexuality, pornography, and equal rights for women; support of huge military budget increases, massive arms sales, and prayer in schools; and silence on problems of poverty, racism, inequality, and injustice.) Nor does the main danger arise from its perceived successes in the electoral process—of helping to put in office a President sympathetic to its views and helping defeat legislators deemed too liberal. The big danger is its desire to move beyond merely influencing the political system and instead to control it. In jubilation James Robison, a television preacher, exclaimed, "We have enough votes to run the country."[4]

One suspects that behind this goal lies yet another—to make America the new Israel. The religious right tends to see this nation as God's chosen people. What idealized America is, the rest of the world should become. To be sure, the country must be purged of its corruptions, but it is nonetheless regarded as the last great platform for world evangelism—hence its image and institutions are to be protected and its power projected, whatever the cost or risk.

Once America is perceived as God's special people with a special purpose, it is only a short step to the conviction that this country must also be the "rod of God's wrath," with the duty to discipline the nations, to punish those which do not conform to what is perceived as God's plan. Thus ever-larger military budgets and an ever more belligerent foreign policy represent no contradiction of faith.

That is the ultimate danger of the religious right. It tends to absolutize the American state and to make absolute commitments to it. This is heresy of classic form. As disciples, we make only one absolute commitment—to God as known in Christ. Everything else, including the nation, is relative.

Of course, the attempt to nationalize God and baptize the state is not new and certainly not limited to America's fundamentalist Protestants. Contemporary Latin America offers numerous examples. In country after country where the masses are demanding justice and change, the elites are resisting, using the military power of the state to crush opposition—which is identified by definition as "godless communism." The argument is inexorable: to favor change is subversion; subversion is motivated by communism; communism is atheistic; atheism must be opposed. Therefore, in the name of Christian duty and of the preservation of Christian civilization, generals assume power; political rights are suspended; justice is forever postponed; privilege is protected. Toward these ends, imprisonment, torture, and murder are adopted as practices, if not policies, of the state.

In its own absolutized national interests, the United States is supporting many such governments with funds and weapons. They are defended on grounds that they are the only and necessary alternatives to communism, chaos, and corruption. That is almost certainly not the case, but even if it were so, from a biblical perspective the fear of an unknown evil is not justification enough to perpetuate a known evil. Surely that is one of the meanings of God calling Jeremiah to announce the defeat of Israel by Babylonia. There is nothing to indicate that the Babylonians were less selfish, or brutal, or unjust than the Judeans. Yet God refused to withhold judgment. As Dom Helder Câmara, Archbishop of Recife in Brazil, put it: "We in the church should have no illusions about communism, but creating a new Nazism cannot be the best way to fight it."[5]

Jesus sought baptism at the hands of a prophet who denounced the pretensions of nationalism. His disciples are surely called to do the same.

When Jesus received baptism, he showed that God's way is always to seek righteousness which creates justice within the nation and beyond. That was what lay at the heart of the call to the prophets from Moses to John the Baptist. In his baptism, Jesus aligned himself with the prophetic task and made it central to the call of all disciples.

BIBLIOGRAPHY

Comblin, José. *The Church and the National Security State.* Orbis Books, 1979.

Miranda, José. *Marx and the Bible: A Critique of the Philosophy of Oppression.* Orbis Books, 1974.

Scott, Robert B. Y. *The Relevance of the Prophets.* Macmillan Co., 1953.

Third World Sermon Notes, 1121 University Ave., Madison, Wis. 53715. A subscription service that focuses on one lectionary passage from each month and addresses issues of global concern. 12 issues annually (mailed quarterly).

2

WHAT KIND OF MESSIAH?

Robert McAfee Brown

Messianic Ministry

Rejection at Nazareth	Isa. 61:1–4	Luke 4:14–30
Suffering Servant	Isa. 42:1–9; 49:1–18	
Astonishing Authority and Healing Power	Job 7:1–17	Mark 1:21–45
	Lev. 13:1–2, 44–46	
Sign at Cana	Isa. 62:1–5	John 2:1–11
Miraculous Catch		Luke 5:1–11
		(cf. John 21:1–14)

During Advent we *anticipate* the coming of a Messiah. During the Christmas season we *celebrate* the coming of a Messiah. During Epiphany we *reflect* on the nature of the Messiah who has come, and we face the risky problem of how we are to *act* on the basis of our reflection.

Whatever clues we had ahead of time about the nature of the coming Messiah don't seem to have helped very much. At least, if the clues were good ones, we read the signs incorrectly. For the Messiah who comes is very different from the Messiah who was anticipated. And the consequences of living in a world where an unexpected kind of Messiah has come are disturbing: life does not promise "more of the same"; rather, the future will be one in which everything must be "turned upside down," as the early Christian community soon discovered (cf. Acts 17:6).

I

Consider the dramatic scene in the synagogue in Nazareth at the beginning of Jesus' ministry (Luke 4:14–30). The episode is familiar to all who have sought to understand Jesus' ministry. But its very familiarity has led us to miss its revolutionary impact, just as the familiarity of Jesus' listeners with the words he read led them to miss their revolutionary impact, until Jesus (apparently not knowing enough to quit while he was ahead) began to explain their meaning. And once his hearers began to get the point, they were outraged.

Here is the hometown boy back home, reading the lesson at the Friday night service. Many of his hearers probably know the words of the passage by heart. But tonight, they come through with new beauty. For Jesus reads them very well. His hearers are charmed by his self-possession, his elocution, the clarity of his diction. The words are familiar ones—words about freeing the captives, liberating the oppressed, bringing good news to the poor. How soothing to hear them on the lips of this fine fellow, Joe's boy, the one who used to work at the carpenter's shop. And when he tells them that the Scripture "has been fulfilled" that very evening, they love it.

Their response has been the familiar response through the centuries. There are noble, powerful cadences in Isaiah's poetry, and Jesus summarizes them well for us. Words of disturbance? Surely not. They are words of assurance, for Jesus tells us that "the acceptable year of the Lord" has begun. And he talks about "good news." It is good news "to the poor," but since we are all poor in the sense of being spiritually impoverished, his words bring us needed reassurance. And all of us are "captives" needing release, captives of neuroses or inner feelings of inadequacy over which Jesus (and Isaiah) promise us victory. So we are soothed.

But then something goes wrong in the tranquil atmosphere in Nazareth. Jesus talks about a drought long ago, and reminds his hearers that God's prophet Elijah did not concern himself with the true believers (like those gathered for worship) but instead visited a widow in Sidon, a foreigner. And during a time of terrible leprosy, another of God's prophets, Elisha, paid no attention to the Israelites, but cured Naaman, a Syrian, another foreigner. Apparently, God's concern doesn't focus exclusively or even primarily on the believers. Indeed, it begins to sound as though those on the outside are getting preferential treatment. What sort of reward for good behavior is that? So, as Clarence Jordan translates Luke 4:28, "the whole congregation blew a gasket."

And the story develops, quite literally, into a cliffhanger. They take Jesus out of the synagogue and up to the top of the nearby hill, intent on throwing him over the side. He escapes, but later on the crowd gets him on another hill called The Place of the Skull, where he doesn't escape.

What happened to shift the worshipers' response so rapidly? Apparently the full implications of what Jesus was saying only gradually seeped into their consciousness. And when they realized what they were hearing, they were not pleased. It began to sound suspiciously like the last being first, and who wants that, particularly if you consider yourself as already first? All that business about the "poor," the "captives," the "oppressed"—maybe he really meant the *materially* poor, the *physically* captive, the *economically* oppressed. And that innocent phrase, "the acceptable year of the Lord," turns out to be not so innocent after all; it turns out to be a reference to the jubilee year, a time when debts were to be forgiven and slaves freed, and when land was to revert to its former owners: a formula, in other words, for social revolution. And this, Jesus says, is the message that "has been fulfilled in your hearing."

What kind of Messiah? One who comes "to preach good news to the poor," and to embody it; one who comes "to proclaim release to the captives," and to work for it; one who comes "to set at liberty those who are oppressed," and not just talk about it: one who comes to inaugurate the jubilee year. A Messiah like that, who needs him? (Unless, of course, you are poor or oppressed or in captivity.) Over the cliff with him.

II

Luke doesn't quote the full Isaiah passage, which has a further emphasis that gives another clue to the nature of the Messiah. Isaiah insists, in a hopeful way, that things are really going to be reversed: those who mourn will be given "a garland instead of ashes [i.e., mourning], the mantle of praise instead of a faint spirit" (Isa. 61:3). Rebuilding is going to be the order of the day, rebuilding out of the ruins, repairs in place of rubble (cf. v. 4).

Things are not going to remain the way they were. There may be a time of devastation, but devastation will not be the last word. You see ruins? There will be new construction. You see imprisonment? There will be open doors. You see mourning? There will be gladness (vs. 3–4). What kind of Messiah? One who brings down our present ways of thinking and doing, but who also promises that new things will emerge, and who exercises a particular kind of power in working toward those ends.

The nature of that messianic power is developed in Isa. 42:1–7, the first of four poems about the Suffering Servant that are found in the postexilic portions of the book. Nobody knows for sure who the author of this part of Isaiah had in mind in describing the Suffering Servant, but it is clear that Jesus took the imagery very seriously as a way to describe his own messiahship; in his crucial exchange with Peter at Caesarea Philippi he teaches his disciples that "the Son of Man [a familiar messianic image of the time] must suffer many things" (Mark 8:31).

The Isaiah passage doesn't initially seem to be about power at all, but about weakness. The Servant isn't going to lift up his voice or break bruised reeds or quench dimly burning wicks (Isa. 42:2–3). But God is going to put the divine Spirit upon the Servant (v. 1), the same Spirit in the name of whom Jesus quoted the other Isaiah passage in the synagogue in Nazareth (Luke 4:18). And "Spirit" in the Old Testament is a very strong word. The Hebrew word *ruach* can be translated as both "breath" and "spirit," and it means precisely "power." Where the Spirit of the Lord is, there is power, whether in the Suffering Servant or in the valley of dry bones (Ezekiel 37) or at Pentecost (Acts 2).

And what will be the nature of this power? What will it do, and for whom? The answer is very clear. Indeed, so intent is the writer on seeing to it that we don't miss the point that the connection is repeated three times within four verses: "He will bring forth justice to the nations. . . . He will faithfully bring forth justice. . . . He will not fail or be discouraged till he has established justice in the earth" (Isa. 42:1, 3–4).

This is certainly an unexpected conclusion to a description of servanthood. We could understand that servanthood might lead to martyrdom. And servanthood might be noble but ineffective. But servanthood as a vehicle for justice? That we do not understand.

So once again, our anticipations about the nature of messiahship are overridden. Messiahship is to be a vehicle for justice, for seeing to it that everyone gets what is due him or her. The rules of the game are not going to be "Might makes right," or "Take whatever you can get," but rather, "Justice is to be established in the earth."

It sounds surprisingly like what Jesus was talking about back in Nazareth. Indeed, there are even some parallels between the two passages, for in Isa. 42:7 we are told that prisoners are to be brought out of the dungeon, i.e., that there is to be liberty for the captives. This is what Jesus' servanthood-messiahship is to be all about—not telling people to become complaisant doormats on which the tough ones can scuff their boots, but to be instruments of justice. To share the Spirit with the people, we can conclude, is to give breath or power to the people.

Just to some people? No, to all people. For the Servant-Messiah is to be "a light to the nations" (v. 7), a theme repeated in a later Servant passage (Isa. 49:6). That is comfort, but also disturbing presence. For it is the same theme that so upset the synagogue crowd in Nazareth. If the message is finally meant for all, perhaps we, its presumed initial recipients, don't have an exclusive corner on it. Present-day Naamans will start crowding in. And that would mean treating everybody else as potential recipients of the message, rather than putting others down or demeaning or exploiting them. The current notion, for example, that America must remain number one at all costs, since presumably God's will can only be done through us, would be cast down; the notion that America is to be supported whether right or wrong, would be displaced; the notion that white people or rich people have inherent privileges, not necessarily belonging to others, would be dismantled. . . . Too bad that crowd in Nazareth didn't get Jesus tossed over the cliff before he had time to spread around such disturbing ideas.

III

So the kind of Messiah Jesus turns out to be *upsets* our expectations. But it does something else. It *outstrips* them. Whatever we could have imagined him to be, he always turns out to be something more. That was certainly his impact on his contemporaries, as some early material in Mark (Mark 1:21–45) makes clear. What are the prevailing words used to describe the reaction of the people to Jesus? Words like "amazement," "surprise," "astonishment." No sooner do they think they have begun to understand him than he surprises them once again. Presumably he knows something about good spirits, but even evil spirits acknowledge him, and obey him! Presumably he wants to get the word around about his healing powers, but he admonishes a cured man to keep quiet about the whole business. It's all more than the onlookers know how to handle.

The same thing happens at the wedding feast at Cana (John 2:1–11). Once again Jesus' presence sends things in an unanticipated direction. Life was no longer predictable when he was around. A host runs short of wine? We've experienced that. A host, in a frantic flurry of concern, realizes he must get more wine? We've experienced that. A host, realizing that the guests are already pretty jolly and their palates have lost their initial discrimination, does get more wine but capitalizes on the occasion to offer second-rate wine? We've experienced that as well. But a wedding feast at which the host saves the best wine for the last? We've not experienced that, and if we were running a wedding reception, we certainly wouldn't be so foolish as to save the best wine until almost no one could tell the difference.

But the Messiah is on the scene. So everything is different, nothing is predictable, all ordinary expectations are overthrown. It's a vivid example of the theme of the corresponding Old Testament passage in Isa. 62:2–5. Here too, everything is turned topsy-turvy. Those who seemed to be the defeated will, in fact, be vindicated. There will be a change of status so drastic that new names will be needed to describe the protagonists. Those who were called "Forsaken" will be called "My Delight"; those who were described as "Desolate" will now be described as "Married" (Isa. 62:4). The image of marriage is invoked to illustrate the dramatic shift of fortunes, due in this case to the power of God. From loneliness to companionship; from isolation to love; from sorrow to rejoicing. Indeed, "as the bridegroom rejoices over the bride, so shall your God rejoice over you" (Isa. 62:5).

This recurring theme of unexpectedness, of sudden reversal, is further underlined in the remaining passages (Luke 5:1–11; John 21: 1–14). Both scenes are by the side of the lake, and both involve the fisherfolk who gathered around Jesus. The Lucan passage describes his initial relationship to them; the Johannine passage describes their final contact with one another. And both center on unexpectedness. In both passages, the fishermen have been down on their luck, and at a word from Jesus a huge catch is made. The first time around, Peter is staggered by this intrusion into his tidy universe. He knew there were no fish out there—and yet there were. So he tells Jesus to go away: "Depart from me!" Who wants a tidy universe unhinged? The second time, they all share the fish together, but again Peter's universe is unhinged; this time there is an abrupt shift from judgment to forgiveness.

There is one other interesting thing about these two final passages. In both of them, the messianic visitation comes right in the midst of where people carry on their daily life and work. Where is the Messiah to be found? Where does the Messiah find us? Not necessarily "in church." Not necessarily in the midst of a so-called religious experience. Not necessarily in some time of retreat and spiritual fervor. Where? Right in the midst of the daily routine, right in the midst of catching fish or failing to catch fish, right in the midst of tidying up the living room, right in the midst of working out a real estate transaction, right in the midst of riding the subway, right in the midst of the ordinary things we do. Who would have thought it so? Aren't Messiahs supposed to be so special that their presence can be discovered only under unusual circumstances? Apparently not. If we miss the presence of the Messiah it may only be because we are looking in the wrong places.

What kind of Messiah has come? These passages, cumulatively, tell us to acknowledge the Messiah on his terms rather than ours: namely, as an advocate of the poor and dispossessed who struggle for justice, not simply with their own resources, but with the stamp of the Spirit of the Lord upon them. We are also told that in the midst of apparent ruin, rebuilding is already going on; that the Messiah isn't the private property of religious people like us, but disturbingly universal in his promises and demands; that all of this comes in ways that will amaze us and cause us to rethink everything we had taken for granted; and that it will be right in the midst of where we are that the incursion of newness begins.

BIBLIOGRAPHY

Brown, Robert McAfee. *Theology in a New Key.* Westminster Press, 1978. See especially Ch. 3, on biblical interpretation.

—————. *Gustavo Gutiérrez.* John Knox Press, 1980. On ways in which new views of God's workings impact our understanding of the world.

Cassidy, Richard J. *Jesus, Politics, and Society: A Study of Luke's Gospel.* Orbis Books, 1978. Delivers what the title promises.

Niebuhr, Reinhold. *The Nature and Destiny of Man.* Vol. II. Charles
    Scribner's Sons, 1943. Helpful on the theme of the difference between the
    Messiah who was expected and the Messiah who came. See especially
    Chs. I and II.
Pixley, George V. *God's Kingdom: A Guide for Bible Study.* Orbis Books,
    1981. Relates Jesus and "the Jesus movement" to first-century hopes for
    change.

3

JESUS' LIFE-STYLE SERMON
AND PRAYER

John H. Yoder

Sermon on the Mount and Plain (including the Lord's Prayer, its personal and political significance)	Deut. 30:15–20 Lev. 19:1–2, 17–18 Job 23:1–7 Jer. 17:5–10	Matt. 5; 6:7–15, 19–34 Luke 6:17–49 (cf. Matt. 7)

It is customary to designate as the "Sermon on the Mount" chs. 5–7 of Matthew, which are presented as one uninterrupted discourse, the first block of such material to be reported at the beginning of Jesus' ministry. Luke 6:17–49, a much briefer passage containing parallel material, is designated as the "Sermon on the Plain." This discourse in Luke also stands as a kind of "platform" statement at the beginning of Jesus' public ministry. We shall be analyzing five fragments of this material, looking at both the Matthean and Lucan versions, *not* to lift from them a catalog of sample statements about proper behavior (although such specimens are given), but rather to see these examples as representative of the mentality and the world vision within which Jesus calls his disciples to a new style of life.

The entire text has come to be the most dramatic specimen of the way in which the presence of Jesus reverses all the otherwise dominant value patterns of a society. For the past century, the understanding of this text in the West has been under the impact of the simple literal argument of Leo Tolstoy, whose intellectual and spiritual conversion came about by taking this text seriously and seeing in it a condemnation of the moral laxity and betrayal of Christendom. In a host of ways, interpreters since Tolstoy have circled around the text, proposing alternative ways to understand its simplicity. We cannot in this connection even survey the variety of reinterpretations that make the meaning more spiritual and more distant, more idealistic, or more symbolic. But we can be warned when we see all this reinterpretation.

This text of the Sermon being neither parabolic nor poetic, our goal should be the most straightforward interpretation possible. We therefore need to direct a special suspicion to traditions of interpretation whose intent or effect is to divert our attention from taking these words of Jesus as a call to us, here and now.

A text we know is most likely to speak to us tomorrow if it says something it did not say yesterday. So it is the interpreter's task to turn a suspicious eye to any well-established convention of interpretation, even the best-intentioned. For this reason the headings of this article are phrased in a tone of critical disentanglement.

I. THE BEATITUDES AND WOES *(Matt. 5:3–11; Luke 6:20–26)*: WHAT JESUS DOES NOT MEAN WHEN HE SAYS THAT THE POOR ARE BLESSED

The hearer's first mental reflex is to transpose "Blessed are those who . . ." into some form of "You ought to be . . ." So Jesus would be promising us God's reward if we would do the right kinds of things and be the right kind of people. Then the Beatitudes would be simply a backhanded oriental way of saying, "These are eight basic virtues."

But that will not work. The things of which Jesus says "Blessed are those who . . ." are not all things that one can by an act of will set out to do. One does not make oneself poor or make oneself thirsty for righteousness, or make oneself mourn, or even make oneself pure in heart. Jesus is describing a set of ways of being, or states, or conditions in which people already find themselves. He is not saying, "If you become thus, you will get a reward for it." He is saying, "There are some people who are already thus: good for them."

The Greek term *makarios,* which is translated "blessed," does not apply to people who are praised or people who get a reward for achievement, but to people who are fortunate, even "lucky." So the reversal of values that the kingdom brings is described in terms of the reversal of the categories of people who will be well off as the kingdom comes. Those who are poor will be well off, because in the great reversal they shall be provided for. Those who mourn will be consoled. And to fill in the contrasts from Luke's version, those who are rich will lose their wealth.

The presupposition of all this is that the coming of the kingdom whose approach Jesus has just announced (Matt. 4:17, "Repent, for the kingdom of heaven is at hand") is something socially real.

To repent, as the exchanges between the John the Baptist and his listeners had already made clear, means not only to confess one's sinfulness, or to be remorseful about one's failures, but to change one's pattern of life in order to reflect a change of worlds or of lords. So the presupposition of the Beatitudes is the proclamation of the kingdom. The Beatitudes are good news because of the kingdom. They are the gospel.

Some people are poor: good for them, for the kingdom is coming and they shall receive it as their inheritance.

Some people are peacemakers: good for them, because in the coming kingdom it will be manifest that they are like God their Parent.

Some people are meek: good for them, for in the coming kingdom their kind will be in charge.

Some of you are rich: too bad for you; you have had all you will get.

The counter-cultural newness and the concrete realism of the good news of the kingdom inaugurate a new age in which things are true that were not true before. Jesus is not merely bringing to the surface some profound common sense about how people can get along better with each other. He is not merely raising by a degree or two the intensity of the general moral idealism with which all good people try, when they can, to be a little more loving. Nor is he escalating the divine demand in an intentionally unrealistic way in order to make us all recognize that we are sinners. For none of those purposes was a Messiah needed.

Jesus is bringing to pass in his person the newness of the age in which God's righteousness is operative among those who hear it proclaimed. The reversal of values is not first of all new information or new potential or new motivation on the moral level: it is first of all a whole new world, in which this radically different style of relating to others "comes naturally."

The "social theme" with which we are to begin is not new information about the good society, nor new motivation to set about building it, but rather the Word that the kingdom is upon us. Is it thinkable that we might take guidance in daily life from another social system than the one we see in place?

II. LOVE OF THE ENEMY *(Matt. 5:38–48; Luke 6:27–36):* WHAT JESUS DOES NOT MEAN IN SAYINGS THAT BEGIN, "BUT I SAY TO YOU"

Some interpreters of the Sermon on the Mount have taken it as the central expression of a fundamental contradiction between the morality of the Old Testament and that of the New. Such an interpretation is understandable, since there are differences between the two Testaments, and since some of them have to do partly with the structures of social justice: with nationhood and the state, violence and the offender. But it would be a mistake to read the six contrasts between the Old and the New, the last two of which are on the subject of violence and the enemy, as if they were meant to dramatize a polarity between the Testaments.

It is said explicitly in the introductory paragraph (Matt. 5:17ff.) that Jesus' intent is "not to destroy but to fulfill" the real meaning of the law. Each of the six specimens, in a different way, exemplifies how the Old is not rejected but radicalized or deepened or clarified in the application made by Jesus. The prescription of the former law, "an eye for an eye and a tooth for a tooth" had not meant so much that vengeance is divinely demanded as that such retaliation as is demanded by the aggrieved and permitted by law must be limited to the measure of the offense and no more. It is this restraining intent which Jesus "fills full" as he sets aside all vengeance and illustrates the abandonment of that kind of response to conflict with the counter strategy of the other cheek and the second mile.

Similarly the commandment to love the neighbor is in no way modified by the Sermon on the Mount; Jesus simply universalizes its meaning by including even the enemy in the category of the "neighbors" to be loved. (The word "neighbor" here, as in most other languages, means anyone with whom we have to do, the representative other person with whom we are dealing, and not a person especially close to us.) There is no person to whom neighbor love does not apply. Specifically the enemy becomes the test of whether our love for neighbor is authentic. Loving those who are close to us is characterized as the morality of "sinners" or "the Gentiles."

The life-style that Jesus rejects is thus not selfishness in the sense of a failure to love anyone, so that the devotion of someone who makes a sacrifice on behalf of posterity or client or nation should be praised as virtuous. The most destructive kinds of selfishness, especially on the level of institutional injustice, are those that have their root in the claim to be altruistic: i.e., that need in the name of some cause, some victim, some human solidarity, to exclude another person or category of people from one's loving concern. The more clear we are that our own intentions are just, that they constitute "rights," or that the hostilities in which we are involved are on behalf of some legitimate victim, the more unquestioning we become about the unworthy means we are ready to use for that higher cause.

It would take little moral profundity to reject purely personal selfishness. What Jesus rejects is every ground for dealing with a fellow human being as if he or she were an exception to the obligation to love. This does not mean, in some idealistic way, saying that we have no enemies or refusing to recognize them as such. It means just the opposite: we are to name the relationship as one of enmity and then to express love within it.

III. Imitation of the Father *(Matt. 5:45, 48; Luke 6:35–36):* What Jesus Does Not Mean by "Be Perfect" and "Love Your Enemies"

The thought that we might be like God the Father is not a frequent one in the New Testament. Small wonder that it has seemed shocking or frightening, so that efforts to interpret such a simple and sweeping phrase have gone in several directions.

One meaning of "Christian perfection" has seen it as a distant target, to be achieved only at the end of a lengthy process of growth and self-discipline whereby the seeker after perfection develops character, sets aside lesser values, and lives only for God and God's cause in a growing wholeness of consecration. Such understandings of perfection have been at home especially in the religious life in mysticism and in the literature of devotion, both Catholic and Protestant.

Another view, more widely represented in middle America, sees "perfection" not as the end of a long process of human effort but as a unique gift of divine grace offered to those who will accept it in faith. The position is represented in those denominations called "Wesleyan," amid continuing debate about how clearly and whether John Wesley, the founder of Methodism, really meant this kind of experience by what he called "perfection."

The two models just named have in common with the evident meaning of the teaching of Jesus that they try to describe something that is possible. The third classical Protestant approach is to see in this text an impossible demand: Jesus calls us precisely to do what he knows we cannot do. He demands of us that we be flawless, sinless. He demands it not because he expects it but because he knows it to be unattainable. He wants to leave us no excuse or escape before the humiliating recognition of our sinfulness. The purpose of moral teaching generally, and therefore also of the Sermon on the Mount, is not first to instruct us but to condemn us, bringing us to our knees, driving us to recognize that we can be acceptable before God only by grace.

Each of these interpretations of "perfection" is solidly rooted somewhere else in the thought and piety of the people who then bring it into this passage. In this text, when taken straightforwardly, the context makes evident that to be "perfect" is something far more simple and, although not easy, not impossible by definition. We are called to be nondiscriminatory in our love just as God does not discriminate. Discriminating in favor of those to whom we are closer is something which the Gentiles, the tax collectors, the sinners do; the contrast is with God, whose benevolence aids the evil and the good (Matt. 5:46), whose generosity is extended to the "ungrateful and the selfish" (Luke 6:35).

Most of our discussions of social justice center upon the debates about what is a desirable goal and who should lead us toward it. Jesus asks a prior question: For whom do we want what we want? Whose welfare do we seek to serve? Do we recognize a moral priority to the needs and claims of our adversaries in the social system? If not, we do not initiate the search for social justice where Jesus does, namely, at the point of the fundamental flaw in our community. That flaw is not that food is scarce, nor that every individual is selfish. It is that we have acquiesced in a truncated understanding of community, according to which certain adversaries are excluded from the range of our mercy.

One of the reasons that the misunderstanding identified above could persist was the tendency in our culture to see love as an emotion whose grasp upon us is prerational, a given kind of empathy or bond with a claim on our sentiments, powerful to move our decisions toward the needs of those whom we "love." The romantic or erotic understandings of love as an irrational drive are only the extreme forms of this. Familial and cultural, ethical and national forms make the same kinds of claim: they affirm a loyalty that is not reasoned but given, a loyalty that by its very nature is part of a wider social self, rather than including adversaries. What Jesus says is not that we have or should cultivate that kind of "love," in the sense of an emotional attitude toward people with whom we have nothing human in common. It is that we should (and can) seek their welfare and serve their needs, whoever they be.

IV. DOXOLOGY AND FORGIVENESS
AS SOCIAL POWER *(Matt. 6:9–15; Luke 11:2–4):*
WHAT IT MEANS NOT TO HEAP UP EMPTY PHRASES

When we lift the "Our Father" or "Lord's Prayer" out of the text of the Sermon on the Mount and take it simply as a standard outline for prayer in common worship, we get the impression of a series of seven requests, each of them meaningful in its own right, but with no special internal connections among them except that they begin with the honor of God and end with our needs. Closer attention, however, gives us a much less scattered impression, and focuses far more upon a commitment to concrete righteousness on the part of the one who prays.

Jewish thought holds that since the revelation of God's holiness had been received most adequately in the form of gracious commands (Torah), therefore to recognize and proclaim the holiness of God is not an action of mere cultic adoration or mystical contemplation. To sanctify the name, to proclaim the holiness of God, is most fittingly to obey God. Especially it means to obey God in a context where obedience has to be a matter of costly choice. "To sanctify the Name" became, in later Jewish thought, the standard designation for martyrdom.

When we take account of the place of parallelism in Hebrew prayer and poetry, we see that the first three "you" petitions probably should be interpreted as three different facets of the same thing. That God's name is sanctified, that God's kingdom comes, and that God's

will is done on earth as in heaven are three formulations of the same
reality for which we pray. Then, instead of a not-very-clearly structured sequence of scattered notions, we have a massive affirmation
that the one thing we ask for globally, as topic sentence or superscrip-
tion of the entire prayer, is the doing of God's will among us, which
is itself the way for "the Name" (Godself) to be glorified. The prayer
(together with the other words of Jesus about prayer in the context,
which are not part of our lectionary scope) turns its back on worshiping God through inner contemplation and ritual ceremony, in favor of
concretely lived out holiness.

Like his listeners and like Matthew, Jesus assumed—as we do not
since the cultural triumph of monotheism—that God's control of history is contested. When addressed to the victorious Sovereign of the
universe and of Christendom, the petition "May your name be sanctified, may your will be done" seems to be asking for something to
happen which can hardly help happening: thus prayer becomes sub-
mitting to and lining oneself up with the way things are. But in Jesus'
world, God's sovereignty is not yet confirmed and God's name is not
yet hallowed. The other gods are still around, and are apparently
winning. To pray, "Your name be hallowed, your will be done" is not
an acceptance of evident reality, not the liturgical celebration of a
settled cosmology, but a battle cry. It is a word of hope in defiance
of the powers.

The first "us" petition directed toward ourselves acknowledges our
dependence upon God to meet our need for bread: a theme to which
Jesus returns later in Matthew 6. The second petition is unique in the
prayer in that it is conditional. There the forgiveness requested corresponds to the forgiveness we have extended to others. This is also
the only portion of the prayer to be commented upon afterward by
Jesus (vs. 14–15). The same point is made as well in Luke 6:37 and in
much of Matthew 18. The duty constantly to forgive is linked directly
with our confession of our own constant need for forgiveness.

Translators and commentators have not yet finished discussing
whether the forgiveness in question is most fittingly understood as
beginning with concrete financial obligations and then extending by
analogy to other offenses and kinds of guilt or "trespass," or whether
it should be the other way around. In either case it is central that
everyone who prays is committing herself or himself to live from and
toward a quality of relationships in which one can be free from the
bondage of past obligations and offenses. Not all debts have to be
paid by me or to me: not all offenses need to be avenged or punished.
We accept from God the grace of remission, and we commit ourselves
to live out that grace as we relate to those who have incurred obligations toward us. It is not enough then to see in this prayer a petition
for social *justice:* it is even more a petition for and commitment to
social *grace,* to liberation from obligations actually incurred through

our weakness and guilt and need. Already in the psalms the pious Hebrews had praised God for not remembering our trespasses: Jesus' disciples commit themselves to be instruments of that same quality of gracious forgetfulness. Does this have something to say about society's treatment of offenders?

The other major theme of the prayer is protection from temptation. The petition is not that we may be made strong to face temptation successfully, but that we be saved from testing. There is no interest in braving the tempter's power, no sense that moral character would be formed or demonstrated by flirting with the edges of evil.

In the Greek one cannot distinguish between "evil thing" and "evil one." Although most translations have favored the former, it might well be that the latter is meant. This would again make two sentences more nearly parallel: "Do not lead us into a time of trial; save us from the tempter." This petition acknowledges vulnerability and dependence in a world predisposed to foster our disobedience.

One last observation is as profound as it is formal. The prayer is consistently in the plural. We pray together for *our* bread and *our* forgiveness and *our* protection from temptation. The agent of Christian petition is the community, not the lonely soul or the moral hero. Likewise then, the sanctifying of the name and the doing of his will on earth as in heaven are collective activities as we pray for and do them.

V. SEEK FIRST THE KINGDOM *(Matt. 6:25–34; Luke 12:22–31):* HOW NOT TO TAKE NO THOUGHT FOR THE MORROW

The concrete meaning of the warnings against preoccupation with material security has been likewise rendered less accessible by some of the short-circuited ways it has been read, sometimes in order to be applied sincerely and sometimes in order to be set aside as utopian. Since the birds and the flowers are fed without their thinking about it, and since the Old Testament reports that the prophet Elijah was once fed by ravens, there are those who think that Jesus was promising some kind of nature miracle as an alternative to sober economic planning. Then obviously such "trust in God" would not be something we could reproduce in our culture. But that was not his point.

The concrete and credible meaning of Jesus' words was confirmed by the life of the circle of disciples who had literally left economic security behind and were already experiencing material support from the common fund. Already in this life, Jesus later told them (Mark 10:29ff.), those who forsake other communities and securities find in the kingdom fellowship new possession and new families. Thus the first impact of the promise that the morrow will take care of itself needs to be the admonition to us to make real among us the new economic solidarity of those who consider nothing their own and who share according to need.

The further logical analysis of what it means to trust God for survival is pointed up by the parallel, already accentuated by Leo Tolstoy and Reinhold Niebuhr, between the renunciation of selfish economic security in Matthew 6 and the renunciation of violence toward the enemy in Matthew 5. Both chapters contain examples of renouncing the habit of thinking from a perspective of control of the situation for good, and the habit of beginning with one's own rights. The most entrenched defenses of inequitable social systems in our time are not the unabashed selfishness of criminal types, but consciously justified "legitimate self-concern" and the assignment to oneself of the responsibility to make sure that things do not come out still worse, whereby people claiming to do justice maintain things the way they are because something else would be worse. "Taking thought for the morrow" is the claim that it is one's right or one's duty to exercise control over others—control first of all over the social system, and therefore control over other persons—in the name of a relative justice which is better than something else one fears, and in which, not so incidentally, one's own rights will be taken care of first.

A pietist or a prescientific social thinker would say more simply that this means not trusting God. A more sophisticated social analyst in our time would add that it means not trusting other people, not trusting to dialogue and conflict resolution and due process; claiming instead that one has no choice but to manipulate, to use nondialogical power, and to accumulate and preserve one's own economic advantage at the cost of wider sharing. "Taking thought for the morrow" is what some call "an ethic of responsibility." We must control events because God won't. Its basic moral mood is utilitarian. It puts security above solidarity. It privileges one's own party in calculating the common good.

Thereby we have backed into a functional definition of what "trusting God" would mean in concrete social terms. It would mean that our calculations of the common good would not begin by privileging one's own perspective, and would not be used to assign to oneself or to one's party the authority to impose one's vision or one's rights on others by authority or superior power. To trust God is then to trust to dialogue and due process, repentance and the common search. Does this have something to say about economic justice and "national security"?

There is a deep commonality between the daring to share that is enjoined for the disciples' economic life and the love for enemy that is commended in the realm of conflict. Both risk themselves at the hand of open process over which one is ready to relinquish control. Proclamation and prayer derived from the coming of the kingdom give reason to trust that such renunciation is not going to be generally suicidal. The heralding of the kingdom (Matt. 3:2; 4:17; 10:7) and the commitment in prayer to its coming (Matt. 6:10) change the calculation of common good. They do not replace sober calculation with blind faith, or social analysis with unthinking obedience. They place realism in a framework of faith and hope.

BIBLIOGRAPHY

Crosby, Michael H., O.F.M. Cap. *Spirituality of the Beatitudes: Matthew's Challenge to First World Christians.* Orbis Books, 1981.

————. *Thy Will Be Done: Praying the Our Father, as Subversive Activity.* Orbis Books, 1977.

Davies, W. D. *The Setting of the Sermon on the Mount.* Cambridge University Press, 1964. Also published in paperback under the less precise title *The Sermon on the Mount,* Cambridge University Press, 1966.

Hunter, Archibald M. *Design for Life.* London: SCM Press, 1953.

Jeremias, Joachim. *The Sermon on the Mount,* "Facet" Biblical Studies Series. Fortress Press, 1963.

McArthur, Harvey. *Understanding the Sermon on the Mount.* London: Epworth Press, 1961.

Minear, Paul S. "The Bible's Authority in the Congregation," *Theology Today,* Vol. 38, No. 3 (Oct. 1981), pp. 350–356. Examines the petitions of the Lord's Prayer.

Tolstoy, Leo. *What I Believe.* Many editions; Oxford University Press, World Classics, No. 229.

4

FOOLS IN CHRIST

Dorothee Soelle

God's Foolishness	I Cor. 1:10 to 2:10
God's Yes; Christ's Aroma	II Cor. 1:18–22; 2:14–16
Servants of Christ and Stewards of God's Mysteries	I Cor. 3:16 to 4:5
Against Immorality (Disciplined Freedom)	I Cor. 6:12–20; 7:29–35; 8:1–13; 9:16–27
	II Cor. 3:1–6, 17–18; 4:1–2
Spiritual Gifts	I Cor. 10:23 to 11:1
	I Cor. 12 and 13

According to Paul, our faith rests "not on human wisdom but on God's power" (I Cor. 2:5). How can we hear this message in a liberating, life-changing way? What is wrong with "human wisdom"? In which sense do we need to be freed from it?

My method of interpretation entails a four-step process of praxis/analysis/meditation/renewed praxis. Since I prefer biblical over hermeneutical-technical language, I call these four steps: (1) To see the Cross. (2) To recognize the Principalities and Powers. (3) To remember the Resurrection. (4) To take up one's bed and walk. An irreversible dynamic occurs in the process of these four steps and, again, "dynamic" is a secular word for what we might better call the Spirit who moves in these phases and transcends where we are and who we are.

Whereas traditional theology starts with the Word in the text, liberation theology starts with the context of our lives, our experiences, our hopes and fears, our "praxis." This is not to deny but to make room for the power of the text and its spiritual quality.

I. To See the Cross

In order to understand our own praxis, we have to listen and to see and to feel. None of it is given. The description has to touch the depth of our feelings. The first question to ask about our praxis is: "Who is

victimized?" Our concern, our worrying, becomes visible in the process. We have to expose ourselves personally and to increase our
vulnerability. The goal of the first step is to make us see the cross.

Christians in the First World have developed a specific form of
division and separation from the human family. I conceive the concept of "apartheid" not only as a political concept of racial separation
in South Africa but as a spiritual concept as well that permeates the
institutions and the lives of First World people. Even our theology is
stained by our living in apartheid because of the simple fact that we
do not allow our brothers and sisters from the Third World to enter
our thoughts and feelings, our singing and praying, our reading of
Scripture, and our theologizing. We use our ideas about family life
and privacy in order to hide ourselves from those we exploit. Living
in the rich countries of the First World means to participate in apartheid through life-style and ideology. How can we move from apartheid to faith?

Our lives have deepest meaning in the overcoming of divisions and
separations. Every created being seeks unification and suffers unconsciously or consciously under divisions, even more so if he or she has
encountered Jesus Christ. The most fundamental divisions in the
church are based on worldly, namely socioeconomic, conditions.
How can we talk about the undivided love of God if we are rich and
become richer at the cost of the poor? How can we give our lives
totally to God's life in the world if we don't allow our vision to
interfere with the dividing powers that be? How can we talk about
unity while our government increases the annihilation potential that
divides the human community into first strikers and second strikers
with a deep death wish and a desire to annihilate the so-called
enemy?

We must "become fools in order to grow wise; for the wisdom of
this world is folly in God's sight" (I Cor. 3:18–19). Paul understood the
wisdom of this world as a philosophical system with diverging
schools but united in support of the prevailing social and economic
order. In Paul's time the name of the order was Pax Romana. It is
impossible to understand any of Paul's writings without an awareness of the real-life conditions of those who lived under the Pax
Romana—the taxed, subjected populace in the provinces under the
Empire's control.

The Pax Romana was a worldwide system that shaped the life-
style of any person subjected to it. Rome was the geopolitical center
of this "peace," as the order was named by those who profited from
it. In the Empire's center there was material abundance and super-
fluity, an unlimited greediness for new merchandise and pleasures.
The corrupt life-style fostered psychological emptiness.

On the periphery of this world in the faraway dominated provinces
there was misery and poverty. The population there, with the excep-

tion of the Romanized elite, was in dire want for the simple necessities, such as water, shelter, and food, not to mention work, health, and education. Psychologically an apathetic helplessness prevailed —a fatalism that is the dark background for what Jesus calls "faith." Jesus' parable of the workers in the vineyard (Matt. 20:1–16), who wait all day long to be hired, precisely mirrors the situation of the poor under Roman domination. Many other texts of the New Testament talk about these landless, propertyless masses, about their hunger and their diseases. Pax Romana means an extreme division between the rich and the impoverished, enforced by legal and military means. When Paul talks about "this" world, we have to picture this sort of misery and unfreedom.[6]

The "wisdom" of the world of the Roman Empire does not care for the poor. It is essentially apartheid wisdom that makes the poor invisible. Roman militarism protected the rich from the enemies on the outside, and Roman wisdom offered a philosophical internal protection that kept those who enjoyed the system blind. But Paul spoke of faith that rests on "divine strength" (I Cor. 2:5), not on intellectual neutrality. The Spirit gives the faithful "God's secret wisdom," which to the powers that be remains nonsense (I Cor. 2:6–16).

My earlier reading of the theme was mainly philosophical. Being a student of theology, I felt confused by the polemical tone against wisdom in this text and I felt puzzled about God's being "foolish." I loved v. 9, though, because of its mystical quality and because of Johann Sebastian Bach's hymn "Wachet auf, ruft uns die Stimme." Quite unconsciously, I overlooked v. 8, which speaks so clearly about the efficiency of the Pax Romana. The hermeneutic I was then using excluded the sociopolitical reality. The idealistic tradition of thought had made me blind to the social and political aspects I now see more clearly.

One of the suggestions of modern learning theory is that we learn only when we unlearn. *Learning the cross means unlearning apartheid.* We unlearn our own apartheid ideology when we learn to read our reality in the light of the crosses by which we are surrounded.

II. To Recognize the Principalities and Powers

When we listen to the cry that comes out of praxis we develop a need for the best available analysis. The second hermeneutical step is to understand, to identify the causes—to name the Beast. The analytical question then becomes: "Who profits?" The literary form is the socioeconomic analysis. We move from the personal experience to the institutional pattern. We make use of other materials and broaden our experiential understanding. We ground our understanding in the depth of the historical process. We begin to recognize the principalities and powers.

"The Bible is a book of hope, concern and solidarity with the poor," as the World Council of Churches' Development Commission reminds us. "Reading the Bible from the perspective of the poor must be stimulated. Many Christian communities, renewed by the Holy Spirit through their openness to the challenge presented by the poor, point to the Bible as crucial for their self-understanding. Despite conflicts of interpretation that sometimes arise when the scriptures are read from the perspective of the needy and oppressed, only in this way can the Bible become the liberating Word of God for those who are living in the base of human society."[7]

The analysis we need is different from a Greek search for wisdom (I Cor. 1:18ff.), which is neutral and above any call to action. If we preach the crucified Christ and discover his cross among the campesinos who are tortured and executed, our proclamation has a different quality than wisdom. It drives us to understand our own imprisonment and it leads us to change our lives. The rich countries live in a permanent and relentless war against the poor nations. During the last twenty years the profit-centered economy has proved its incompetence to deal with the problem of hunger. Instead of feeding the hungry, we in the First World arm ourselves against them. Under the pretext of the east-west conflict, we escalate the arms race as the major dynamism in the north-south conflict.

There is no unification, because there already is war now. "The bombs are falling now," as Mobilization for Survival, a U.S. peace group, states. Militarism protects multinational capitalism, which uses racism and sexism as helpmates. The new political doctrine of national security, instead of stressing an international balance of deterrence, underlines the global master plan of the Trilateral Commission, which consists in: unity by silencing the oppressed, peace without justice, suppression and regulation of those who thirst for justice. There is the "fatal aroma that brings death" or "a deadly fume that kills" around Caesar's imperium (II Cor. 2:16). Christians are the catalysts who bring out the odor!

To the scientific observer the talk about the crosses around us is of no specific relevance. "For the message of the cross is sheer folly to those on their way to destruction" (I Cor. 1:18). This is more true today than at any other time in human history because of the role of scientific productive force, with its suicidal attacks on the human race and its search for better methods of overkill. In God's eyes, this world's wisdom is foolish (I Cor. 1:20–21). The text points to the principalities and powers of the military-industrial complex right before our eyes. Around 30 million people work for the armaments industry, 20 million work in the armies, and more than 400,000 scientists and technicians work for the laboratories of armaments industries.

Those who don't work for death, don't believe in death, don't pay for death, and don't prepare the nuclear holocaust—those peace minorities are considered to be fools. But this leads to the third step of our hermeneutical journey through the text.

III. To Remember the Resurrection

The narrative and the analysis together constitute the context. We should withstand the temptation of leaping too early into the text, which then would be a "leaning on the everlasting arms" without foundation in the historical and institutional realities. In order to dialogue with the Word of God and the praxis of the prophets and Jesus, we need the clearest possible understanding of our own praxis. When we delve deep enough into our own situation, we reach a point where theological reflection becomes necessary. We then have to "theologize" the given situation. We read the context so long (steps I and II) that it cries out for theology. As we go deeply enough into our own sociohistorical context, we become aware of our need for prayer, for hope, for stories of people who have been liberated. We discover the inner necessity of theology in a given situation of human anguish that has potential for unfolding theological meaning. We have to reach this point of no return where we learn anew that we do need God. We come to this theological point through worldly analysis of our situation.

The third step is meditation. The verb is "to remember." We read the Bible out of our thirst for justice. We search in Scripture and tradition for help. We look for those parts of the tradition which at least speak to our despair. The literary form now is exegesis, and the goal is to "re-member" ourselves; to remember that we are children of Life and not of Death. We remember the resurrection—God's power and wisdom in the crucified-risen Christ (I Cor. 1:22–25; 15:24ff.).

Who is the crucified Christ to us? How is the crucified rabbi of Nazareth related to the crucified Christ? And who else is related to this Christ of faith? As Martin Luther said, we must tug or draw Christ into the flesh—and he meant historical flesh, i.e., into what is happening to people today. When Luther uses this expression, he directs it polemically against those who do not want to bring Christ into the concrete day-to-day flesh, but who spiritualize him instead, so that Christ has nothing to do with the peasants' sons and daughters tortured to death in El Salvador today. To draw him into flesh means to bring him down out of the abstract, the remote, the merely pondered, into the reality that is ours to live.

But if we try to do this, we will run into some difficulty with Paul's text. At least I stumble over the famous v. 22 in I Corinthians 1. Maybe I am as critical as Paul is of the Greek search for wisdom; but I do need "signs." Signs have to do with flesh, with experience, with

visibility. There is a deep desire for signs in any group or congregation. I doubt whether without this thirst we could be Christians. Why
then is Paul critical of the Jewish request for signs? Is this not early
anti-Judaism which finally led to anti-Semitism? The danger of
spiritualizing the gospel is more clear to us now than it could be to
Paul. We do not want to separate our faith from its Jewish roots. Can
we live in hope and with faith without some crumbs of bread, some
occasional visibility, some signs of God's kingdom today?

Obviously Paul was overwhelmed by the one great sign, namely,
Christ's resurrection. But we need to see more of this resurrection
than just one empty grave two thousand years ago, and to do more
than resign ourselves heroically to the dark night of Good Friday we
are living through. Dialoguing with Paul about the question of his own
Jewishness, I would ask him about signs of Life, right here. Getting
into a theological dialogue with Paul makes me aware of my own
needs and teaches me to pray.

The lectionary reading on God's foolishness ends with a reference
to the fathoming, revealing Spirit (I Cor. 2:10). Paul's own Jewishness
and need for "signs" comes in again by the back door through the
Spirit. If we pray for the Spirit, we pray for signs. If the scientific mind
needs proof and uses falsification criteria, fools in Christ need signs
and stories. To give an example: The hunger strike of Bolivian mothers and wives for the jobless miners in 1977–78 ended with a victory:
the government released fifty-two political prisoners and gave in to
the demands of the miners. This is a "sign," not a proof. It sustains
our hope, it encourages us, it does what the Spirit always does. But
it is not a formula for hunger strikers, nor a generally applicable
strategy.

IV. To Take Up One's Bed and Walk

How then does it happen that "God's folly surpasses human wisdom and God's weakness surpasses human strength" (I Cor. 1:25)?
The fourth step on our way from human wisdom to divine strength
is a renewed praxis. What the theologian should learn here is to
dream and to hope. Our imagination has been freed from original
sinful bondage, and we are empowered to envision alternative institutions. We become agents of change. Prayer and action become our
doing. The literary form is now the creative envisioning. We find new
language.

Only this last step accomplishes the text and makes us both readers and "writers" of the Bible. We say to each other, "Take up your
bed and walk," which is a necessary step in any liberation theology.
"People should regard us as servants of Christ and stewards of God's
mysteries. The prime requisite of stewards is fidelity" (I Cor. 4:1–2).
We are fellow workers in God's service (I Cor. 3:9). If the deepest

mystery is God's foolishness, our acting has to share the same quality.

What does it mean to be a fool in Christ today? It means resistance.
Ignazio Silone writes: "We are saved today by freeing our spirit from
resignation to the existing disorder. Spiritual life has always meant
a capacity for sacrifice. In a society like ours a spiritual life can only
be a revolutionary life."

The existing disorder corresponds to the prevailing unbelief. The
existing disorder means to rape the earth, to lead a war of annihilation against the poor, to betray the spirit through the godless dream
of individualism, to disconnect the people from each other. The most
natural response to these facts is resignation to the existing disorder.
Many people do not consider faith to be an alternative because of the
ambivalence of the established churches on all of these issues.

A conscientious spiritual response to these facts is possible, however. It is a response that comes out of a different vision of life,
handed down to us from the biblical tradition, and a more daring
interference with the powers that be. It seems that from the side of
the citizen of the First World the concept of resistance becomes more
and more relevant toward the end of the twentieth century. "Trust in
God and resist" becomes the new imperative. To create resistance
groups inside the belly of the beast is the missionary task. To follow
Christ at least up to Gethsemane—if not, as some have done, to
Golgotha—is the way.

The historical situation in Europe changed when NATO decided,
in December 1979, to "go nuclear." There is no way to have an unchanged theological situation; the first mission commandment of
Jesus was given when he sent the disciples out with the message,
"The kingdom of heaven is at hand." The following imperatives are
rules for resisters today: "Heal the sick, raise the dead, cleanse lepers, cast out demons" (Matt. 10:8). Those who do so are the true
followers of Jesus: they raise the dead apartheid folk, they conscien-
tize them, they cast out the demons of militarism. The church being
on the side of the resistance groups could provide them support and
encouragement. Churches then would understand themselves as civil
rights movements for peace and justice.

We have to unlearn our worldly apartheid wisdom and to learn
God's foolishness in the struggle. We have to unlearn our obsession
with power and success. Christ was a loser after all, in the same
sense as those who oppose more nuclear weapons development. I am
thinking of groups like the Women at the Pentagon; or the Plowshare
Eight, who destroyed two Mark 12 A warheads in a General Electric
plant at King of Prussia, Pennsylvania; or those who withhold 50
percent of their income taxes as an act of boycott for the sake of
peace.

In West Germany, church groups have circulated a statement entitled "To Live Without Weapons," which has already been signed by tens of thousands. The declaration states:

> I am prepared to live without the protection of military weapons. I wish to speak up in our state for the political development of peace without weapons . . .

Peace cannot be made by one nation or state alone. Christians who understand themselves in an ecumenical sense (must) think and behave irrespective of national borders. They learn to see others, not as capitalists or atheistic socialists, but as people beloved by God. They reduce anxiety and help to build trust. In no other way is peace possible.

There are different forms of resistance and noncooperation that express God's foolishness today, but the "no" to "this" world of murder and self-destruction is common to all the diverse groups. If we don't teach and live resistance as Jesus did, we will die, as victims of preemptive strikes, or psychically in the midst of our apartheid fortress.

Our goal is the unity of the church and of the human community. The Old Testament readings from Isaiah point to the unity of the church and the human family as a whole. But these readings are not just utopian dreams about a time after ours. We have to read them in the light of God's foolishness and not only in the light of wisdom's despair.

Christ unifies us, not as do conferences that create consensus out of compromise and exhaustion, but through the cross. The crosses we keep ourselves so busy to avoid come down on our neighbors. If we look for the spiritual reality grounded in Jesus Christ who loved all things and did so with his whole being, there is one way to find unification—namely, in the struggle, in the cross, in resistance.

BIBLIOGRAPHY

Brown, Robert McAfee. *Theology in a New Key.* Westminster Press, 1978.
Cardenal, Ernesto. *The Gospel in Solentiname.* 4 vols. Orbis Books, 1982.
Soelle, Dorothee. *Choosing Life.* Fortress Press, 1981.
————. *Beyond Mere Obedience.* Pilgrim Press, 1982.

B. A WHOLE APPROACH

EPIPHANY

Eunice Blanchard Poethig

Epiphany marks the dramatic moment when Christ confronts the world's darkness with light. The story of the Magi signals "Danger ahead" as God announces: "This is my Son"; "The kingdom is at hand"; "Follow me." The unsettling results are vividly spelled out in the Scriptures, and the implications of that revelation for the human family have been explored in the preceding essays. The texts for the Sundays after Epiphany are among the most widely used both in preaching and in Christian education. They call for a fundamental altering of our lives and a commitment to be a part of God's new people.

In the ancient Eastern church, the feast of Epiphany celebrated Christ's birth and baptism, and the coming of light into this world's darkness. When the feast was introduced into the Western church in the fourth century it became the feast of the Magi and the celebration of the mission to the Gentiles.

There is an advantage to the daily-life quality of church life in January and February, in the four to eight weeks after Epiphany. As churches prepare their year-end reports and hold their annual meetings, they might look at what they are doing in the light of Epiphany. The texts make clear Christ's "program" for ministry. They invite a congregation to set those words over against the social-political-ethical-spiritual realities of our times, reflect on its own involvement in these issues, act to resist evil, and join in the ways of salvation.

The New Testament readings in the lectionary provide the story line. They begin with Jesus as a revelation of God's good creation and of God's loving presence among the people of this earth. Epiphany texts make clear that in God's sight there are no distinctions that make some people clean and others unclean, nor differences that leave some people outside the circle of God's concern. The story line moves from the coming of the Magi, to Jesus' baptism by John, to the call of the first disciples and the beginning of Jesus' ministry. The readings include the lead stories from the four Gospels, each suggesting a distinctive way to understand the ministry of the Messiah.

The Old Testament readings are chosen to make clear the scriptural origins of the Messiah images and expectations and the specific customs and texts used in the New Testament readings. Old Testament and New Testament texts are paired to illustrate that Jesus fulfilled the promises made to the people of Israel.

The Epistle readings are a "book study" of I and II Corinthians over the three-year cycle. Although these readings are not specifically linked to the Gospel and Old Testament readings, they offer a look at issues in the early church and thereby provide a provocative contrast both to the Gospel story and to ours.

Epiphany and the social themes. Epiphany marks the recognition that Jesus came to all people. His mission (and therefore, ours) was also a "mission to the Gentiles." This is really an archaic way of saying that God made a world without barriers of hostility between people and that the church is expected to be a sign of that wholeness. Not only is the door open to welcome the Magi/strangers of the world who come to worship; the Messiah also walks the roads of Galilee where he can deal with local people, city priests, Roman soldiers, and Greek tourists.

As Walter Owensby shows, in being baptized by John, Jesus linked himself to the prophetic tradition. The announcement of the kingdom meant that a rule of righteousness was at hand. However, it was not to be economic and social justice only for Jews, or a time of international political or religious power. It was to be a time of peace for the human family.

But in his baptism Jesus was linked not only to the prophetic tradition but to the tradition of kingship in Israel. Prophets anointed kings with oil (I Kings 19:15–16) and God would take the king as son (II Sam. 7:14). It was the responsibility of the king to be righteous, and he had the power to be just. Jesus' baptism with water in the River Jordan also recalls Joshua, who led the new people of Israel across the Jordan into the Promised Land. Jesus, the new Joshua, would call a people into service in a new community.[8]

Jesus is the anointed one, the Messiah. But what kind of Messiah! Robert McAfee Brown describes the implausible combination of Messiah-as-servant, and bringer of justice for all nations. The difficulty people had with Jesus' form of messiahship is told in each Gospel's opening stories of Jesus' ministry. The reversal of expectations is made most explicit in the teachings found in the Sermon on the Mount in Matthew and their parallels in Luke. John H. Yoder points out the reversal of categories of those who will be well off in the kingdom. The most difficult concept of all is that no limits can be placed on love. Those who love best do not protect their own well-being through the use of the economic and political powers of society. They can ask only for daily bread, and God's forgiveness, and protection from temptation.

Such people are fools in Christ, says Dorothee Soelle in her essay on I and II Corinthians. The key to understanding how the wise of this world make decisions is to ask: Who profits from their decisions? Because of their separation from real communication with the poor of the world (a form of apartheid), the wise misuse their positions of privilege. The poor are pitted against the nuclear-fueled power of the wise. Fools in Christ provide signs and stories of resistance—and, therefore, hope.

MISSION TO THE GENTILES

Worship. Epiphany means not only that Christ is revealed to the world but that God is in the world revealing the world to us. It is in this world setting that we meet Christ. Multiple images of Christ combined with the strong Argentine rhythms of the tune of "We Meet You, O Christ"[9] make it clear that we mean a world of many nations and many life settings. Pablo Sosa, an Argentine musician burdened by love for his people, wrote the music while at a small gathering of international musicians and worship leaders at Bossey in Switzerland. An Epiphany feast can reduplicate that experience with an international dinner, the sharing of song and story from our many international neighbors and congregations of different social or racial makeup, and a service that recognizes that in the church there is no Jew or Gentile, only Christ's body.

Education. What does Christ look like? A group of Filipinos explored that question by looking over a collection of pictures of Messiah Jesus. First they chose Sallman's head of Christ, but further reflection led them away from that image. Finally they chose an abstract painting of a crown of thorns which somehow conveyed both the pain and the glory. They made this the center of a montage, surrounded it with other pictures, placing closest to the center those that they felt to be most important. One person insisted on including cutouts from the newspaper of faces she thought showed Christ. A Japanese Messiah was retained only on the outer edge because they knew they had to deal with that image, though it made them uneasy. A Filipino madonna was near the center. Forty-five minutes of choosing, rejecting, critiquing, and compromising had changed the images of Christ in the montage, and the images of Christ in the heart's eye of the participants. They could truly say, "We meet you, O Christ, in many a guise"!

Action. The members of Hope Church in Wheaton, Illinois, have seen Christ in the faces of the Cambodian community in their midst. They have discovered that while federal assistance programs have been drastically curtailed, economic, health, and language problems remain to be solved. The pastor of Lake View Korean Church is busy finding apartments, jobs, and schooling for immigrants from "home."

Members of several congregations and regional church bodies rejoice at the defeat of a state bill that would have made it illegal to employ persons without immigration papers.[10]

Adult Bible study. The texts are not just about the mission *to* the Gentiles, but about the mission *of* the Gentiles to the church. Read from that point of view, what are the roles of the Magi, the Egyptians, and the part-foreign King Herod? What do foreigners and immigrants want? What gifts do they offer? What problems do they and you encounter?

Matthew 2 is also about becoming a special kind of foreigner—a refugee. Jesus became a refugee so that the story of the exodus could be reenacted, Matthew tells us. Is being a refugee always a salvation experience? Is our church a refugee? a refugee camp? or a border patrol?

When studying these questions, the groups should be as diverse as possible. Participants may identify with different characters in the story and answer from that perspective. The goal, however, is an analysis of one's own church and its role in the ever-present question of the relationship between the world's peoples.

BAPTISM AND THE CALL OF THE DISCIPLES

Worship. Recapturing the Messiah images of baptism radicalizes our understanding of the rite. A Messiah (Jesus=Joshua) is one who is chosen by God ("My son") to lead the people, a choice confirmed by the anointing (baptism) of that one by a prophet (John). The Messiah is not only expected to rule justly according to the covenant, but has the power to do so.

The images of a radical social understanding of baptism are made more explicit in Gal. 3:26–29. It is through baptism that all become "sons" of God, or heirs of Abraham. "Sons" in this sense means "rulers," a term Jesus redefined to mean "servants" in Luke 22:24–27. When we are united in Christ there are no categories of Jew, Greek, male, female, slave, free. Christians not only are expected to live as people of the Messiah's kingdom but, having been anointed as he was, have the power to do so. Through the use of Scripture, commentary, and prayers based on these images, the service of baptism can be the rite of entrance into a community that shares the promised power to live in peace and righteousness.

Education. The community of disciples goes with Jesus where he goes, as illustrated by the life of Martin Luther King, Jr., whose birthday is celebrated on January 15. There are many resources suitable for a program or an intergenerational unit on his life and the continuing issues in the civil rights movement.[11] Check local sources for materials, speakers, current racial justice issues such as voting rights legislation, open housing in the suburbs, the rise of the Ku Klux Klan, the urban school system, and jobs.

Action. "Struggling with People Is Living in Christ." This is not only the name of a book of stories about civil rights issues in Asia. It is a brief statement of the basis of action for baptized Christians.[12] Besides our ongoing participation in the struggle, letters on behalf of those imprisoned for their action are important. Names and action suggestions can be obtained from Amnesty International and The Church Committee on Human Rights in Asia.[13]

Adult Bible study. The action/reflection method of Bible study[14] helps to expose the socially conditioned nature of our understanding of our baptism and to liberate our interpretation of the text. The first step is to identify the meaning of baptism for you (discussion, stories, drawings). Next, ask how baptism came to mean that for you (who told you, what was your experience?), and were there options that were excluded? The next movement is input from an "expert" (speaker, book, audiovisual) to study the meaning of the texts. In the fourth movement, the group reflects on the social context of the texts and asks how that has affected the understanding of baptism and the call of the disciples. The final job is to put it all together as a guide to our discipleship.

MESSIANIC MINISTRY

Worship. The lead story in each Gospel's account of Jesus' ministry suggests that liberation is to take place among the people now—not in some future end time—and that the Messiah is after more than freedom from Roman oppressors. Using congregational drama for the Old Testament and New Testament readings will help worshipers get into the events. Divide the congregation and give instructions before beginning. It may be necessary to write out the parts.

Pastor: "The Scripture readings are Luke 4:14–30; Lev. 25:10; Isa. 61: 1–2; and Jer. 34:8–12, 17. Let us attend to readings of the word."
O.T. Readers: (Lev. 25:10)
N.T. Narrators: (Luke 4:14–15)
Nazareth Congregation: (Luke 4:16–17)
Jesus and O.T. Readers: (Luke 4:18 read simultaneously with Isa. 61:1)
Jesus and O.T. Readers: (Luke 4:19 read simultaneously with Isa. 61:2 up to "God")
Nazareth Congregation: (Luke 4:20)
Jesus: (Luke 4:21)

[Continue to specify the parts up to v. 29]

N.T. Narrators: (Luke 4:30)
O.T. Readers: (Jer. 34:8–12, 17)
Pastor: "May God give us insight into this biblical testimony."

In an informal setting some people may mime the drama with slow, broad movements. This miming could be followed by discussion using adult Bible study methods suggested under Theme II.

Education. Salvation could not come to the people of Nazareth, because to them Jesus was only a carpenter's son. Later Jesus would point out the value of the widow's mite. The Least Coin Offering, originating with Asian women in 1946, shows the value of least things in making the kingdom real. A church supper provides the setting where the congregation can live through the experience. Start with the story through slides or page 35 of *Circle of Prayer.* [15] Asian women wanted a way all Christian women could work together for reconciliation and could participate equally in building up a fund for peacemaking. Each time a woman prays, she sets aside the least coin of her country. An international committee of women decides the use of the money.

At your supper, take up an offering of the least coin each person has. Dedicate the offering with one of the stories and prayers from *Circle of Prayer.* Choose a representative committee to decide what to do with the offering.

Action. What are women doing in your community to bring about the liberation of women? List your local organizations focused on women's economic needs, women's professional organizations, rape counseling, battered women, midwifery programs. Choose one issue and become involved. How does becoming involved in one group's efforts for liberation help us understand Robert McAfee Brown's description of servanthood as an avenue for justice?

Adult Bible study. What can a lectionary study group learn about the different visions of the Messiah from the Gospel of Mark's lead-off story in Mark 1:21–45 (or from John 2:1–12; Luke 4:14–30; or Matthew, chs. 5–7)? What unique theological views become clear as the Gospels are compared? What can be learned about the settings and needs of Mark's community? Luke's? John's? Matthew's? Different people need different kinds of liberation.

THE SERMON ON THE MOUNT

Worship. In the kingdom, the world's value systems are turned upside down. This good news suggests a liturgical dance in three movements. The first movement celebrates the good fortune of those who are pure in heart, poor in purse, righteous and persecuted, meek and mournful. The second movement is the battle cry against the evil that keeps God's will from being done on earth, and the third expresses the new economic solidarity of the kingdom fellowship and the risky love of the enemy. Let this dance of hope be done by a special group, or in a community dance that lets the nimble-footed bring along the more fearful steppers.

Education. How do you learn a new set of values? By being that which is blessed—a peacemaker, or poor, or persecuted for righteousness' sake; by living a life that benefits others. Field trips, work camps, involvement in action around an issue, visits—these are ways to get acquainted with those who are blessed in the kingdom, though that may or may not be the way they view themselves! Studying the Sermon on the Mount or the Sermon on the Plain experientially is a start on being part of the messianic ministry. If trips are impossible, simulation games are a good alternative.[16]

Action. While working toward a new international economic order that more adequately reflects God's value system, congregations can check their own life-styles. Excellent life-style change resources for adults, children, and intergenerational groups have been developed ecumenically.[17]

Adult Bible study. Yoder urges a straightforward interpretation of the Sermon texts, an interpretation that speaks to us today. *Your Kingdom Come*[18] offers a reading of the Lord's Prayer that is based on the fact that most of the world's people are poor. The kingdom is theirs. This is the context for our mission as the church of Jesus Christ.

FOOLS IN CHRIST

Worship. Henri Nouwen calls prayer the "most radical and revolutionary act . . . , the act by which barriers of fear are broken down, the act by which we can enter into a world which is not of this world."[19] Developing a disciplined prayer life is essential if fools in Christ are to confront the powerful wise, and to hear the cries of the victimized.[20]

Education. If Epiphany is the season when God through Christ illumines the world's darkness with startling light, then I Corinthians would connect that darkness to the conceits of human wisdom. The education of Christian fools consists in being able to see clearly who is victimized by a situation and who benefits, and to take the side of the victimized.

To test Soelle's claim that much of the rich countries' brainpower is being used in the military economy, analyze your university's grants, your local and regional economic base, the use of nuclear research. Examine the impact of this militarized economy on the deterioration of "civilian" industry, and on unemployment. How does military spending and the concentration of intellectual skills in this area affect social services, world peace, feeding and housing the world's population? Translate your research into a program for community groups or for cable television, or put it on videotape for use by home discussion groups.

Action. Take some action to stop the transfer of money, technology, and expertise from the civilian sphere to the military. Work on a local issue in cooperation with other concerned groups (e.g., the American Friends Service Committee, Mobilization for Survival, SANE, and denominational and ecumenical peacemaking programs) or work with an ecumenical group that focuses on the needs of particular countries in Asia, Africa, or Latin America.

Adult Bible study. The first two steps of Soelle's Bible study method were used in the Education section of our discussion: Ask who is victimized and who profits ("To see the Cross" and "To recognize the Principalities and Powers"). The Action section is an example of the fourth step ("To take up one's bed and walk"). The third step ("To remember the Resurrection") explores the relationship of the crucifixion and the resurrection to what is happening to people today. After a study group has dealt with militarism, it may use these four steps to explore "Christian foolishness" in response to other problems Paul discusses in Corinthians, such as human sexuality, cultural/religious differences, sacrificial giving.

Life in Christ is life in the liberating struggle. We need stories as signs of hope. The signs are all around us, today's epiphanies through which Christ shatters the darkness and declares: "The kingdom is at hand. Follow me."

III. LENT–HOLY WEEK

READINGS

Sunday or Day	Year	First Lesson	Second Lesson	Gospel
Ash Wednesday	A	Joel 2:12–18	II Cor. 5:20 to 6:2	Matt. 6:1–6, 16–18
	B	Isa. 58:3–12	James 1:12–18	Mark 2:15–20
	C	Zech. 7:4–10	I Cor. 9:19–27	Luke 5:29–35
1st Sunday in Lent	A	Gen. 2:4b–9, 15–17, 25; 3:1–7	Rom. 5:12–19	Matt. 4:1–11
	B	Gen. 9:8–17	I Peter 3:18–22	Mark 1:9–13
	C	Deut. 26:1–11	Rom. 10:8–13	Luke 4:1–13
2d Sunday in Lent	A	Gen. 12:1–8	Rom. 4:1–5 (6–12), 13–16a	John 3:1–17 or Matt. 17:1–9
	B	Gen. 22:1–2, 9–13	Rom. 4:16–25	Mark 8:31–38 or Mark 9:1–9
	C	Gen. 15:1–12, 17–18	Phil. 3:17 to 4:1	Luke 13:31–35 or Luke 9:28–36
3d Sunday in Lent	A	Ex. 17:3–7 or Ex. 24:12–18	Rom. 5:1–11	John 4:5–26
	B	Ex. 20:1–17	I Cor. 1:22–25	John 2:13–22
	C	Ex. 3:1–15	I Cor. 10:1–13	Luke 13:1–9
4th Sunday in Lent	A	I Sam. 16:1–13	Eph. 5:8–14	John 9:1–41
	B	II Chron. 36: 14–23	Eph. 2:4–10	John 3:14–21
	C	Josh. 5:9–12	II Cor. 5:16–21	Luke 15:1–3, 11–32
5th Sunday in Lent	A	Ezek. 37:1–14	Rom. 8:6–11	John 11:(1–16) 17–45
	B	Jer. 31:31–34	Heb. 5:7–10	John 12:20–33
	C	Isa. 43:16–21	Phil. 3:8–14	John 12:1–8
6th Sunday in Lent, when observed as Passion Sunday	A	Isa. 50:4–9a	Phil. 2:5–11	Matt. 26:14 to 27:66 or Matt. 27:11–54
	B	Same as A	Same as A	Mark 14:1 to 15:47 or Mark 15:1–39
	C	Same as A	Same as A	Luke 22:14 to 23:56 or Luke 23:1–49

Sunday or Day	Year	First Lesson	Second Lesson	Gospel
6th Sunday in Lent, when observed as Palm Sunday	A B C	Isa. 50:4–9a Zech. 9:9–12 Isa. 59:14–20	Phil. 2:5–11 Heb. 12:1–6 I Tim. 1:12–17	Matt. 21:1–11 Mark 11:1–11 Luke 19:28–40
Holy Week Monday		Isa. 42:1–9	Heb. 9:11–15	John 12:1–11 or Luke 19:41–48
Tuesday		Isa. 49:1–7	I Cor. 1:18–31 or I Tim. 6: 11–16	John 12:20–36
Wednesday		Isa. 50:4–9a	Heb. 12:1–3	John 13:21–30
Maundy Thursday	A B C	Ex. 12:1–14 Deut. 16:1–8 or Ex. 24:3–8 Jer. 31:31–34	I Cor. 11:23–26 I Cor. 10:16–17 Heb. 10:16–25	John 13:1–15 Mark 14:12–26 Luke 22:7–20

Good Friday	A
	
	B
	C
		Isa. 52:13–
		  53:12
		
		Lam. 1:7–12
		Hos. 6:1–6
			Heb. 4:14–16;
			  5:7–9
			
			Heb. 10:4–18
			Rev. 5:6–14
				John 18:1 to
				  19:42 or
				  John 19:17–30
				Same as A
				Same as A

Easter Eve Vigil		Ex. 14:15 to 15:1 Ezek. 36:16–28 Dan. 12:1–3	Acts 5:29–32 I Cor. 5:6–8 Rom. 6:3–11	Luke 24:13–49

N.B. This listing of Holy Week readings follows the Consensus Lectionary. It may also be used in connection with F. Herzog's exposition of "Passion Week" readings on pp. 159 ff. The readings listed on p. 159 follow the "Lectionary for the Christian Year" in the Presbyterian *Worshipbook,* and may be more appropriate in congregations that observe the Sixth Sunday in Lent as Palm Sunday.

A. Thematic Essays

1

TRUE REPENTANCE
AS A MORAL IMPERATIVE

Gayraud S. Wilmore

True Repentance	Joel 2:12–18	James 1:12–18 and	Matt. 6:1–6, 16–18
(including	Isa. 58:3–12	additional chs.	Mark 2:15–22
Ash Wednesday)	(Amos 5	II Cor. 5:16 to 6:2	Luke 5:29–35;
	Mal. 3)		13:1–9; 15:11–32
	Zech. 7:4–10		

Between the reality of sin and the possibility of redemption there is the moral imperative of repentance. Our hearts condemn us (I John 3:20), but it is not only with our hearts, but with our whole beings that we must repent. God is greater than our hearts and "knows all things," but not even God interferes with our right and obligation to repent of sin.

Sin, repentance, and forgiveness form a triad of conditions which describe, in Christian terms, what it means to exist in history under the sovereign Lordship of the God revealed to us in Jesus Christ. When we put this triad on a time frame the mediating ethical role of repentance becomes evident. Consider, therefore, the following way of stating the matter theologically.

In our rebelliousness we have done violence to our own human nature and to the creation with which we should have been in harmonious partnership. That is essentially the meaning of the past. That is the history of the world which, in fact, is the history of sin. In the present we continue to reap the effects of this sin sown in the past. We cannot change the past, but we can repent of it. The future, on the other hand, remains open and hopeful because the God who hears prayer and accepts our repentance, each day at a time, also redeems us for eternity. Although we must experience judgment—the "day of the Lord" of which the prophet speaks (Joel 2:1) —we find assurance in the promise of forgiveness, by the miracle of a costly, unmerited grace. This means that, notwithstanding its radical corruption, humankind's potential for the future is unlimited. That is the basis for Christian hope. *Now,* however, *today, this moment,* is the time for the action that is repentance! The meaning of the present is that God is giving us time to repent, to fill out in moral action the blank space between sin and forgiveness, the past and the future.

Repentance connects a sinful yesterday with a hopeful tomorrow —with God's forgiveness. If we were born in sin and hope to die knowing that we are forgiven by the atoning sacrifice of Christ—both sin and grace being in some sense inescapable—the moral initiative, nevertheless, returns to us most forcefully in the necessity of repentance. If there is something profoundly involuntary about the way God's law operates to condemn and the grace of Christ operates to forgive, there is certainly nothing involuntary about repentance. We must assume that God cannot save us unless we repent today—not only in word but in deed.

Repentance is, therefore, a much-neglected but fundamental doctrine of the Christian faith. It is first and foremost a moral act, because it involves the acknowledgment of a moral imperative and specific wrongdoing instead of a general feeling of remorse about human sinfulness. It is secondly an act of the will, because it involves a decision to turn around and go in a different direction with one's life and behavior. It is thirdly a social act, because it involves an open admission of guilt to an injured person or persons, and a willingness to make restitution.

I

The passages from Joel (2:12–18) and Isaiah (58:3–12) teach that true repentance involves an honest and specific facing of what is wrong in our lives. It is not enough blandly to assume our common sinfulness as human beings, yawn through the General Confession on Sunday mornings, receive the Words of Pardon, and then go on about our usual business because it is, after all, God's nature to forgive. From this perspective all that is necessary is that we come back next Sunday and repeat the ritual all over again.

This is not to say that ritual is unimportant in authentic religion. There is no real religion without some form of ritual behavior. "Return to me," says the Lord through the prophet Joel, "with all your heart, with fasting, with weeping, and with mourning." Both outward and inward expressions of godly sorrow for our misdoings are appropriate and each completes and authenticates the sincerity of the other. The congregation is commanded to assemble before God as a worshiping community with tears of contrition and unfeigned sorrow because of its sin. This is precisely why we are commanded to rend our *hearts* rather than our garments (Joel 2:13).

But the essence of repentance is neither heartrending assemblies nor individual fasting, but to turn from every kind of oppression, to remove the yoke that our selfish way of life has placed upon the necks of others, to share bread with the hungry and provide shelter for the homeless (Isa. 58:6–7). The word of the Lord to Zechariah tells us to look out for widows and orphans, show hospitality to strangers, and in every way to express our true repentance with kindness and mercy (Zech. 7:9–10).

Every week many millions of Americans go to churches and synagogues to confess their sins. Many would say that in the context of worship they sincerely repent of them. But we fail to see that sincere repentance is lacking whenever we simply feel generally sorry about our behavior but are doing nothing about it. True repentance begins when we begin to look squarely at the specific ways in which we are implicated, individually and corporately, in the suffering of others and determine to desist from our hurtful actions.

Nor is it necessary to begin with the people of Africa, Asia, and Latin America, although their needs are certainly great and American development aid is only 0.24 percent of our gross national product. Actually we are only thirteenth among eighteen nations assisting the developing areas of the world.

But we can begin with the poor, hungry, overpowered people at home—the marginated underclass of the metropolitan areas in which most Americans now reside (without ignoring the other Americans in rural hollows, migrant camps, tenant farms, and designated reservations). It is one thing, for example, to rebuild the cities for business and industry, or for the middle-class suburbanites who now want to return to the downtown area, but it is quite another thing to rebuild for the people who never left—the people who still live in the core of our cities and should be the beneficiaries rather than the victims of urban renewal.

> And your ancient ruins shall be rebuilt;
>   you shall raise up the foundations of many generations;
> you shall be called the repairer of the breach,
>   the restorer of streets to dwell in.
>
> (Isa. 58:12)

The prophet Isaiah speaks here of urban renewal in the context of repentance! But we need to read what he says in terms of the neglected poor, the elderly, and the ethnic minorities who have traditionally been shunted aside to make room for gleaming cultural centers, skyscraper office buildings, or pleasant townhouses and condominiums. The reclamation of the downtown areas of most of our central cities has been in the interests of the commercial and cultural elite, not the masses of our people. (Similarly, new land developments displace many of the people who most need access to land to live sufficiently.)

II

The Greek word for repentance, *metanoia,* means literally to make a U-turn on the road of life and move in the opposite direction. Although the word "repentance" is not mentioned specifically in the lectionary passages from the Epistles it is clear that what is called for is not some superficial, momentary attitudinal change that cannot stand the test and makes us vulnerable to enticement by the sinful desires of our hearts (James 1:12–14). On the contrary, true repentance is precisely that radical turning-about, that transformation of thought, attitude, outlook, deed, and way of life that the apostle Paul speaks about as "a new creation." The old having passed away when we reversed our direction, now everything in the ambience of our experience becomes new in a new, reconciled relationship to God through Jesus Christ (II Cor. 5:17–18).

In the early church, Christians expressed this new relationship to Christ and to one another by pooling their resources, selling their possessions, and distributing the proceeds "to each as any had need" (Acts 4:32–35). Living in the kind of world in which we live, most Christians would find that kind of communalism economically impracticable today. We can, however, reverse our life-styles and start living in the opposite direction from the "getting and spending" consumerism that makes it impossible for others in the world to reach even a level of material sufficiency.

Dr. Shiro Abe, chairperson of the Japanese Christian Social Work League, wrote in the May-June 1981 issue of *Church and Society:*

> Although 75 percent of the world's population lives in developing countries, the people of these lands use only 15 percent of the world's energy. . . . The cost of daily necessities for one American would maintain 100 persons in India for the same length of time.

A just and sustainable future for all the people of the world today requires that some of us must decide to live on less and, at the same time, *advocate and press for those national political and economic decisions which will lead to the redistribution of the goods and services of this world.* That is not a pipe dream of soft-headed liberals. It is a scientifically proven possibility for Christian people in the richest nations of the world. We need to present our governments with goals and policies that will attend to the basic needs of all people in an ecologically sustainable way and begin to show to our brother and sister citizens who may owe no allegiance to Christ that, by our own reduced personal and family consumption, and our commitment to basic human entitlements, we Christians are prepared to lead the way.

This is what it means, in this complex world at the end of the twentieth century, to repent of our sinful and selfish ways and to return to the Lord who is the only legitimate owner of the earth and the fullness thereof (Ps. 24:1). This is also what it means to experience the radical, internal transformation of *metanoia,* so that we become ambassadors for Christ in a world of ill-gotten and maldistributed gain—God making his appeal to alienated and impoverished millions through us (II Cor. 5:17–18).

III

Jesus admonished his disciples that when they fasted or otherwise deprived themselves for religious purposes related to guilt and penitence they should not try their best to look as self-effacing and put-upon as possible. Just the opposite, he said: "Anoint your head and wash your face, that your fasting may not be seen by men but by your Father who is in secret" (Matt. 6:16–18). We should, in other words, beware of practicing our repentance in public in order to get credit from those who may be impressed by how pious we are.

Repentance is something one does before God rather than the public. Yet it is also a *social* act in the sense that what Jesus is telling us is that it makes a significant difference what our repentance communicates about our true disposition and motive. He does say, of course, that we should not let our left hand know what our right hand is doing, to give alms in secret in order to be rewarded in secret. But we have to understand the real purpose behind this injunction.

What our Lord is speaking against is prideful display, arrogant vanity, and hypocrisy. He is addressing that spurious, ostentatious religiosity which offends those who need help by parading our philanthropy, rubbing their noses in our good deeds, making them the dehumanized objects of our self-righteousness, rather than someone who has a right to share what we have so freely received.

So while the Gospel passages seem to make repentance a transaction between only God and ourselves, they actually emphasize its social nature by showing what difference it makes how others perceive what we are doing when we repent. Does our almsgiving remind people of how much we are sacrificing for them, or do we quietly, unpretentiously, and with a good will, do what we *ought* to do, because our path crosses "paths of wretchedness and need" and we want to share God's goodness with the least of Christ's sisters and brothers? The spirit with which we give has much to do with the methods and procedures we choose for dispensing charity—be it public or private.

Repentance also means admitting our guilt and responsibility to those we have offended, and making restitution to the best of our ability.

And Zacchaeus stood and said to the Lord, "Behold, Lord, the half of my goods I give to the poor; and if I have defrauded any one of any thing, I restore it fourfold." And Jesus said to him, "Today salvation has come to this house." (Luke 19:8–9)

It is too easy for white Americans to dismiss the sins of their ancestors who, upon the backs of red and black people during 244 years of slavery, amassed the great fortunes their sons and daughters enjoy today. Gordon C. Bjork, in the June 24, 1968, issue of *Christianity and Crisis,* wrote: "The estate of one generation in our society is passed to the next after the subtraction of liabilities incurred. By the same logic the debts incurred by our white forefathers in the deprivation of Negroes by slavery and discrimination call for the repayment of debts from our massive inheritance."

Many Christians today would recoil from such an interpretation of repentance. Yet it is too easy for white Christians to say about the past, "We're sorry about that," and then to repudiate affirmative action programs in education and employment; disavow any reason why private and public agencies should compensate the oppressed for their many handicaps and for the special privileges lavished upon the oppressors; and support massive budget cuts in social programs that were designed to mitigate some of the institutionalized effects of past policies and intended to help groups at the end of the race to catch up with those of us who had an unfair start.

The repentant person, and the repentant church, wants to make amends. The truly penitent mood opens up new moral vistas so that new insights and fresh illuminations come to help the penitent make atonement to the person or persons who were wronged, to the society or ecological order that was violated. Jesus said that when we bring our gifts to the altar and remember that someone has something against us, we should set our gifts aside and first make amends to that person, and then return to the altar and offer our gifts. Under most conditions repentance requires restitution. Godly sorrow for sin requires finding our brothers and sisters and being reconciled with them before we ask God for forgiveness.

IV

The story of the prodigal son, with which the lectionary completes this inauguration of the Lenten season, brings us full circle to the main actor in the drama of redemption—to God by whose righteousness we are convicted of sin, led to repentance, and graciously pardoned through the atoning death of Christ. This is undoubtedly the main lesson, but there are several other lessons that bear upon the social ministry of the church that we might draw from this familiar parable —the excessive nationalism which assumes that there is some way of claiming and dividing up the world's energy apart from the interdependent needs of all humankind; the consequences of squandering the limited ecological cargo aboard Spaceship Earth; the similarity of the older brother's situation with that of Anglo-Saxon America when a tide of people of different colors and traditions tests the sincerity of our invitation to "wretched refuse" and "huddled masses yearning to breathe free."

Statistics over the past decade show that only 892,000 Europeans became Americans, but there was an increase in the immigration of Asians from 362,000 in 1970 to 1.5 million in 1980; of Africans from 33,000 to 87,000; of South Americans from 219,000 to 266,000. What will the older brother have to say about the radical changes about to take place at the old family homestead? (In 1981, the answer was Poles, yes; Haitians and Salvadorans, no!) It is in how policies work for people that we must learn to think about the meaning of repentance in the context of our postmodern world, so warped by ideological rigidity and institutionalized racism.

The parable of the prodigal suggests these and other ethical implications we might draw from an exploration of inheritance, desertion, dissoluteness and waste, repentance and redemption, envy and righteous indignation. But the central message of Luke 15:11–32 is God's grace and forgiving love for the wayward and repentant child, the joy in heaven over the return of one sinner who was accounted dead and is alive, who was irretrievably lost and is found. The message is the grace of a loving Parent who is willing to accept those who truly repent and restore them to full membership in the communion of the saints, the kingdom of heaven.

But let us be clear that grace does not excuse the church from those ethical actions which are the bedrock of the Judeo-Christian faith— from the liberating justice and compassion exemplified in the life and teaching of Jesus and the great prophets who preceded him. It is no accident that John the Baptist preached the baptism of repentance as the first act of moral restoration and that Jesus began his own ministry with the same words: "Repent, for the kingdom of heaven is at hand" (Matt. 4:17). The kingdom could be entered only by sinners who repented. Its promise to those Jesus called to follow him was no different than the earlier promise the prophets made to Israel:

> If you take away from the midst of you the yoke,
>   the pointing of the finger, and speaking wickedness,
> if you pour yourself out for the hungry
>   and satisfy the desire of the afflicted,
> then shall your light rise in the darkness
>   and your gloom be as the noonday.
>
> (Isa. 58:9–10)

Following Jesus required a similar repentance, a similar moral courage and self-discipline. Since the rich young man had fulfilled all the commandments from his youth, only one thing more stood between him and eternal life. Jesus said: "One thing you still lack. Sell all that you have and distribute to the poor, and you will have treasure in heaven; and come, follow me" (Luke 18:22).

But the final word is not about our ability to live up to the requirements of the rigorous morality Jesus demands. The final word is that if we repent (with all that we now understand repentance to mean) and do the best we can, God will do the rest. God will run to meet us when we are still a great distance from home. God will send for the best robe, the ring, the shoes, and kill the fatted calf. By an amazing grace that we can never measure or merit we will be forgiven and received back into the household—for we are those who were dead and through repentance are alive again, we were lost and are found.

2

JESUS' TEMPTATION, TRANSFIGURATION, AND TRIUMPH: THE POWER OF WEAKNESS AND THE WEAKNESS OF POWER

Paul Lehmann

Jesus' Temptation	(Use O.T. linkages not found in the lectionary)	Matt. 4:1–11 Mark 1:12–15 Luke 4:1–13
and Transfiguration		Matt. 17:1–9 Mark 9:1–9 Luke 9:28–36
and Triumphal Entry	Isa. 50:4–7 Zech. 9:9–12 Isa. 59:14–20	Matt. 21:1–11 Mark 11:1–11 Luke 19:28–40

The crucial happenings concerning Jesus of Nazareth, recorded in the Gospels and remembered by the church, are Jesus' Temptation, Transfiguration, and Triumph. In turn, and taken together, they center upon power. The temptation centers upon a power decision; the transfiguration centers upon the focus and consequence of that power decision; and Jesus' triumphal entry into Jerusalem on Palm Sunday celebrates a power confrontation. At issue is a radical (root) shift in the experience, meaning, uses, foundation, and purposes of power. The line is drawn on the boundary between the power of weakness and the weakness of power.

The calendar, according to which the church calibrates its memories for the nourishment of its faith and the liberation of its hopes, assigns this "power line" to the 1st, 2d, and 6th *threshold* Sundays in Lent. The two Sundays immediately following the beginning of the Lenten season on Ash Wednesday concentrate upon the temptation and the transfiguration. As if in haste, the church, following the Gospels, loses no time in getting from the beginning to the turning point of the power struggle under way. In similar haste, the triumphal entry of Jesus into Jerusalem, which is a focus of the 6th Sunday in Lent and the beginning of Holy Week, moves with almost breathtaking swiftness to the crucifixion and resurrection. These *threshold* Sundays

underline the beginning of the end, designed to spell out the end of
the beginning.

A Theology of Power. Power, as Bertrand Russell remarked, "is to
society what energy is to physics."[1] This means that power is the
principal characteristic of social interaction. It denotes the capacity
to effect changes in the behavior of people in their relations with each
other.[2] As the capacity to effect change, power in society and energy
in physics are analogous. Unlike energy, however, the phenomenon
of power intrinsically involves another factor. This is the factor of
sanction. Implicitly or explicitly, power claims *validity,* or *right,* or
authority in effecting the changes that the exercise of power has
brought about. The coinherence of the "authority factor" and the
"change-effect factor" in the use of power means that power is a
political as well as a *social* reality. To put it another way, *power* and
accountability are inseparable. Thus, it is not accidental that the
question of authority or accountability should have come to the top
of the agenda of the power confrontation at the center of Jesus'
triumphal entry into Jerusalem (Mark 11:27–28).

The *weakness of power* is its vulnerability to the temptation to
claim that what it does validates its *right,* or *authority,* to do what it
does. Power is self-justifying, on its own warrant and beyond accountability. Translated politically, this means that the stability and security established by power are the proof of its rightful possession and
use. The power of weakness, on the other hand, is its trust that what it
does will be validated by a power not its own, which effects in social
interaction the changes that bear self-evident accountability. Translated politically, this means that the accountability of power signals
its authority, and thus also its trustworthiness. The possession and
use of power derive their warrant from the purposes to which they
are instrumental. The weakness of power is its ultimate reliance upon
the self-justifying claim that the purpose of power is power.

The *power of weakness* is its ultimate reliance upon the purpose
of power. The code words of the weakness of power are "law and
order." The code words of the power of weakness are "justice and
freedom." The weakness of power is its appeal to "law and order"
in order to conceal its arbitrariness. The power of weakness is its
readiness to risk disobedience, and even anarchy, for the sake of
justice and freedom, which are indispensable to a world and society
fit for being human in.

The dynamics of power in action are such that the tyranny inherent
in the arbitrariness of power is sooner or later destroyed by the
justice and freedom intrinsic to the human use of power. On the other
hand, the risk of anarchy, which is inherent in every struggle for
justice and freedom against the primacy of law and order, shadows
that struggle with the temptation to convert risk into policy, and thus,
anarchy into tyranny. As a perceptive observer of the French Revolu-

tion noted: "All revolutions begin with a vision of a new order of freedom and justice in human affairs, and all revolutions end by devouring their own children."[3]

The powerless are not inherently protected against the temptation to convert risk into policy, and thereby to practice the self-justifying arbitrariness of the powerful. Nor are the powerful inherently denied the prospect of law subordinated to justice and order subordinated to freedom. As the powerless are bearers of a righteousness not their own (Matt. 11:5; Luke 7:22), so the powerful are bearers of an unrighteousness from which they can be set free (Mark 10:25; Matt. 19:24; Luke 18:25). This is why the power question is the focus of the Temptation, Transfiguration, and Triumph of Jesus; and why what is going on in the wilderness, on the mountain, and in Jerusalem makes all the power difference in the world.

With notable clarity and force, the cluster of texts that direct our attention to these events converge upon each other, owing to a logic of power of their own. The sense and range of what is happening to Jesus under the blandishments of the devil, in the momentous conversation with Moses and Elijah, and amid the frenzied adulation of the people upon his entrance into the city—these texts affirm Jesus as a person at the center of whatever it takes to be and to stay human. His personal history is rooted in the history and destiny of his own people, and, together with them, the history and destiny of all peoples are offered and promised a humanizing journey toward human fulfillment. This fulfillment coming their way includes nature and history, individuals and communities; and it bears their secret and sense—the mystery and meaning, the point and purpose of who they are and are coming to be.

Of course, there is drama going on! But Jesus is neither a phantom nor a hero. He is a concrete, flesh-and-blood human being, whose struggle in the world for the human point and purpose of the world draws to him—in acceptance or rejection—all sorts and conditions of people. In and through that struggle, Jesus is identified as the Messiah, "the anointed of the Lord," and as such the bearer and active presence of the Creator, Redeemer, and Perfecter of the world (Heb. 12:2). "Jesus Christ," as Blaise Pascal, the renowned seventeenth-century mathematician, declared, "is the end of all, and the center to which all tends. Whoever knows Him knows the reason of everything."[4]

I. THE TEMPTATION
Matt. 4:1–11; Deut. 26:5–11; I Peter 3:18–22;
cf. Mark 1:12–15; Luke 4:1–13

The terse account in the Gospel of Mark (1:12–13) sets the framework of the narrative. The Spirit drives Jesus into the wilderness, where he remains for forty days and nights in the company of wild beasts. There he is tempted by Satan and ministered to by angels. The fuller account by Matthew amplifies Mark's stark report of a power conflict going on. The Spirit and Satan are polarized in opposition; Jesus and the angels are joined in need. Jesus is exhausted by the struggle; the angels stand by him in his extremity. For the angels are the bearers of the divine solicitude in and for all persons, places, and things in the world. It is no accident, as Andrew Greeley has noted, that when the church gave up on the angels, Hollywood took them over.

The conflict is vastly more critical than the question: "What is Jesus going to do with his life?" He is not a young man in search of a vocation or goal for his life. These familiar moralizations trivialize the intensity of the power decision by which Jesus was being confronted. The power decision was centered upon a commitment to weakness as against strength, to obedience against domination, to self-giving against self-realization, to responsibility against self-determination, to purposed creativity as against imaginative ingenuity. The human and historical secret therein unveiled is as follows: Weakness *so* chosen *is* strength, whereas strength *so* vaunted *is* weakness. Obedience *so* chosen *is* freedom, whereas domination *so* coveted *is* bondage. Self-giving *so* chosen *is* self-fulfilling, whereas self-realization *so* pursued *is* tormenting. Responsibility *so* chosen *is* fulfilling, whereas self-determination *so* consuming *is* self-defeating. Creativity *so* purposed *is* rooted in and nurtures trust, whereas imaginative ingenuity *so* cultivated *is* rooted in and nurtures tantalizing restlessness.

This human and historical secret of power is pointed to and pointed up by the setting of the temptation and by the resources upon which Jesus drew in his refutation of Satan. The wilderness echoes the bitter and trying wanderings of his ancient forebears on the way from their deliverance from bondage in Egypt to the Land of Promise. The wilderness is the horrendous and haunting place of decision and destiny of diverse times and terrains in the long story of the covenanted people of God, from Noah to Abraham to Moses to Elijah, and to Jesus himself. Whether it be the forty days and nights during which rains flooded the earth (Genesis 7–9), or the forty days and nights during which Elijah pursued his lonely way from the desert to the mountain of God (I Kings 19:8), or the forty years of wanderings that almost turned the exodus around, it is this history which floods in upon the forty days and nights which Jesus spent in the wilderness, being put to the test by God and putting the devil to flight.

In the accounts of Jesus' temptation, the words "Satan" and "devil" are interchangeable. They denote the persistence, intensity, ultimacy, and immediacy of power. At this level, power is experienced as a human decision so basic that destiny or destruction, fulfillment or frustration, humanization or dehumanization of life in this world hang in the balance. On the edge of *this* decision, Jesus draws upon the one sure resource of power at the disposal of weakness in face of insuperable power odds.

The *first* temptation strikes at the core of bodily survival. Jesus is hungry. "If you really are who you claim to be (i.e., the Son of God)," says the devil, "command these stones to become loaves of bread." The certification of power is its capacity to do whatever the human condition requires, and to deliver on the spot. To this illusion of power, masquerading weakness as strength, Jesus replies by citing the Scriptures on which he has been brought up: "It is written, 'Man shall not live by bread alone, but by every word that proceeds from the mouth of God' " (Matt. 4:4). It is the book of Deuteronomy (8:3) which sets the devil back in the power of the experience and the remembrance of history.

The *second* temptation offers the promise of bodily survival in the power of spiritual credibility. The test of the Temple is the power of miracle, i.e., of the unexpected, the unpredictable, and the unconventional, to confirm the truth and the value of ultimate power claims. "The devil . . . set him on the pinnacle of the temple, and said to him, 'If you are the Son of God, throw yourself down' " (Matt. 4:5–6). In so saying, the devil himself exposes the subtle and insidious pervasiveness of the weakness of power making a show of strength. The devil, too, can quote Scripture: in this instance, Ps. 91:11–12. "For it is written, 'He will give his angels charge of you,' and 'On their hands they will bear you up, lest you strike your foot against a stone.' " Liturgy is a time-honored mask worn by the weakness of power in the endeavor to confuse and confound the power of weakness. And once again Jesus draws upon the book of Deuteronomy (6:16): "Again it is written, 'You shall not tempt the Lord your God' " (Matt. 4:7). Whenever miracle is made an invitation to believe, or claimed as a proof of the truth of faith, we put the Lord our God to the test. For to give primacy to miracle over covenanted trust, responsibility, and freedom in human life is to exalt the self-justifying weakness of power over the self-fulfilling self-giving in self-surrender that inspires and informs the power of weakness in the world.

The *third* temptation proposes the guarantee of bodily survival and spiritual credibility through the subjection of accountability to power. All challenges to power are discredited as contrary to the stability and security indispensable to human fulfillment in the world. The ultimate weakness of power is exposed by the addiction of power to glory and to the fascination with its own splendor and success. A radical and ultimate inversion of loyalty and value becomes the order of the day. Evil is celebrated as good; lie as truth; and the ultimate destruction as the ultimate fulfillment. "Again, the devil took him to a very high mountain, and showed him all the kingdoms of the world and the glory of them; and he said to him, 'All these will I give you, if you will fall down and worship me.' Then Jesus said to him, 'Begone, Satan! for it is written, "You shall worship the Lord your God and [God] only shall you serve" ' " (Matt. 4:8–10). The reply was shaped by Deut. 6:13.

In citing Deuteronomy, Jesus is not proof texting, but confounding the devil with a radically different perception and practice of power. This power difference is rooted in, and has been shaped by, the history, memories, and hopes of a people in covenant with a God whose power is authenticated by purposes designed for human freedom and fulfillment through trust and responsibility. Deuteronomy 26:5–11 ("A wandering Aramean was my father . . .") transmits and preserves the most significant summary recital of this story in an immemorial confession of faith. Through cultic repetition of this creed, God's acts in the midst of and for the sake of the people of Israel are celebrated; and the people are reminded that they have been chosen to make known in the world how and why it is that the power of weakness unmasks and confounds the weakness of power at every turn of the road. Thus: "History becomes word and the Word becomes history. . . . The Old Testament is of the opinion that ever and again . . . the glory of Yahweh's providence has become completely visible, that what happens can be recognized as a 'sign,' indeed as a miracle."[5] From the "wandering Aramean"—via Jesus' decision in the wilderness *against* enslavement enticingly offered as freedom, and *for* freedom won through suffering and the risk of life —to the steadying encouragement of Christians under persecution to consider their sufferings in the light of Christ's sufferings (I Peter 3:18–22), the critical rejection of the weakness of power in the power of weakness is underlined, affirmed, and sustained. The reference to "the spirits in prison," of I Peter 3:19, suggests Rev. 20:7, where at the end of Christ's thousand-year reign, Satan is said to be "loosed from his prison" for the final power showdown.[6]

It is, of course, easier to repress the weakness of power and to deride—and even persecute—the power of weakness. It is easier to succumb to the power wiles of the devil, and to convert the lure of commerce, culture, and preeminent security into policy, than to risk trust in the power purposed for deliverance from oppression, for the righteousness which sets right whatever is not right in the world, and for the reconciliation which through justice makes for human freedom and fulfillment. The weakness of power is the special provenance of tyranny; the power of weakness is the special providence wherein and whereby those who are called, and faithful to the one hope of their calling (Eph. 4:4; Heb. 3:1–11; 12:1–4), persevere unto their life's end, and until the end of the ages, in converting the love of power into the power of love.

II. The Transfiguration
Matt. 17:1–9; Gen. 22:1–2, 9–13; Phil. 3:17 to 4:1;
cf. Mark 9:1–9; Luke 9:28–36

The focus and consequence of this power decision are pointed to and pointed up by the transfiguration of Jesus. The scene shifts from the wilderness to "a high mountain apart" (Matt. 17:1). The wilderness, too, is a place *apart*. But unlike the wilderness, where Jesus' only companions were the wild beasts and the devil (and, after the struggle, the angels), on the "Mount of Transfiguration" Jesus finds himself in the company of the memorable trio of his disciples, Peter, James, and John; and in the presence of Moses and Elijah. The angels are replaced by "a voice from the cloud," which identifies who Jesus is, and who really is "in charge"—in the wilderness *and* on the mountaintop—in contrast to each powermonger who "plays with the bigness of his littleness . . . till unwish returns on its unself."[7]

Mark's Gospel has grasped both the prospect and the enormity of this power shift. Mark notes that Jesus "was transfigured before them, and his garments became glistening, intensely white, as no fuller on earth could bleach them" (Mark 9:2–3). Matthew says that "his face shone like the sun, and his garments became white as light" (Matt. 17:2); and Luke reports that "the appearance of his countenance was altered, and his raiment became dazzling white" (Luke 9:29). The ecstatic tone of these descriptions has suggested and reinforced a tendency in the church to interpret the transfiguration of Jesus as a mystical experience. The stress lies upon an overpowering and transforming nearness of God to a human individual that exceeds all perception and comprehension, and that exudes a mysterious and bewildering identification of the divine with the human in what is going on. But this mystical interpretation obscures the meaning of the transfiguration texts.

In the Eastern Church, the Feast of the Transfiguration is called the "Feast of Taborian" because the "high mountain" was identified with Mt. Tabor. Although the Roman and Protestant churches do not concur in this Eastern identification of the place, they have, until recently, concurred in the designation of the feast between Trinity and Advent, on August 6. It has now been advanced to an octave between Epiphany and Lent. Nevertheless the earlier date is worth pausing over because one of those Deuteronomic happenings through which "history becomes word and the Word becomes history" fell upon the 6th of August 1945. On that date, an atomic bomb was dropped on the Japanese city of Hiroshima by the United States Army Air Force. It is doubtful that President Harry Truman and his military commanders and advisers—in their eagerness to bring the Second World War to an end—thought of the Feast of the Transfiguration. What can scarcely be doubted, however, is the coincidence between that awesome instant of power—in its weakness, vaunting its self-justifying strength—and the transfiguration of Jesus. Hiroshima radically changed the face and the force of power in the world.

On that "high mountain apart" when Jesus "was transfigured before them" (Matt. 17:1–2), the secret of the transforming and fulfilling power of weakness over against the futility and fatality of the weakness of power was being exposed and loosed in the world. Jesus' conversation with Moses and Elijah, the identifying voice from the cloud, and the disciples alone with Jesus after all, underline the *political*—in distinction from the *mystical*—focus and consequence of what was going on.

The "voice from the cloud" echoes not only the baptism of Jesus by John in the wilderness (Matt. 3:17) but, more trenchantly, that momentous ascent of Mt. Moriah dramatically described in Genesis 22. Abraham's extraordinary trust in the power of weakness did not yield, even when confronted by the risk of sacrificing his only son as God asked, "as a burnt offering upon one of the mountains of which I shall tell you" (Gen. 22:2). In so doing, Abraham unmasked the weakness of power from that day to this. At the precise and ultimate moment, when the risk of trust is exposed as the point of intersection between trust and obedience, then and there God provides the sacrifice, in celebration of God's glory, and lets the Son go free. The arbitrariness of power, with its self-justifying pretensions to self-evidence, is rejected; and the death-dealing chill of human cruelty in blind obedience is displaced by the ingression of power purposed for giving, sustaining, and fulfilling human life. On the Mount of Transfiguration, God's only Son does not go free. He goes instead from there to a criminal's death, so that the power of sin, death, and the devil may be broken, and that the end of the beginning may be perfected by the beginning of the end.

On that "high mountain" where Jesus was transfigured, Moses and Elijah are the bearers of this ingression.[8] Upon them converge the two formative motifs of the transfiguration event: (1) the heaven-earth-glory theme; (2) the Messiah-suffering-vindication theme. The first is the reality theme; the second is the redemption theme. The first is the presence (or truth) theme; the second is the power (or life) theme.

Only Luke notes what the conversation between Jesus and Moses and Elijah was about. It concerned the imminent exodus and vindication of Jesus. They "spoke of his departure, the destiny he was to fulfill in Jerusalem" (Luke 9:31). This accords with Mark's assignment of priority to Elijah over Moses in the dynamics of what was going on. When Mark (9:4) tells us that "they saw Elijah appear, and Moses with him," and that on the way down from the mountain Jesus implicitly identified himself with John the Baptist, he all but lets the messianic secret out, in a marked break with Jewish Elijah belief, and in a sharply drawn line between the power of weakness and the weakness of power. What *they* did to John, *they* are already conspiring to do to Jesus. And they *will* do it. So Elijah is John the Baptist and Jesus is Elijah.

Correlative with this messianic-redemption theme is the presence-reality theme. Jesus is not only *like* Elijah and Moses; he is also *different* from them. Not only does Jesus join Elijah and Moses in the accelerating tempo of the end of the beginning and the beginning of the end, but he, unlike them, is in control of the new order of things and at the work of clearing the old order out of the way and getting the new order under way.

There is a fundamental difference between *political messianism* and *messianic politics.*[9] There is a difference between the seizure of power by force in order to establish a safer or a new order of human affairs and the unyielding pressure upon established power, already under judgment for its default of order, by the power already ordering all things in a new and humanizing way. In either case, the Law (Moses) and the Prophets (Elijah) identify the focus, context, and conditions of Israel's—and through Israel, everyone's—participation in the humanizing activity of God. "Of absolutely central significance in this activity, for all the relationships of human life . . . is . . . righteousness."[10]

The righteousness of God means God's presence in the midst of humanity, setting right what is not right in the world, establishing justice in the power of the divine purposes. This power and these purposes divide those who "live as enemies of the cross of Christ" from those whose "commonwealth is in heaven, and [who] await . . . the Lord Jesus Christ" (Phil. 3:18, 20). Those who glory in their shame, and whose minds are set on earthly things, are at the other end of the spectrum from those who trust and hope that "our lowly body" will be changed "to be like his glorious body, by the power which enables him even to subject all things to himself" (Phil. 3:19, 21). This power and these purposes divide those whose end is destruction in the weakness of power from those who—in the power of weakness—"stand firm in the Lord" (Phil. 3:19; 4:1).

In this passage, Paul the apostle documents from his own experience the focus and direction of his own faith and hope, and invites Christians across the centuries to share in his discoveries and expectations. For "with the Christ-event, history has become an ellipse with two foci: the Christ event and the Parousia, or the day of God's final victory. . . . And even where this confidence is shaken by the perilous events of [Paul's] life (II Cor. 1:9; Phil. 1:19–26; 2:17), the hope persists that 'not much time is left' (I Cor. 7:29) and that the true 'commonwealth' of the Christian is heaven, from where Christ will imminently return (Phil. 3:20–21)."[11]

III. THE TRIUMPH
Matt. 21:1–22; Mark 11:1–11; Luke 19:28–40;
Zech. 9:9–12; Isa. 50:4–7; 59:14–20;
I Tim. 1:12–17; Phil. 2:5–11; Heb. 12:1–6

This strong sense of a foreshortened future is difficult for contemporary Christians to grasp. There is a growing awareness on every hand that we are caught up in a "time of troubles" (Toynbee); and in darker moments there is a strong sense that the end of the beginning has come upon us. But that these dark forebodings signal the beginning of the end is a confidence shared—despite the Lord's clear proscription of this information—rather more by those who claim to be "on the Lord's side," and thus "to know the times and seasons" (Acts 1:7), than by those who have learned from the swift pace of the consequence of Jesus' transfiguration that the imminent triumph of the end which is beginning is no "glory train" to the heavenly commonwealth.

On the Mount of Transfiguration, Peter had suggested, with the silent consent of James and John, that it would be very agreeable to prolong the wonder that had overcome them. Perhaps Moses and Elijah would return for further conversations. Hence Peter offered to "make three booths here" (Matt. 17:4). After all, it was that time of year; the celebration of the Feast of Booths or Tabernacles (or Succoth) had come around again. The Tabernacle of the Presence had sheltered the companioning Presence of God, who had delivered the Israelites from Egypt and watched over them in the wilderness. At harvest end each year, there came to be a celebration of thanksgiving for the sustaining fruits of the year and for the entrance upon a new year and a new beginning.

Although leafy palms were chiefly associated with the Feast of Booths and Passover, they were also evocative of nationalistic recollections, aims, and hopes. When Judas Maccabeus rededicated the Temple after its profanation by the Syrians (164 B.C.), the Jews brought palms into the Temple (II Macc. 10:7). When Jesus, in turn, enters Jerusalem and is received by the people with palms and shouting, nationalistic stirrings are at work.[12] Indeed, these actions have political overtones. "The crowds that went before him and that followed him shouted, 'Hosanna to the Son of David! Blessed is he who comes in the name of the Lord!' " (Matt. 21:9.) The shout echoes Ps. 118:26, significant in the worship in the Temple upon the entrance of the people to give thanksgiving for deliverance. And though the Gospel accounts of Jesus' entry into Jerusalem do not identify the "leafy branches" that were cut from the trees and spread out (Matt. 21:8) before him as *palm branches,* the association of royal palms with this triumphant occasion is more than plausible.

These royal associations, with their political signs, raise a puzzling question about Jesus' transfiguration and triumph. Why did Jesus, who refused Peter's urging to tarry on the Mount, go up there in the first place, instead of going at once from "his own country" (Matt. 13:54), i.e., Galilee, to the city to celebrate the Feast of Tabernacles? The question is the more intriguing since, after the momentous happening on the Mount, Jesus seems bent upon making haste to get back to Galilee (Matt. 17:22) and then on to "Judea beyond the Jordan" (Matt. 19:1), and from there "up to Jerusalem" (Matt. 20:17–18) for the Passover Feast.

A clear answer to this question is that Jesus had affinities with an ultranationalist party called the Zealots.[13] Jesus' stricture against violent men who seek by violence to seize the kingdom of heaven by force (Matt. 11:12) may well be applied to the "New Right" today, as indeed this stricture is more than a hint at a warning to the Zealots in his day. Jesus' proclamation of the kingdom of God was vulnerable to co-option by the ultranationalists whose "Maccabean revival" he was suspected of encouraging. Instead, then, of going to the city for the Feast of Tabernacles, Jesus went to the mountain to sort out the thrust and consequence of his messianic destiny. On the way down from the mountain, he swore his disciples to secrecy about his identity and commitment (Matt. 17:9), only to unveil it all on the eve of the Passover.

So palms and power do go together. But not in the accustomed and expected way. The consequence of the messianic focus of the transfiguration was a power confrontation between Jesus and the existing authorities. Jesus' entrance, mounted on a donkey, signaled a widening gap between his view of the power at work in what was going on and that of the "law-and-order people" and of the crowd. The clue to what was really happening had long before been pointed to by the prophet Zechariah (9:9–10).

Thus, *how* Jesus Christ should be acclaimed makes all the power difference in the world. At issue is power held and used for nationalistic security, grandeur, and prestige *and* power purposed for the guardianship of the poor, the lame, the weak, the defenseless. At issue is power, the possession and use of which signals a gap between authority and accountability, a gap filled by the rhetoric and practice of self-justification; *and* power, the possession and use of which are the sign that authority and accountability are coordinate: two sides of the same coin.

Jesus' entry into Jerusalem is a triumph for him because it is the beginning of his vindication. The power decision that marked his victory over the devil in the wilderness, and that led to the messianic confirmation on the Mount of Transfiguration, now begins to put existing authority and power to the test. The possession and use of power, which from the beginning has ruptured the purposes for which the world and human life were made, has come to an end. Events have overtaken the possession and use of power, which has ignored its passion for self-justification as its fate-ful weakness; divorced authority from accountability; and spawned bondage, oppression, and injustice everywhere. The beginning of the end has set free, *in* the world and *for* the world, the power whose weakness is its passion for justice, liberation, and human wholeness, and whose accountability is its authority. The victory of messianic politics over political messianism has begun, and its triumph is sure.

The Gospel accounts of the temptation and transfiguration of Jesus, and their roots in the reality of Old Testament experience, are brought, through their cognate Epistles, to bear upon the perils and sufferings, the faithfulness and trust of those who have been delivered from the weakness of power in the power of weakness. So, I Timothy joins I Peter and Philippians, and underlines the power victory in the power confrontation anticipated from afar by Zechariah and set in operation with Jesus' entry into Jerusalem (I Tim. 1:12–16).

When it comes to power, the power shift identified in the Temptation, Transfiguration, and Triumph of Jesus comes to this:

> We had fed the heart on fantasies,
> The heart's grown brutal from the fare.[14]

Our enmities overwhelm our loves, and our only hope is in a Love beyond ourselves. Therefore, "To the King of the ages, immortal, invisible, the only God, be honor and glory for ever and ever. Amen." (I Tim. 1:17.)

3

DIMENSIONS OF COVENANT: PARTICULAR, UNIVERSAL, AND MESSIANIC

Rosemary Radford Ruether

God's Covenant		
with Humanity	Gen. 1:6ff.	Rom. 5:12–21
	2 and 3	
with Noah	9:8–17	I Peter 3:18–22
with Abraham		
Call	12:1–7	II Tim. 1:8–14
Covenant	15:5–12, 17–18	Phil. 3:17 to 4:1
Testing	22:1–14	(Rom. 4:13–25)
		Rom. 8:31–39

The Christian tends to start with universality and then move to particularity. Because the stories of the covenant with Adam and with Noah occur earlier in the biblical texts than the story of the covenant with Abraham, we tend to think that the later stories developed after and out of the earlier ones. God first made a covenant with all humanity as descendants of Adam and renewed it after the flood in the covenant with Noah and his descendants (Gen. 9:8–17). God chose a particular people as the special vehicle of revelation.

In reality, in the development of biblical thought and in the development of human experience generally, the reverse is the case. Human groups first define their own particularity, demarcating it over against other human groups. Then they may gradually grow to more inclusive concepts of human groups together and, finally, to a sense of humanity as a whole. We are far from having outgrown this basic particularism of human identity today! The fundamental starting point for the Hebrew Scriptures is the covenant of God with Israel as a particular people chosen from among other peoples to have a special covenanted relationship with God.

I

The concept of covenant is based on the practice of tribal confederations or pacts for mutual defense. The confederation of Israel was made up of a group of tribes that came together for mutual defense, uniting themselves under the one cult of Yahweh. They were not originally one tribal group, but came from diverse backgrounds, finding a common interest in defense against the more powerful peoples of the cities and the plains.[15]

The legend of a common descent from one ancestor, Abraham, was a means of giving this group of tribes a sense of unity. In exchange for a loyalty so total that Abraham would leave his own homeland and even risk the death of the only son of his old age, God promised him many descendants and a land that would stretch from the Nile to the Euphrates. The many tribes of Israel, covenanting together under Yahweh, saw themselves as those many descendants of Abraham (Gen. 12:1–17; 22:1–14).

Several ideas are interwoven in the Hebrew covenantal concept; these include election, the law, and the land. The covenant is a free gift of God's grace. God chose the people of Israel, not because they were the best or the most mighty people in the Near East, but solely because God loved them. Their loyalty to God is a response to this free gift of the covenant.

The covenant implies mutual responsibilities. God gives the people commandments. Contrary to what some Christians have understood, reading back from Pauline theology, the Jewish conception of the law is not one of "good works" whereby Israel "earns" its relationship to God. The relationship to God is already given as a gift. Law lies under the covenant. It is the *way* that the people are to walk to express their covenantal relationship with God. Even though the people may sin and break their covenantal relationship with God by unfaithfulness, God remains faithful to the covenant. Sometimes the Scriptures even use the image of God as a mother to express this unbreakable fidelity of God to the people. As a mother does not forget the child of her womb, so God will not forget her relationship with Israel (Isa. 49:14–15).[16]

With the commandments comes the promise of the land. These nomadic ex-slave people shall become heirs to the land between the sea and the two great rivers of the Middle East (Gen. 15:18). They shall become a great people, no longer harried by their enemies. The prophets develop the critical side of these ideas of commandments and covenant. The misfortunes that befall the people at the hands of their enemies are punishments God visits upon them to chastise them for their infidelity. Their ultimate punishment is that of exile, loss of the land, and slavery under foreign powers.

But these punishments are provisional. God has not forgotten the covenant. Chastisement is itself a call to repentance. When the people turn, heed the commandments, and keep their side of the covenant, God will fulfill the promises. The people will return. The land will be restored. The people will cultivate their fields in peace and prosperity.[17]

Thus, as in so many ideas of Hebrew religion, covenant has its unfulfilled dimension which is projected upon the future. The promises of the covenant point toward an expanding horizon of hope. The people's conversion to full fidelity to God, and God's fulfillment of the promises of the covenant, becomes an ideal future. It becomes the Shalom of God, the time of God's reign, when every threat of internal infidelity and external menace is overcome, when the land is held in security and peace.

II

In the time of Jesus of Nazareth, these ideas of covenant were seen by groups of Jews as increasingly inadequate. Palestine had experienced successive conquests by great Near Eastern imperial powers: the Persians, the Greeks, and then the Romans. It had become a small province within the great Roman Empire that stretched from the Euphrates to the pillars of Hercules, from coastal North Africa to the misty lands of Britain. How could such a small people continue to imagine itself the apple of God's eye, or to think that human history turned on its particular fortunes?

The Jews themselves had become dispersed throughout this empire. Colonies of Jews were to be found in all the great cities of the Middle East and even in Greece and Rome. Some of these cosmopolitan Jews wished to allegorize their ancient traditions. The Temple was really the cosmos, and the Promised Land the homeland of the soul. The Torah expressed the natural law of universal ethics written on the consciences of all humanity. The particular expressions of the Jewish religion were simply the concrete form of this universal religion of humanity. Stoic philosophy viewed all persons as siblings under the universal parenthood of God.

Paul belonged to this cosmopolitan Jewish intelligentsia, anxious to overcome the offense of Jewish particularism. However, in his conversion to faith in Jesus as the Christ, he found a new, more powerful, way to express his quest for universalism. The ancient covenantal expectations had moved toward eschatological hope. It seemed to some apocalyptic groups of Jews that the inveterate human tendency to sin demanded a new and final dispensation of God's commandments that would implant them in the human heart once and for all. A new Moses would arise, who would teach a new and spiritual Torah. The people of Israel would finally understand and heed God's will, and the promises of God's messianic reign would be fulfilled (e.g., Jer. 31:31–34).

For Paul, Jesus the Christ was the solution to the dilemma of the ever-unfulfilled obedience of Israel to the demands of the covenant. God does not demand that the people fulfill a certain set of commands before God completes the promise. On the contrary, humanity is incapable of such obedience. Through the sin of its first ancestor,

Adam, humanity shares a common sinful nature. God fulfills the promises of the covenant by providing humanity with a new nature. Jesus is that new humanity through which fidelity to God will be implanted in the human heart as a new spiritual nature. This new covenant, like the old, cannot be earned. It is a free gift of God. It has been given to us even when we were sold under sin (Rom. 5:12–21).

This new covenant also abolishes the particularity of the old covenant. The difference between Israel and the nations is overcome. Paul reinterprets the old story of the covenant of God with Abraham. The promise that Abraham will be the father of many nations means all the nations of humanity, Jew and Gentile. The promise is given before the law. Fulfillment of the promise does not depend on fulfilling the law, but is a free gift. Those who are spiritual children of Abraham and heirs of the promise are those who, like Abraham, are justified through faith (Rom. 4:13–25).

Christians tend to assume that Gen. 3:1–24 is the basis of a doctrine of original sin that is basic to biblical theology, viewed through the lens of traditional Christian theology. But, in fact, the sin of Adam and Eve appears as a legend in the early chapters of Genesis and was never used in Old Testament thought, nor in the early Christianity of the Gospels, as the basis of a concept of the sin of the first ancestors. This idea emerged in certain forms of Judaism, but has never been adopted as a Jewish theological tenet. Paul's development of this idea made it central to Christian theology.

For Paul, Jesus embodies the new, spiritual and eschatological covenant, open to all, transcending the present sinful condition of humanity. The particularity of Israel, its peoplehood, land, and commandments, came to represent, for Paul, this sinful condition of humanity now superseded by Christ. The church is the new, spiritual and universal Israel that has superseded the old particularist and carnal people of the law. It has rescued humanity from the dilemma of the human condition. This interpretation of Jesus as the embodiment of the promise of the new covenant solved, for Paul, the contradiction between particularity and universality, carnality and spirituality, mortality and eternal life.

III

However, we Christians who live almost 2,000 years later cannot rest with simply repeating the Pauline formulas. Many new historical situations have developed. Christians have become a great imperial people spanning many nations. The view of Judaism as the old, superseded humanity and religion has been translated into two millennia of religious odium and racism. It has spawned a history of pogroms, culminating in the Holocaust. Biblical thought is not authentic if it merely repeats old formulas, revelatory in their time, but now misleading. It must respond to new historical conditions. The history of anti-Semitism, culminating in the Holocaust, is such a new condition that demands new reflection.

Is it appropriate today to speak of Israel (i.e., Jews) as the old, superseded humanity, over against the church as the new, universal and spiritual humanity of God's promise? Doesn't this distort Paul's thought by turning what was, for him, an internal dialectic of his own identity into an external opposition of historical groups? Christians appropriate the positive side of universality and eschatological hope and project upon the Jews the shadow side of human failure. In this way Christianity makes Jewish identity a paradigm of perfidy, but also loses the prophetic tradition of self-criticism.[18]

Israel was a small people embracing many tribes. Christians are a large people embracing many nations. But they are still a particular historical people. To claim that they are the one universal people, the sole means by which one is a child of God and heir of the promise, is an ethnocentric imperialism. Such a claim denies to others the right to their own identity and relationship to God through their own history.

Rabbinic Judaism and its adherents have had a different way of relating particularism and universalism. They have seen the covenant of God with Adam, renewed in the covenant with Noah after the Flood, as the universal covenant with all humanity. This universal human covenant does not cancel out the particularity of God's covenant with Israel, but gives each its place. The Noachic covenant carries with it its universal obligations. These are the basic laws of human decency and justice of people toward each other. Monotheism is also implied in the Noachic covenant, because humanity can only be one if there is one God who created us all.

But the particularity of the covenant with Israel remains. The Torah lays special and higher obligations upon Jews, as an expression not of special privilege, but of special obligation. Other peoples are not called to the Torah obligations. They may be saved through fulfilling the obligations of the Noachic code. One does not have to be a Jew to be saved.

Some Jews and Christians have tried to rethink the relationship between the covenant with Israel and the new covenant in Christ in ways that amend these traditional patterns. For example, some say that the old covenant is still valid, but particular to the people of Israel, and that Christianity is the way this particular covenant is universalized and extended to the Gentiles.[19] While this pattern might solve the relations of Jews and Christians, it is doubtful that Moslems or Buddhists would be satisfied with this viewpoint, which discounts the validity of their identities.

It seems that Paul's problem of particularism and universalism, history and eschatology, is not yet solved. We are still particular people with distinct historical identities, each of which demands that it be taken seriously as a framework of meaning and identity before God. Moreover, each of these identities carries residues of demands and hopes that have not yet been fulfilled. We need a new understanding of universality that can affirm the many particular peoples without trying to submerge one into another, and still affirm our kinship in one humanity. Each of these identities carries obligations that do not negate other people, but which are the self-critical goad to become our authentic selves. In this sense, the members of each people exist in the covenant with their particular ancestor, rooted in universal humanity and pointing forward to their true selves. Abraham, Adam, and Christ are paradigms of these three dimensions of covenant: particular, universal, and messianic.

IV

Western European and American societies, through a distorted and secularized version of Christian universalism, have become imperialist and colonialist societies. The dominant identity of privileged groups has projected itself as the only authentic human identity, the norm for being human. To be Christian was the only authentic way of being religious. European Christian nations saw themselves as having a divine mandate to conquer and absorb all other peoples into their culture/religion.

This imperialism was extended to many other characteristics of the dominant group. Only the European language of the conquering groups was civilized. Others must forget their own languages and histories and identify with the language and history of the conquerors. Indians learned to think of themselves as Spanish; Indonesians as Dutch; Africans as English or French; and so on. To be white, male, and of the privileged classes allowed one to exercise the rights and privileges of the culture and the state. Other people remained invisible. Their stories were not a part of the public culture. They could not go to the universities, enter public life, define their own identities, or defend themselves.

However, for some two hundred years this European and American extension of its own universal and messianic ideals has engendered its own contradiction. Conquered religious and racial groups, and also women, have begun to rise up against this imperialism and claim their own share in the universal humanity. Males cannot define women's identity. Whites cannot define black identity. Europeans cannot define Third World identity. Each people must recover its own suppressed history and define its distinctive ways of being human in the light of its particular realities.

Black theology, feminist theology, Latin-American liberation theology have become the ways in which Christians in these groups have begun to reflect theologically upon this history of injustice and suppression.[20] Each looks forward to a new culture where each can become visible and self-affirming, in a new global system which dismantles privilege and unprivilege, and in which all groups have their place in the sun. This is the new way of reflecting on the meaning of the coming of God's Shalom.

Some people have condemned the minority theologies as a contradiction of Christian universalism. There cannot be black theology, feminist theology, Latin-American theology. There must be one theology for everyone. But this is to fail to understand that the dominant theologies have masked the imperialism of the dominant identities. They have acted as though white, male, and European experiences were universal. Only by recognizing the particularity of the dominant identities, and accepting the right of the subjugated groups to become self-defining, can we work through to that authentically universal humanity which still eludes us. To affirm our common humanity in the covenant with Adam is to struggle to overcome the heritage of sexism, racism, and colonialism.

The covenant of God with creation calls us to go beyond even the quest for human solidarity. It calls us to ask about our covenant with nature. Rapacious relations with nature, polluted skies and waters, also reflect the false claims of some groups to use the resources of the earth at the expense of others. We cannot create a more just social order without asking about a more sustainable relationship with the skies, the waters, and the soil, which are the matrix of created existence.[21]

The covenant with Adam within the covenant of creation leads us back to the beginning and toward the future. It is a mandate to become a people living in justice and harmony with each other and the world. The covenant of creation, reaffirmed with Noah, is like a rainbow of hope over the world, pointing us forward to that time of promised fulfillment. This is the time when, as Jesus taught us, God's kingdom comes, God's will is done on earth. This is the mandate and promise of the covenant with Abraham, pointing back to Adam and Noah, and forward to Christ.

4

THE COVENANT AT SINAI: RESPONSE TO GOD'S FREEDOM

Bruce C. Birch

Sinai Covenant

Basis for the Pentateuch	Deut. 26:5–11	
Moses' Call	Ex. 3:1–8, 13–15	I Cor. 10:1–12
Wilderness	Ex. 17:3–7; 24:12–18	
Ten Words	Ex. 20:1–3, 12–17	
In the Promised Land	Josh. 5:9–12	

Included in the Old Testament lectionary readings for the Lenten season are a number of passages that have to do with the establishment of God's covenant with Israel at Mt. Sinai. Covenant is the major image through which Scripture understands the concrete implications of salvation for religious and social community. Covenant is a special focus of the Third Sunday in Lent, where the Old Testament reading for each year of the three-year cycle is a covenant passage. For Year A, Ex. 24:12–18 gives the narrative account of Moses' ascent onto the sacred mountain, where he will receive God's law. In Year B our reading is the Ten Commandments, found in Ex. 20:1–17. For Year C the selection is the story of the call of Moses, Ex. 3:1–15, which is the key to understanding the events of Israel's story from Egypt to Sinai, especially in the social implications of those events. In addition to the readings for the Third Sunday in Lent, Year C includes for the First Sunday the important creedal statement from Deut. 26:5–11. This creed is recited at the offering of firstfruits and is in effect a recalling and renewing of the covenant relationship between Israel and God.

It is important to note that the lectionary has included readings on the Sinai covenant before we encounter the story of Israel's deliverance from bondage in Egypt—which, of course, is the reverse of the biblical order. In Exodus the central salvation event of deliverance from bondage is followed by the establishment of covenant, which grounds the experience of salvation in concrete sociopolitical history. In the lectionary the exodus event does not appear until the Easter Eve Vigil and on Easter Sunday. This juxtaposes the central salvation experience of the Old Testament with the resurrection as the central saving event of the New. The effect is to change the mood of the covenant readings earlier in Lent from response to anticipation. These passages now anticipate the goal of liberation in the formation of faithful community. Liberation is not only *from* but *for.*

The few covenantal passages in Lent are enough to expose the major themes associated with covenant in the Old Testament. Above all else, covenant is a relational matter. In the dynamic relationship of covenant we learn more clearly who God is and what kind of community is called into existence by that God. Each of these covenantal partners must receive full focus. It is in the covenant theme that we see most clearly the necessary interconnections in the Hebrew faith between sacred and secular, religious and social, divine and human.[22]

I. COVENANT AS WITNESS TO THE CHARACTER OF GOD

1. The most striking aspect of the divine to which covenant points is the *freedom of God.* It is God who initiates covenant, but not because God is compelled to do so. God has entered into relationship out of sovereign freedom. "It is because the LORD loves you" (Deut. 7:8).

Paul van Buren, in an especially helpful treatment of the freedom of God,[23] has suggested that this freedom is seen most clearly in God's choosing of Israel (the promise to the ancestors), God's creation of the world, and God's liberation of Israel from Egypt. None of these central acts were compelled or necessary. They can only be accounted for out of God's free action for the sake of relationship.

Two of these three witnesses to God's freedom are seen in our lectionary passages. Exodus 3 is the beginning of the events that lead to God's liberation of Israel from the hands of the oppressive Pharaoh, but when this God is revealed to Moses it is as the God who has already freely entered into relationship with Abraham and Isaac and Jacob through the promise (Ex. 3:6, 15). God announces the divine intention to liberate Israel (3:8), but it is not because of Israel's merit or God's obligation. The reference back to the ancestors makes clear that this is a new act of divine freedom based only on a promise freely given. Salvation by the hand of this God is to be understood as unconditional, unearned, and unexpected. Deuteronomy 26:5ff. shows Israel's memory of promise and deliverance in precisely this way, as actions of God's grace, not achievements due to Israel's righteousness or importance. The promise of relationship and the experience of liberation are gifts of God.

Those concerned for the social implications of faith have sometimes undervalued the biblical notion of God's freedom. Walter Brueggemann has reminded us that the liberation of Israel from Egypt was not only the overturning of an oppressive social system but the disclosure of an alternative to the state triumphalism of Egypt's religion. "In place of the gods of Egypt, creatures of the imperial consciousness, Moses discloses Yahweh the sovereign one who acts in his lordly freedom, is extrapolated from no social reality, and is captive to no social perception but acts from his own person toward his own purposes. At the same time, Moses dismantles the politics of oppression and exploitation by countering it with a politics of justice and compassion. . . . The participants in the Exodus found themselves . . . involved in the intentional formation of a new social community to match the vision of God's freedom."[24] Formation of alternative community in covenant is accompanied by an alternative understanding of the divine.

2. God not only has freedom but has chosen to use that freedom to enter into relationship. Freedom alone could result in the picture of an aloof, uncaring God. This is not at all the picture in our covenantal texts. Instead we see a God whose freedom has been used to become vulnerable to human experience. This *vulnerability of God* is what James Wharton has called God's freedom *for* Israel alongside God's freedom *from* Israel.[25] To put it simply, God has chosen to care about people, and that care is seen particularly in relation to those who are oppressed and suffering.

Exodus 3:7 is one of the classic texts for this theme. Here God not only cares about the oppression of the Israelites in bondage but identifies with them and even participates in their suffering. God sees Israel's plight and acknowledges the cry of complaint that comes from Israel.[26] The most remarkable statement comes in the last phrase (foreshadowed in 2:25): "I *know* their sufferings." The Hebrew verb *yd'* ("to know") means far more than the cognitive knowledge our word implies. For the Hebrews "to know" meant a total involvement with and experiencing of that which is known. This is one of the beginning points of a Judeo-Christian conception of a suffering God. God participates in the pain of those who suffer. The ultimate expression of this is the crucifixion. This text is extraordinarily appropriate to Lent, when one of the main themes should be the vulnerability of God to those who suffer—and, by extension, the vulnerability required of God's community.

On the basis of God's caring, God acts to deliver. Identification with Israel's suffering does not mean God's acceptance of Israel's condition (Ex. 3:8). This caring leads not only to God's liberation but also to the formation of community in covenant. Although the lectionary selection omits it, v. 12 clearly indicates that God's deliverance is to result in a return to Sinai, where covenant community is to be formed. Exodus 24:12–18 is the story of the establishment of this relationship to God in social as well as religious terms, a relationship already envisioned in the call to Moses in Exodus 3. Covenant is our reminder that God's salvation is the beginning of a spiritual relationship with God that is to be expressed in concrete social terms.

3. If we were to trace the covenant themes from our lectionary passages on through the days of the kings and the prophets, we would find there a witness to the *fidelity of God*. Our passages are the beginning of that story of God's faithfulness. Israel can choose to break covenant and therefore sever the relationship, but God's love and the offer of that relationship are never withdrawn. It is a permanent and unconditional offer initiated freely by God.

The Hebrew word for this covenant faithfulness is *hesed*, "steadfast love." Psalm 136 expresses it best by using the refrain over and over, "For [God's] steadfast love endures forever." Deuteronomy 26:5ff. is a recital of Israel's experience of that covenant faithfulness of God. The fidelity of God to the freely given covenant relationship becomes the basis in Israel's faith for justice, righteousness, and peace (shalom). These qualities can only exist in history if they are based in a radically free God who is not limited by history, yet is trustworthy in relationship to that history. Any attempt to locate justice and its related qualities in the social order itself is destined to fail, for even the most noble attempts at just community experience brokenness. Israel's own history is eloquent testimony to that. Even the covenant community fell into patterns of oppression and privilege. Hope was possible because God in whom justice rests was free and faithful. Thus, the prophets could announce both judgment and hope in the name of that covenant God. Wherever the attempt is made to limit or domesticate the freedom of God or to suggest that God is not faithful in caring (e.g., the nihilistic claim that justice is purely relative), you can be certain that privilege and oppression in the social order are not far behind.

II. COVENANT AS CONTEXT FOR FAITHFUL COMMUNITY RESPONSE

Covenant at Sinai is the occasion for the community's response to God's liberation in the exodus event. Israel has known God's saving grace. How were the people to live in acknowledgment of that grace? Relationship had been established by God's free initiative. Surely such a relationship transforms and makes new the life of the people.

Covenant finds its basis in the liberation of exodus. As Ex. 20:2 acknowledges: "I am the LORD your God, who brought you out of the land of Egypt, out of the house of bondage." Whatever else covenant is, it is an act of response to God's freedom in behalf of Israel. The salvation experience cannot stand alone as an end in itself. Exodus challenges Israel to use its freedom to choose for God. American Christians have often given in to the temptation to proclaim salvation without calling to covenant. We have settled for exodus without Sinai, resurrection without Pentecost. Biblically this separation of God's saving and liberating activity from the work of community-building (social and religious) is impossible.

1. Covenant was a *context for the remembrance of liberation.*
Deuteronomy 26:5ff. and Ex. 20:2 show the seriousness of Israel's
memory. These texts are probably reflective of formal liturgical moments in which the keeping alive of the liberating memory of Israel
was an important covenantal task. How else is the community to
trust in God's liberating action in moments when that liberation
seems impossible or far off?[27] Memory is the root of hope.

Remembrance of exodus in Israel was not only a matter of hope,
it was a matter of humility. Over and over again in the Old Testament
texts Israel is admonished in a manner similar to this: "You shall
remember that you were a slave in the land of Egypt, and the LORD
your God redeemed you" (Deut. 15:15). All is the gift of God. Even its
deliverance was not because of unique status before God, but simply
because God loved this seemingly insignificant band of slaves (Deut.
7:7–8).

The community of faith from biblical times onward has been
tempted, when it experienced prosperity, to take pride in its own
efforts and worth. Blessing is regarded as an achievement. Covenant
was the context for Israel's remembering of its own roots among the
dispossessed. Such remembrance was a corrective to pride and self-
sufficiency.

2. Covenant is the term used to identify what appears biblically to
be the *formation of an alternative community,* a new social/religious
reality among the nations of Israel's time.[28]

The religious focus of this community is on the alternative vision
and experience of a radically free God. We have already discussed
this aspect of the covenant understanding earlier. The human community of Israel holds forth the memory of this God's liberating activity and forms itself in a manner that reflects God's activity in its own
life. The people of a liberating God must become a liberating community. James Wharton expresses this well: "God's style of relating is
marked by covenant love, covenant justice, covenant goodness, covenant faithfulness, covenant truth, covenant 'delight in the other.'
When Israel responds to God in faith and trust, these same qualities
emerge as Israel's style of relating defined by God in Torah, elicited
by God from Israel, but to be chosen freely by Israel as the style
appropriate to loving God with heart, soul, and might."[29]

In short, God's freedom *for* Israel was to be reflected in Israel's
freedom *for* others. Jesus' summation of the greatest commandment
in the unity of love of God with love of neighbor (Matt. 22:34–40) is
indeed an accurate summation of the Old Testament understanding
of covenant relationship (Lev. 19:18). As has long been recognized,
the Decalogue itself moves from commandments dealing with relationship to God (1–4) to those dealing with the neighbor (5–10) as
equally part of the basic community obligation (Ex. 20:1–17).

3. Because God in deliverance has identified with the powerless, the alternative community of covenant was also called to *special concern for the dispossessed*. In Israel this was understood very radically. Love and care for the dispossessed was not an optional act of voluntary piety. It was at the heart of what it meant to be God's people. Even as God knows and shares our suffering, we can know God through our identifying with the pain and need of others (cf. Jer. 22:16).

Concern for the dispossessed in Israel was not allowed to remain abstract or individualistic. At Sinai, Israel was called upon to begin the task of embodying its experience of God's deliverance in a community where love of God would be intimately bound up with love of neighbor. Israel was liberated *from* oppression and suffering, but it was liberated *for* community and mutual responsibility. The central question Sinai poses for those concerned with bread and justice in our modern world is this: How can hope move from proclamation to embodiment in social systems?

The law codes are a primary witness in the Old Testament to the seriousness with which Israel took this covenantal task of social formation. The law codes of Israel represented a radical reordering of the social systems and religious practice of Israel's time. These legal materials are greatly misunderstood and undervalued in the modern church. We tend to think of the law as rigid and confining. Indeed, it can become that when separated from covenant, as with some of Jesus' opponents. But in the Old Testament there are so many different law codes precisely because Israel knew that the task of concrete embodiment of covenant understanding in religious and social systems must go on anew in every generation. Each collection of legal material represents a new taking up of the struggle for faithful social formation.

Much could be learned from this material and from the call of the prophets to return to these tasks of social formation, but selections from the case law of Israel and from the prophets are not part of our lectionary selections for Lent.[30]

What has been included, however, is *the Decalogue* (Ex. 20:1–17). This is one of the foundational documents of Israel's covenantal tradition and the cornerstone of all Israel's efforts to give concrete expression to covenant community in the social order. Unlike Israel's case law, these ten "words" are expressed as negatives. They are prohibitions with no effort to describe particular contexts for application or penalties for violations. In fact, they cry out for the formation of case law as the necessary next step.

Walter Harrelson, in an important recent work,[31] has helped us to understand the importance of the Decalogue as a defining of the initial boundaries within the covenant community. These prohibitions point to the "path that leads to death" and those things that undermine free and whole relationship to God and others. Except for the fact that they include an explicitly religious dimension, they are for Harrelson analogous to the general statement of rights found in such documents as the U.S. Bill of Rights and the Universal Declaration of Human Rights. They are the noes that the Israelite faith community says to the tendency to compromise with the influences of other cultural pressures. From the statement of those boundary concerns Israel can continue in its case law to flesh out whole systems of faithful covenant community.

The church in our time very much needs to appropriate the images of Sinai as well as those of exodus. We must become involved in working for social structures that embody God's demand for justice and righteousness. The stress of Sinai is upon corporate as well as individual action. The call is for systemic care rather than for episodic concern. The crises facing this world with its limited resources and its great gap between rich/powerful and poor/powerless cannot be forestalled by Band-Aid responses to crises while the need for whole new structures of justice goes unnoticed. The biblical word is clear: we cannot seek our own salvation without seeking that of our neighbor, and we cannot minister to the anguish of our neighbor's soul without ministering to the anguish of our neighbor's body. We have been called into covenant by the action of the free, caring God. Exodus frees us from the forced labor that builds the Pharaoh's cities, but Sinai calls us to the covenantal labor that is necessary to build the just community.

BIBLIOGRAPHY

Birch, Bruce C., and Rasmussen, Larry L. *Bible and Ethics in the Christian Life.* Augsburg Publishing House, 1976.
_____. *The Predicament of the Prosperous.* Westminster Press, 1978.
Brueggemann, Walter. *The Prophetic Imagination.* Fortress Press, 1978.
Harrelson, Walter. *The Ten Commandments and Human Rights.* Fortress Press, 1980.
Hillers, Delbert R. *Covenant: The History of a Biblical Idea.* Johns Hopkins Press, 1969.
McCarthy, D. J. *Old Testament Covenant: A Survey of Current Opinions.* John Knox Press, 1972.
Van Buren, Paul. *The Burden of Freedom: Americans and the God of Israel.* Seabury Press, 1976.

5

TOWARD THE BREAKPOINT— AND BEYOND

Walter Brueggemann

Hos. 2:2–23; Jer. 31:31–34; Isa. 43:16–21;
II Chron. 36:14–21; Ezek. 37:1–14

These texts are best understood with reference to a "breakpoint," a time of deep discontinuity in personal experience and social cohesiveness. They bear witness to the collapse of an entire life world. The result is total displacement in every dimension of life. And then they begin to bear witness to the surprise of new life that emerges out of the breakpoint (Doomed Kingdom/New Covenant). Beyond the breakpoint there emerges a new social possibility given only by the mercy of God.

I

The most comprehensive statement about the breakpoint among these texts is in Hosea 2 (vs. 2–23). We may begin there by paying attention to the structure of the text. The structure of this extended poem will give us a model out of which to consider the other texts in this cluster. This text is easily divided into three poetic movements:

1. Verses 2–13 are a harsh statement of judgment that Yahweh will work against God's special people. These verses assert that an end is coming to Israel in its present form. A collage of reasons is given for that end. All the reasons concern distorted and destructive faith.

2. Verses 14–15 anticipate an "in between" moment, in which Israel is helpless and hopeless. Nonetheless, Israel experiences transformation because of God's unexpected intervention. Of course this moment of helplessness is not first of all understood as "in between." It is, rather, discerned as an ignominious social end. There is hid in this moment the strange way in which God works newness where none has been expected. God's newness for Israel is visible precisely in a moment of resourcelessness. But God's newness is characteristically hidden and not advertised. And the Bible regularly mumbles about that unexpected working of newness, because it does not know

what to say. The reality of God's transformation lies beyond our language and our rationality.

3. Verses 16–23 lyrically announce a whole new beginning for Israel in which communion with God is completely restored and the good blessings of life are assured. Communion with God, blessings in creation, harmony in history are now identified and anticipated with specificity.

Two observations can be made about the structure and movement of the text. First the movement of the poem itself seems to correspond to the historical experience of Israel as a political entity. The poem likely is an imaginative engagement with the crisis of 725–722 B.C., when Samaria (the capital city) and the entire Northern Kingdom was destroyed after a long siege by the Assyrians. In one poem the prophet dramatizes the whole history of Israel, even the future that is not yet known by the historians. Thus:

Before 725	*725–722*	*After 722*
Hos. 2:4–13	vs. 14–15	vs. 16–23
the dread collapse	destruction and	new possibility after
and failure	hopelessness	the disaster

Everything is funneled toward and out of the breakpoint of vs. 14–15, which is the dramatic center of the text. In that moment Israel's landed security is voided and Israel is again in a place of dependence and resourcelessness. The old identity as a nation-state is now nullified.

It is the function of the poem to take the listener through the entire historical experience, so that imaginatively Israel is led again through its whole life from the pre-land days, and into the land again. The poem is commonly dated well before 725, so that the breakpoint is an anticipation. And the future possibility of vs. 16–23 is a radical hope well beyond the breakpoint and well beyond the historical data. The poet speaks about such a future not because of visible data, but because he knows of God's relentless commitment to Israel. When the poem is seen to be structured this way, we can observe that the prophet-poet is not simply being descriptive or flatly commenting on what is, but is creating a scenario of a future breakpoint that is sure to come. Thus his poetry invites Israel to an alternative imagination of the future that undermines the dominant, mistaken perception of the present.

Second, the structure of the passage invites Israel to imagine itself on both sides of the breakpoint, both before and after the disaster of 725–722, both before and after vs. 14–15. Thus interpretation might well begin at this central point and move in both directions. The poem asserts that the situation after the break (vs. 16–23) is both continuous with and discontinuous from the situation before 725 (vs. 2–13). Thus:

Before the Disaster	*After the Disaster*
"did not know" (Hos. 2:8)	"know the LORD" (v. 20)
"grain, wine, oil" (v. 8)	"grain, wine, oil" (v. 22)

The new future cannot be understood apart from the old situation. The new situation is full restoration of what had been hoped for and lost in the old. But it is equally the case that the new situation will be quite unlike the old. The old situation is one of a doomed kingdom, a social system under the harsh, inescapable judgment of God. The new situation, by contrast, is one of ready, joyous, fruitful, responsive covenant. Indeed, the old situation of Israel is doomed precisely because it is not covenantal. In the old, doomed kingdom they "did not know," i.e., did not acknowledge, the covenant Lord, did not recognize the only giver of life. In the new age they will know the name of the giver and will answer God faithfully. In the old situation there is loss of grain, wine, and oil, a loss of energy, a termination of the good life assured by creation. In the new covenantal situation, the covenanted earth will "perform" as blessed creation. The historical community will prosper because creation now functions faithfully. (In 4:1–3, Hosea suggests that the creation is dysfunctional when Israel does not keep Torah.)

The contrast between the two situations is total. The future is unexpected and surprising, not to be derived from the old fickle arrangement. The breakpoint is and can only be when Israel is resourceless, alone with Yahweh. Everything depends on that time alone with Yahweh, at Yahweh's mercy, abandoning every other prop, all other gods, all alternative forms of security. And it is that terrifying breakpoint with the collapse of false supports which permits new life given freely by God.

II

When that grid of *old situation / breakpoint / new situation* is fully established, then the other texts in this cluster can be seen according to the same model. Most interesting is II Chron. 36:14–21. Note that it serves to end the book. Indeed it serves to end the entire historical recital of the Chronicles. And in the Hebrew order of texts, this is the very last paragraph of the entire Hebrew Bible. That is where the canon closes! This is historical narrative come to a sorry end. The doomed kingdom is harshly judged. The movement of the text is the same as in Hosea 2. The difference is that while Hosea speaks of the Northern break of 725–722 B.C., Chronicles is preoccupied with the Southern break of 587 B.C. and the failure of the David enterprise. But structurally and theologically the issue is the same. The doomed kingdom is the royal-urban system of Judah. With its monarchy and Temple system, it sought to secure itself. But it has been unresponsive to the expectations of Yahweh, unwilling to repent and reorder public life, and so sure to perish.

The text includes only the first two of the structural elements we have found in Hosea 2. That is, there is only a hint of the third element of a new covenanted community. But even in this truncated form, there is a deliberate move from the *old situation* to the *breakpoint of nullification.* The move is dramatically expressed in the phrase used twice, "had compassion" *(hamal):*

"because he had compassion" (II Chron. 36:15) warning before the breakpoint, prior to 587	"therefore he . . . had no compassion"(v. 17) the breakpoint of 587

Because Judah was unresponsive to the Lord of compassion, the time for mercy passed. And then Judah had to deal with the Babylonians (Chaldeans), who were sent by Yahweh and who had no compassion. They had let the time for compassion pass in their recalcitrance, and now came harshness in the form of an occupying army with imperial ruthlessness.

With the Babylonian army came the breakpoint of Yahweh. The situation was now hopeless and beyond recall. This writer does not have the wherewithal or the courage to say much about any new situation. The end is too massive and overriding. The disobedient society runs against the sovereign God and must be destroyed. There had been mercy (v. 15). Indeed, the entire history of Judah had been one of mercy. The mercy was a warning that Judah must change or die. In that statement about the warning persistently given in the prophets, the text summarizes the entire preexilic history (cf. II Kings 17:12; Zech. 1:1–6). For purposes of this text, that entire historical sequence consists in and exists for the sake of the warning.

But God's compassion is rejected. "Therefore . . ." (v. 17). It is a massive, overpowering "therefore." History takes a turn even as does the rhetoric. The text, like the history itself, moves abruptly to the second point, the disastrous collapse of the whole social system. King and Temple are helpless to prop it up. Having rejected the compassion of Yahweh, now Israel receives none from Babylon. Everything is ended. The entire network of meaning and values (in the form of Temple furnishings) is now confiscated and transported away. The glory has indeed departed.

The final paragraph of II Chronicles (36:22–23) hints at a third element, a new beginning. It is only a hint, barely mentioned. But it is important structurally. The narrative reports the "stirring of the spirit" (v. 22). And when the spirit stirs, there is possibility beyond collapse. The spirit has the chance to evoke genuine newness. So we may go beyond our designated verses for this hint and hope. The new possibility of vs. 22–23 is understated. But it serves the same function as Hos. 2:16–23, to receive a newness from God. This muted anticipation is given with the concreteness of a historian, linked to Cyrus and the Persian Empire (cf. Isa. 44:28; 45:1). To the extent that it has such imperial specificity, this hope is unlike the more lyrical anticipation of Hosea. But the concreteness is most restrained. It is enough to show compassion to the ones without compassion (cf. Hos. 2:23, where the point about new compassion is made in a similar way). That these texts, poem and narrative, can move beyond "no compassion" is not to find hope in the social system. It testifies rather to God's utter freedom "to show mercy on whom I will show mercy" (Ex. 33:19), even on this people just rejected.

III

But it remained for the three great poets of the exile to articulate the coming newness in all its fullness. Now they have put behind them what is old and failed. No need to excoriate Judah further. That point has been made both by the poets and by the invading armies. Now, with exquisite nerve, these poets speak Israel out of exile and into a new context in which God's generous rule is at work. They speak words that create a new, faithful Israel (Rom. 4:17). Structurally these three anticipations function like the third scene of Hosea 2, to articulate with power the new world after Yahweh has moved the people into and beyond painful discontinuity.

1. Jeremiah 31:31–34 is the text best known to Christians, with its links to the new covenant in the Eucharist (Luke 22:20; I Cor. 11:25), and especially with its explicit use in Heb. 8:8–12; 10:16–17. Clearly the early church understood this great promise as linked to the future given by Jesus.

But our purpose is to see how this oracle of anticipation functions for the sake of the new covenant community. This Jeremiah who could speak so poignantly about the judgment and end (cf. Jer. 4: 19–26; 7:27–34) has the faith and resources now to speak beyond the end, in utter amazement about God's new age. God's new age is not dependent upon the old Israel. But it includes that precious Israel. The fresh covenant soon to come will be characterized by full obedience to Torah, by utter forgiveness, and by readiness to acknowledge Yahweh's rule. Notice that in Jer. 31:34 there is the same "knowing of the LORD" anticipated in Hos. 2:20. This new covenantal, humane, Torah-shaped rule displaces every destructive rule of greed and death.

2. The Ezekiel form of anticipation in 37:1–14 is likewise known in the Christian tradition because it serves to anticipate the resurrection of Jesus. The restoration of life here promised is not that of a dead man out of the tomb (not even Jesus), but a new epoch in Israel's history when the community fully responds to the power and pur-

poses of Yahweh. The resurrected One promised here is the faithful community upon whom the winds of God's spirit blow afresh (cf. II Chron. 36:22, where the wind of God blows for the sake of new community). The reality of death, the collapse of social reality, is real. But it is not the last word. Because God's freedom is at work in the public life of Israel, a new people is promised. A new political reality is to be given. What is anticipated here is not remote from "the kingdom" about which Jesus told stories, a people willingly under the rule of God. Both Old and New Testament have as their central anticipation a new public community genuinely responsive to Yahweh's purpose. To that these texts bear witness.

3. As the promise moves from Jer. 31 and Ezek. 37 to Isa. 43:16–21, the assertion of a coming alternative from God becomes more bold and strident. Now it is cast as a promissory speech of Yahweh, who is identified as the one who causes exoduses, who makes new social communities possible. God is able to intrude powerfully against imperial arrangements and make way for new social experimentation.

But even though God is here identified as one who causes exoduses, Israel is now urged to forget the old that has been judged and dismantled (v. 18). Now the old disobedient past characterized in Hos. 2:2–13 and II Chron. 36:14–21 is overridden. God has moved on. And Israel in its imagination is now authorized to move on as well. Israel is now brought by the poet to a new situation, not to anguish in chagrin, but to hoping and waiting and anticipating with buoyancy. The newness will bring all of creation under God's rule—the land, the animals, the water supply, and this people—as a form of praise to God. In every way these three poets announce a new social possibility that is contrasted with the old, recalcitrant one.

IV

We may now observe that all five of these texts can be ordered according to the same evangelical shaping of reality:

Doomed Kingdom	*Null Point*	*New Covenantal Community*
Hos. 2:2–13	vs. 14–15	vs. 16–23
II Chron. 36:14–16	vs. 17–21	(vs. 22–23)
		Jer. 31:31–34
	Ezek. 37:1–2	vs. 3–14
		Isa. 43:16–21

Note that in the configuration of the entire cluster, there is a tilt to the new. These texts do not linger on the judgment of the old. But they presume it. The nullification of the old is very much a part of their hope for newness from God.

The details of exposition of these texts are of course not unimportant. But those details are best understood in the light of this characteristic movement of God's work among us. In different ways these texts bear witness to three convictions:

1. The old social order, disobedient and unresponsive as it is, is under God's judgment and must be nullified. It can be propped up only so long. But because it will not heed a warning and turn, it will disappear. That much is sure. This is a startling affirmation, because we are wont to believe that somehow we can sustain ourselves and endlessly find ways to secure ourselves. These texts assert that no such arrangements can finally resist God's verdict upon a disobedient creation. This is a bold point, because it affirms, against every pretension to autonomy, that answer must be given to God.

2. There will be a new social reality wrought by God out of the hopeless shambles and ruins of what has been. This is a sure affirmation in all these texts. It is an equally staggering statement, because such promise lies beyond our reason and our definition of possibility. It does appear to be impossible (cf. Mark 10:27). We do not really believe in such a radical newness, because we doubt that God is such a free agent. And yet that massive expectation is the only ground for continued caring about the shape of human community.

3. The move from the doomed kingdom to the new covenanted reality is not an easy or a ready one, so that we can move unperturbed from the one to the other. There is a waiting, both in hope and hopelessness, at the "null point." With Hosea there is *wilderness* to which we submit. With Ezekiel there is a season of *dry bones* during which we do not know if there will be a raising. With Isaiah in Babylon, there is an *exile.* The season of God's newness will not be rushed or predicted or programmed. It will not follow readily on the heels of the death. It requires us to wait and not be in control. So there is *an assurance* in the structure of the argument made in ancient Israel. But there is an *inscrutability* as well, for our faith is not in an automatic process or "passage," but in the free God who is Lord even of the processes of death and new life. Finally, we must wait upon the Lord who will not be forced or presumed upon.

V

These texts are set for us in the season of Lent. We ponder the death and resurrection of Jesus. And we think through the discipleship to which those events summon us. The texts link rather easily to the narrative of Jesus we have before us. In his own person Jesus now embodies the movement we have found in these texts; i.e., it is Jesus the innocent sufferer who is brought to death for the sake of the doomed kingdom. It is Jesus the condemned Messiah who takes the role of the troubled city. It is Jesus (in the memory of the church) who "descends into hell," who embraces the wilderness, enters exile. It is

Jesus who from Friday to Sunday lives in God's Nullity. And it is Jesus who surprises us with new life, who is the embodiment of the covenantal social reality of the new age. With Jesus, as with Israel, none of this is automatic. All of it depends on the will and mercy of the Holy God. All of it depends on the responding faithfulness of Jesus.

We grow so accustomed to the story that we miss its startling assertion. It is startling and unacceptable that the Messiah should die (cf. Mark 8:32). And yet the cup is to be drunk (Mark 14:36). It is equally startling that this dead one now abandoned is raised to new life, with all authority, because the power of all that is old and dead cannot hold him (Acts 2:24).

This Jesus in his death and resurrection becomes the embodiment, model, and paradigm of the way it is with social reality in relation to the rule of God. This movement in the life of Jesus is caught in the hymnic assertion of Paul (Phil. 2:5–11). Jesus is asserted as the Lordly one who is emptied to death and exalted to full authority. Jesus also moved, in utter faithfulness to the null point of obedient death, and so was raised to new life as the Lord of the covenanted community.

It is that season of discontinuity which marks our own Lenten reflections on the cost and joy of discipleship! It is scandalous that the Messiah should be obedient to death, even more scandalous that the Holy City should be destroyed. Lent is for reflection upon and embrace of the reality that this One sent by God enters the nullity. And we sing songs of victory because the nullity is broken. In the risen Jesus, new social reality has become for us a concrete possibility.

VI

It is important, before we finish, to make a move to contemporary reality. These texts all speak about a doomed social reality and a surprising new social reality. The former is marked by disregard of God's purposes. The latter is expected to be fully covenantal. The texts boldly assume that the coming and going of kingdoms and nations, cities and empires, is the proper arena for God's rule. Such an assumption is difficult for us in a social setting that assigns absolute dignity to present social reality and that correspondingly reduces God's rule to private, "spiritual" matters.

The voice of these texts requires *two transformed theological convictions* on our part. First, the coming and going of the nations is not beyond the scope of God's rule. God's purposes finally will not be mocked (cf. II Kings 19:16). God's freedom will not be circumscribed. And derivatively, if God's Lordship does have such significance, the nations and social groups are not absolute or ultimate, but are provisional, answering willy-nilly to God's just and sovereign will. One is struck in these texts with the effortlessness of God who is able to dispose of a wayward people and the ease with which God forms a new people. It is not in doubt. God will end and begin according to God's nonnegotiable purposes. God readily does what God intends —and none can resist it (cf. Isa. 14:24, 27).

Of course, that God's way is effortless does not mean it is without anguish. For what God is freely able to do is not what God in passion and compassion may prefer to do. (On this point Hos. 11:8–9 is decisive.)

Any move to contemporaneity depends on those two transformed theological insights. And those insights do not come easily for us in our modern consciousness. We too are prone to assign absoluteness to national communities, and we too are inclined to reduce God's rule to "safer," more obvious matters. Nonetheless, the move depends on establishing an analogy to the doomed kingdom. What is the shape of the doomed kingdom in our experience, which stands under judgment? One must proceed neither easily nor hastily, and in any case only tentatively. But surely that harsh recognition of judgment applies to the system of exploitation and self-serving aggrandizement in corporate consumer capitalism. That is how it appears to this North American Christian. Perhaps in other contexts it would surge to awareness differently. But one can test it out by reading the text again with such a reference in mind.

We propose that the impingement of the texts upon the imagination of the church is by way of a daring analogy. Every such analogy is both bold and tenuous. The analogy is not in the mind or intent of the original poets. But the texts have a life of their own. They rush toward our own circumstance and require us to reexperience our own life. We dare to draw an analogy because it strikes us as overwhelming in its parallel. It will not do to choose up sides and argue about the analogy. It will be much better to ponder, to probe, and to test to see if our imagination is illuminated by the linkage.

The military-industrial-technological network is a comprehensive system not only of power but of meaning and value. That loosely wrought network, like ancient empires, claims to be self-contained, absolute in its authority, answering to none other. It genuinely believes and teaches as its credo that the system is indeed the solution. And whoever doubts that is excommunicated. As with every such pretense to absolutism, there is an absence of self-criticism, an unwitting practice of exploitation. When the holiness of God no longer makes us and our systems provisional, the worth of the neighbor is predictably jeopardized. What appears as a means of security, either in the East or in the West, may be seen as a rash of disobedience and so a rush to death. The social system of death stands under harsh judgment, incongruent as it is with God's covenantal purposes.

If the analogy be sustained, the poetry suggests that we are headed toward a nullity. This entire pretension of security and prosperity will fall. Indeed, there are signs that the judgment of God has begun. Loss of security, loss of meaning, loss of life-support systems, will render us utterly resourceless. One does not need to be excessively apocalyptic to enter the texts in this way. As in the old world of Israel, so now in our world, hints of the dismantling abound. Just as the Messiah must not die, so we wish our life world would endure unbroken. But it is beginning to erode and we sense our helpless futility in the face of it.

Now if the poets of the gospel do not lose heart, we may stay with the analogy of the text long enough to speak yet a hope beyond the painful data. Out of the dismay of collapse, God will work a newness. God will create what does not exist and what we cannot conjure, a community of covenant in which the dignity of each person is guarded, in which networks of justice and freedom function. The beginning is as incredible as the ending. And we are left to ponder if the poem will bear that much traffic when brought close to our experience.

Perhaps the text requires lesser analogies. Perhaps we might speak of the dismantling of the church or of some other "known world" of defunct meaning. The poem may be turned in many directions. But its central claim is relentless. God will rule. Therein lies our sharpest concrete dread, for we are caught in pretensions where God surely does not rule. And therein lies our only ground for hope, for we do know that we are made for public covenanting, and for nothing less.

Two things happen here as usual, as we ponder an analogy. The Lent of our life world presses us in anguish. The Easter of God's new covenant seems unlikely. It always is unlikely—until it is given.

6

PASSION WEEK
Frederick Herzog

Day of Holy Week	Year	First Lesson	Second Lesson	Gospel
Monday		Isa. 42:1–9	Heb. 9:11–15	Luke 19:41–48
Tuesday			I Tim. 6:11–16	John 12:37–50
Wednesday		Isa. 50:4–9a	Rom. 5:6–11	Luke 22:1–16
Maundy Thursday	A	Ex. 12:1–14	I Cor. 11:23–32	John 13:1–15
	B	Deut. 16:1–8	Rev. 1:4–8	Matt. 26:17–30
	C	Num. 9:1–3, 11–12	I Cor. 5:6–8	Mark 14:12–26
Good Friday	A	Isa. 52:13 to 53:12	Heb. 4:14–16; 5:7–9	John 19:17–30
	B	Lam. 1:7–12	Heb. 10:4–18	Luke 23:33–46
	C	Hos. 6:1–6	Rev. 5:6–14	Matt. 27:31–50
Easter Eve Vigil		Ex. 14:15 to 15:1 Ezek. 36:16–28	Rom. 6:3–11	

Understanding Passion Week involves major Christological commitments. Modern faith sees Jesus often as the lonely sufferer. The believer feels loneliness together with Jesus: "My God, my God, why hast thou forsaken me?" (Matt. 27:46). For many today the outcry tells not just of the experience of the absence of God, but of the absence of any experience of God.

The modern view of the cross has been shaped by many currents of thought, such as existentialism and personalism. Two thirds of humankind—the poor and the oppressed—are, however, frequently tuned out in these perspectives, which view death as the terminal point of our own existence.

Jesus' death makes us aware of our captivity to despair and failure. "Cancer of the soul" (Philip Wylie) sensitizes us to the downward trend in our life. It is betrayed by anxiety in us, and the self-deception in which we tell ourselves that we are not afraid.

In the modern mode we are not all that quickly able to find meaning in Jesus' death. Viewing it on the foil of eschatological expectations in Jesus' environment, Albert Schweitzer expressed the gift of one modern argument quite vigorously: Jesus, assuming himself to be the Son of Man, "lays hold of the wheel of the world to set it moving on that last revolution which is to bring all ordinary history to a close. It refuses to turn; and crushes Him. Instead of bringing in the eschatological conditions, He has destroyed them. The wheel rolls onward, and the mangled body of the one immeasurably great Man, who was strong enough to think of himself as the spiritual ruler of mankind and to bend history to His purpose, is hanging upon it still. That is His victory and His reign."[32]

Orthodox Christology could not possibly agree. Its view is that the cross is not an accident of history, but God's will from the foundation of the world for the atonement of the world's sins. It is God's self-sacrifice. Both the orthodox view and the modern approach primarily address the individual. A radically social dimension does not appear to be part of either one.

From exegetical considerations at one point one has to unpack the implicit Christology of the biblical texts. One has to take the risk of saying a new thing in an odd way. Holy Week does not present us with a choice between a meaningless mangled body and a meaningful sacrificial body. Besides modernity and orthodoxy, there is the witness of the primitive church, which does not make mention of Jesus' cross apart from the resurrection (cf. I Cor. 15:17–19).

In Passion Week we dare not tear the mangled body and the sacrificial body away from the resurrection body. What happened in the first Holy Week was already imbued with Easter and Pentecost. God's continuing presence in the crucified One was already a real moment of resurrection on the cross: "And I, when I am lifted up from the earth, will draw all [persons] to myself" (John 12:32).

According to the flesh (cf. II Cor. 5:16), we see nothing but a mangled body on the cross. Yet there is a reason why this scaffold sways the future, as we sing in a hymn. From beyond the dim unknown God invades the shadows of this cross and makes the body on it the reality that gathers in also all the poor and oppressed, all the losers as well as the lost. In the cross God reaches our conscience, turns around our fear of death, and constitutes a new humanity. In Jesus, God did not take on humanness in the abstract, general human nature. God took on specific human nature. In the outcast Jesus, all outcasts are present.

I. The Social Body

The meal at which Jesus shows his disciples the meaning of his death stresses what God is doing in Jesus' body. The text of I Cor.

11:17–34 has to be seen in the context of the abuse of Holy Communion in the primitive church of Corinth at that moment. Paul enjoins the Corinthians to see the death of Jesus as "for you." In this Jesus body, God is present. Thus it is the center of how members relate to each other.

Taking up the point of the disorder of the Corinthian church while celebrating the Eucharist, Tissa Balasuriya observes: "The Eucharist had no meaning if it was not egalitarian and building real community. Paul has a severe judgment on those who desecrated the Lord's Supper."[33] In Paul's view, the crucial issue for the celebrating congregation is "discerning the body" (v. 29). Christians have to understand what the body of Christ is about—for the order and justice of community life.

Paul focuses on the crucified body. Yet this body at the same time is imbued with the resurrection body. Communicated in the meal is not a sheer individual body, but the corporate body through which God expresses solidarity with all persons, the losers as well as the lost.

It may seem too simple when Balasuriya writes: "All were to be equal in the believing community and this was to be symbolized by the Eucharistic meal."[34] We can say this only if the resurrection has already made the mangled body the social body in which all are equal because of God's prevailing presence in it as reconciler and liberator. In this sense *the Lord's Supper is the justice meal.*

Orthodoxy and modern theories of the atonement do not pay primary attention to the relationship between the "one who is hungry" (v. 21) and the other members of the congregation. But Paul wanted us to see ourselves as part of Christ's social body—inclusive humankind.

A new Christology is emerging in a reconsideration of Scripture. The new understanding grows out of discipleship. God's presence in Jesus among the disciples in Galilee and Judea already involved participation in a new body. But as this Jesus went to the cross and finally hung on it, there was present through God's power every person in her or his brokenness, especially those who had been excluded from communion before, the poor and the outcast as well as the lost.

At the time, that also included the Gentiles. In Ephesians the mystery of Jesus as the person in whom God unites all humankind is described as making out of two former enemies, Jew and Gentile, the person and the nonperson, one new humanity. In the body of Jesus on the cross this new humankind is real (Eph. 2:16; cf. Gal. 3:28).

But could not all of this have been without death? Not in the least. God in solidarity with the lost and the losers takes on the brokenness and usurpation in which all of us live on account of sin. Temporal and eternal isolation is overcome and the usurpation of God's power and the rights of the neighbor are undone—swallowed up in the victory of the social body where no one is left to herself or himself. "The wages of sin is death" (Rom. 6:23). By taking death upon himself, Jesus through the real presence of God enables God to take death into Godhead and thus to undo it, bringing the enmity to an end (Eph. 2:16). Here the social body emerges fully. Death is swallowed up in victory.

In the resurrection body as social body the walls between human beings come tumbling down. It begins in the body on the cross. I Corinthians 11:23–32 offers the texture for grasping Christ's body as social body.

II. THE SOCIAL SELF

The more theory-like reflections of I Cor. 11:23–32 are backed up by concrete situations in the life of Christ embodying social selfhood, as reflected in John 13:1–15. The foot-washing undergirds the view of the Lord's Supper sketchily recorded in I Corinthians. Jesus' body is the outward expression of the "social self." He is the social self, not without the body. The social self is not a disembodied idea. In the breaking of the bread and the sharing of the cup the social body comes through forcefully as expression of the social self. The true body of Christ is no longer apart from communal reality. The actual Christopraxis of Jesus gives rise to eucharistic thought. What Jesus does in the breaking of the bread and the sharing of the cup is grounded in the foot-washing.

The gist of the matter is that in Jesus' life, God is incarnate. The foot-washing draws together all of Jesus' signs and actions prefiguring the cross. In it, social selfhood gets embodied as the inner ground of the social body. Before Jesus constitutes the universal body on the cross in the broken body and the shed blood, he embraces all of humanity.

The passage, John 13:1–15, begins with the pungent words: "Before the Passover festival, Jesus knowing that his hour had come to leave the world and to go to the Father, having loved his own who were in the world, he loved them to the end." In *Liberation Theology* (1972) I tried to grasp the gist of this thought in terms of the social self: "We have referred to *agape* . . . as costly love . . . concretized in signs and specific events. Its mystery is that for the first time we are radically *being loved.* Descartes defines himself as *cogito, ergo sum.* Now we can state the reason behind our claim: we can love, because we have been loved. Because of this love, *we are.* The Cartesian formula thus reconstructed would read *amor, ergo sum* (I am being loved, therefore I am). Even better: I am being loved, therefore *we* are, *amor, ergo sumus.*"[35]

On the little Latin phrase of Descartes hinges a lot of Western thought. It sums up the individualistic selfhood aspirations that have become dominant in the West. In Jesus, in the inner heart of things, we do not meet a sheer private person, but rather a corporate self in which God constitutes all of humanity as one community. Here God personally is also a communal self.

What the foot-washing embodies is this new reality of God among humankind—a selfhood we otherwise do not know, the social self. In Jesus' day, foot-washing was the lowly service of a slave. After traveling dusty roads, feet needed washing. Jesus used the "social institution" to dramatize who he was as social self. He stooped lower than a shoeshine boy who, as it were, only takes dirt off the shoes. As he stooped down he embodied the truth "that he had come from God and was going to God" (v. 3). God is made known in a church that did not make him known.

The washing of the disciples' feet concretizes social selfhood. There is nothing virtuous about lowliness as such. The point is that God realizes the social self in history exactly as the point where humanity is at its lowliest and not corporate at all. God constitutes humankind in a new way. On the cross the social self is fully embodied. "It is finished" (John 19:30). God has become an outcast personally. The darkness of the human condition, with its utter despair and the plight of the loser, has been embraced by God personally.

In the documentary film *A Day Without Sunshine,* which tells the plight of the American migrant worker, there is one worker who has tattooed on his arm, "Born to Be a Loser." It is for the losers that God also battles, incorporating them in the selfhood of the true child of God—Jesus.

III. Passover and Passion Week

The Passover of the Jewish community tells a story different from the foot-washing. Exodus 12:1–8, 11–14 makes us sensitive to other "passion weeks," in this instance the suffering of the children of Israel in Egypt and their redemption from Egypt.

An explicit connection between Christ Jesus and the Passover doctrinally is found only once in the New Testament: "For Christ our passover has been sacrificed" (I Cor. 5:7; cf. Rev. 5:12). The analogy was especially helpful for Jewish Christians who understood the sacrifice of Jesus as fulfillment of Israel's practice of Passover. What the killed paschal lamb was for the redemption of Israel in the exodus, the cross was for redemption at the end of time.

Christians have become accustomed to think of Christ's death as passover and to derive Christological benefit from this analogy. Yet for any Christology we need to keep in mind that redemption is going on also in other communities. God does not offer the divine gift as an exclusively "Christian" thing. The Passover points to the liberation of a whole people—something we hardly consider in our Christology. Redemption witnessed to by the Passover has vast corporate dimensions. It functions also as a political event. Christ as passover has all too often been understood as a private affair between the individual and God.

Christology of the social self outwardly expressed as social body will carefully acknowledge the integrity of Israel's tradition. It will not celebrate the superiority of Christianity. Even such a great liberal mind as that of Friedrich Schleiermacher held the conviction, "which we assume every Christian to possess, of the exclusive superiority of Christianity."[36] Christianity is not superior. God is superior.

The different ways to God are part of God's mystery. Yet we do not have to hold Lessing's "Parable of the Rings" view to come to grips with the issue: "The genuine ring no doubt got lost. To hide the grievous loss, to make it good, the father caused three rings to serve for one."[37] The genuine ring is not our religion, or anyone else's, for that matter. The genuine ring is God's work. God is the way to God in all losers as well as in all lost.

Christians do well in Lent to ponder "the wideness of God's mercy" and to learn from the Passover tradition to broaden the notion of redemption. God is at work to bring about "the healing of the nations" (Rev. 22:2). Any new Christology will be accompanied by modesty. Redemption does not come in different qualities. But as Christians we believe that we see it most clearly in the social selfhood of Christ. It is through Christ Jesus that God offers redemption to us. But even Christ Jesus today "we see through a glass darkly" (I Cor. 13:12).

BIBLIOGRAPHY

Balasuriya, Tissa. *The Eucharist and Human Liberation.* Orbis Books, 1979.
Boff, Leonardo. *Jesus Christ Liberator: A Critical Christology for Our Time.* Orbis Books, 1978.
Hellwig, Monika K. *The Eucharist and the Hunger of the World.* Paulist/Newman Press, 1976.
Herzog, Frederick. *Justice Church.* Orbis Books, 1980.
Robinson, John A. T. *The Body.* (1952) Westminster Press, 1977.
Sobrino, Jon. *Christology at the Crossroads.* Orbis Books, 1978.

B. A Whole Approach

LENT–HOLY WEEK

John H. Westerhoff III

The penitential season of Lent is among the oldest and most familiar in the church's eternal cycle. All too frequently, however, it has become a time in the liturgical year to support privatized introspection and self-denial, to encourage escape from our sociopolitical, economic problems, and to increase participation in institutional church life. Typically, parish life in this forty-day season has communicated and sustained a theology of individualism and human depravity resulting in a fatalism with regard to sin and its effects, or the conviction that the world is fundamentally evil and we humans are incapable of making a significant contribution to the transformation of life and history.

Nevertheless, Lent with its historic message remains an essential element in the yearly cycle of the Christian faith and life. A sound liturgical theology of Lent acknowledges sin (a fact some others would prefer to ignore), but Lent, faithfully understood, emphasizes the promise of redemption, is painfully conscious and passionately concerned about oppression and injustice, yet offers a hopeful (not sentimental) vision of the world and of human possibilities.

Recovering the season's meaning. Each year the holy season of Lent comes to us with its call to prayer, fasting, and almsgiving. In the Christian tradition, to pray is to turn toward God, listen for God's call, and discern God's will for social and personal life; to fast is to turn away from superfluous needs and to abstain from all that estranges us, potentially or actually, from God, our true selves, all humanity, and the natural world; to give alms is to turn our attention to the concrete needs of others and to seek their good through a ministry of caring action.

Lent asks us to reflect on our common life in church and society from the perspective of our baptismal covenant and to repent of our failure to live up to it. As a sign of God's covenant with us, we promise to continue in the apostles' teaching and fellowship, the breaking of bread and the prayers; we promise to persevere in resisting evil and, whenever we fall into sin, repent and return to the Lord;

we promise to proclaim by word and example the good news of God in Christ; we promise to seek and serve Christ in all persons, loving our neighbor as ourselves; and we promise to strive for justice and peace among all peoples and respect the dignity of every human being . . . all with God's help. (See *The Book of Common Prayer,* 1979).

Themes in the story line. Consistent with this liturgical understanding of the Lenten season, the themes in this ecumenical lectionary begin with a call to repentance. While we cannot change the past, we can turn toward a new vision, make restitution for the past, and act on behalf of an alternative future.

The second theme focuses on weakness and power. While we are all called to be persons of power and to use our capacity to effect change responsibly, power can be an occasion for sin or grace; it can be used on behalf of self-serving domination over others (sin), or in a self-giving obedience to God's will (grace). We are continually tempted to seek the first and in the name of Christianity to engage in a politics of messianism. Lent is a time to reflect on our use of power and to commit ourselves to the powerful weakness of messianic politics.

The third theme announces God's covenant with all humanity, a covenant promising justice and peace, equality and freedom, unity and the well-being of all to all who do God's will.

The fourth theme concerns the obligations and responses of those who live in God's covenant; that is, it reminds us that at the event of exodus and the giving of the law God identifies with the poor, hungry, oppressed, suffering and hurt, all those who are denied God's will for them. Lent is a time to reflect on how faithfully we have kept the covenant and acted with God on behalf of those with whom God identifies.

The fifth theme, which speaks of the emergence of new life beyond the breaking point, helps us to deal with the ambiguity of not always knowing exactly what is God's will, yet to accept the vulnerability of giving up control and security so that we might trust new possibilities and adopt alternative life-styles.

Because of space limitations, the sixth theme—that of anticipating Christ's power—was not developed in a separate essay that utilizes passages from the Epistles and John. But the subject of Christ's power is central to our interpretation of Temptation, Transfiguration, and Triumph. Palm Sunday/Passion Sunday is the time to return to this theme, utilizing insights from the last section of Paul Lehmann's essay.

The seventh and final theme affirms that we were born to die, to die to live. Holy Week reminds us that Christian life involves us in a servant body which with the eyes of faith sees the presence of God's reign and lives sacrificially for the good of all people.

1. REPENTANCE: A MORAL IMPERATIVE

Worship. Use a litany of penitence appropriate to your community at an Ash Wednesday liturgy. Aspects of repentance that should be considered include repentance for our blindness to human need and suffering; our indifference to injustice, exploitation, cruelty, and oppression; our waste and pollution of God's creation; our lack of concern for those who will come after us; our false judgments and uncharitable thoughts toward others; our prejudice toward those who are different from us; our love of worldly goods and comforts; our pride of race, class, creed, or nationality; our encouragement of competition, individualism, and aggression; our lethargy toward violence; our acceptance of impotency; our commitment to military might as the way to peace.

After each confession the congregation may pray: "Accept our repentance, merciful God." At the close the officiant may pray: "May the Almighty God grant us forgiveness of all our sins and the grace of the Holy Spirit to make restitution and live a new life, walking in the way of Christ. Amen."

Nurture. Well in advance, gather a season-planning group to prepare for Lent. As a group write an original, relevant litany of penitence using the model provided above. Place each statement on a separate piece of newsprint and put all the sheets on the wall where everyone can see them. Put a line down the middle of each paper, dividing it into two sections. Together or in small groups write in each lefthand column specific acts engaged in by your congregation during the past year that are illustrative of this particular sin. Continue by listing those acts which your congregation neglected to perform.

Next, return to each sheet and in the righthand column (next to each sin) write in at least one action that your congregation can perform to demonstrate the fruits of repentance. Write an announcement for the church bulletin explaining what you have done and inviting the congregation to review it with you after the Sunday service.

Witness. On the Sunday before Ash Wednesday, having made an announcement in the church bulletin, place your newsprint sheets in the parish hall for everyone to examine. Under each put a sign-up list for persons to write in their names, addresses, and telephone numbers if they wish to become part of a group whose members will demonstrate their repentance for some particular set of sins by joining with others in the actions listed. After persons have signed up, organize groups to engage in these actions. Later the activities of each group can be shared with the total congregation.

Adult study. Gather a group together to work on an Ash Wednesday liturgy. Share in reading the assigned lessons from a variety of translations. In small groups have persons explore each possible lesson with the help of a commentary. Share your findings. From those provided choose one from the Hebrew Scriptures, one from Paul's letters, and one from the accounts of the Gospels; choose those which you believe best fit together and best speak to your situation.

Take time now to meditate on each lesson. That is, in silence be present to the text, close your eyes and image it, put yourself into the text and open yourself to God's revelation. Share your experiences and discuss what you believe God is saying through this lesson to your congregation about your corporate behavior during the past year. Be particularly conscious of your responses to the poor, hungry, oppressed, hurt, and discriminated-against in your community. Together help to write a short homily on these lessons or a one-page bulletin insert to share with the congregation at the Ash Wednesday liturgy.

2. THE WEAKNESS OF POWER: THE POWER OF WEAKNESS

Worship. The suggested liturgy for this week is a devotion known as "The Way of the Cross." It is based on a custom widely observed by pilgrims to Jerusalem: the offering of prayer at a series of places in that city traditionally associated with Christ's passion and death. See the 1979 *Book of Occasional Offices* published by the Church Hymnal Corporation of the Episcopal Church. There is also a small paper edition, *The Way of the Cross,* published by the Liturgical Press, St. John's Abbey, Collegeville, Minn. 56321.

The Way of the Cross is a pilgrimage of fourteen stops or stations. At each station is found traditionally a pictorial representation; at each there is a reading and prayers. As the pilgrims move between stations, either the Trisagion ("Holy God") is changed or hymns such as the Stabat Mater ("At the Cross Her Station Keeping") are sung.

Nurture. This event is planned for a Friday night and all day Saturday. On Friday night divide your participants into fourteen groups. Assign each group a station. Ask each group to make a pictorial representation for their station, to create a drama based on their assigned reading, and to decide where in your community that event in Christ's life is still being experienced. For example: (1) "Jesus condemned to death"—where injustice is manifested; (2) "Jesus takes up his cross"—where there is agony and shame; (3) "Jesus falls the first time"—where danger is encountered; (4) "Jesus meets his afflicted mother"—where grief is experienced; and so forth.

Saturday morning, in silence, go in cars to each of these places in your community. Be silent and present to each for a few moments and move on. When finished, return to your meeting place and go on The Way of the Cross. At each stop observe the pictorialization, dramatize the story, and lead a meditation taking everyone back to the places you visited.

When finished, ask persons to name the station where they felt closest to Christ. Have persons divide into these new groups and ask them to determine what they can do during Lent to bring Christ's healing power to that place in your community. At a closing Eucharist let each group make that commitment as their offering.

Witness. Share your fourteen group commitments to mission and ministry with your congregation and seek others to join each group for the purpose of action. Take, for example, station 3 ("Jesus falls the first time"—where danger is encountered). Perhaps for your congregation the place of danger is the city streets. In this case you might offer to accompany anyone, especially older persons who need to go out alone, or offer to shop for those who are frightened.

Adult study. Bring together your church officers or the members of an official church body such as the session, board of deacons, or vestry. Have them prepare by reading the assigned lessons and the commentary by Paul Lehmann.

When you begin, divide your total group into three small groups. Have each group prepare to dramatize a contemporary version of Jesus' temptation, transfiguration, or triumph. Share these dramatizations. Then discuss and make a list both of the ways power was used and of the ways power might have been used by your congregation during the past year. Based on this listing, strive to agree on how power and its use is understood by your congregation. Compare and contrast this understanding with that communicated in the lessons you dramatize. Then ask the question: for what do we hope our congregation will be known in our community, and how shall we use our power more responsibly? Move the group to action resolves.

3. GOD'S COVENANTS

Worship. Celebrate a Jewish Seder at your church. A particularly appropriate version is Arthur Waskow, *The Freedom Seder: A New Haggadah for Passover* (Holt, Rinehart & Winston, 1970). An abbreviated form of this seder can be found in John Westerhoff, *Inner Growth/Outer Change* (Seabury Press, 1979), pp. 84–94. Another excellent resource with planning helps and interpretive material is *Seder: For Christian Participation,* an adaptation by Jack Lundin, CCS Publishing House, P.O. Box 107, Downers Grove, Ill. 60515. Also copies of the *Passover Haggadah* in packs of five are available from Argus Communications, 7440 Natchez Ave., Niles, Ill. 60648. The text for a *Feminist Seder,* published by Mother Jones Press, is available from Sherry Flashman, 505 Bay Road, R.D. 1, Amherst, Mass. 01002.

Nurture. Following the seder the participants might discuss their experience and then proceed with the following suggestions. (Or following this session a seder can be celebrated or planned for another date.)

Prepare a dramatization of the story of Abraham. Use this account to initiate a sharing of all you know about the Jews as God's chosen people. Next show the filmstrip *Ages of Anguish,* which is about the persecution of the Jews and anti-Semitism. (It can be purchased from Argus Communications, 7440 Natchez Ave., Niles, Ill. 60648.)

Witness. Ask each household in your group to identify a Jewish family in your community. Invite them to visit you or visit them. Explain that this is the time when Christians reflect on their lives, confess their sins, make restitution, and change their behavior so as to be more merciful and just. Explain, also, that you are concerned about anti-Semitism and how the Christian church encourages or perpetuates negative attitudes toward Jews. Ask them to help you understand the prejudice they have experienced and how Christians may have contributed to it.

Adult study. It is suggested that an evening be planned for all the adults in your congregation on the subject of covenants and that you invite, if possible, a rabbi and members of his or her congregation.

In preparation both groups should study the assigned passages. If no Jews are able to be with you, compare a Christian commentary on these texts with a Jewish commentary such as *The Torah: A Modern Commentary* (New York: Union of American Hebrew Congregations, 1981). When you gather, share your understandings. Be particularly sensitive to the Jewish interpretations of the implications of being in covenant with God. What do Jews believe is the relationship between God's covenant with Noah and God's covenant with Abraham? Is there an advantage to being a Jew? What are the obligations and responsibilities? Consider what insights their understandings provide for a Christian's interpretation of their covenant with God.

Move to a discussion of Jewish-Christian relations, with particular reference to anti-Semitism. Seek to discover ways your congregation might act to bring about more positive relationships. Consult: "The Declaration on the Relationship of the Church to Non-Christian Religions," in Walter Abbott (ed.), *The Documents of Vatican II* (Herder & Herder, 1966); and Rosemary Radford Ruether, *Faith and Fratricide: The Theological Roots of Anti-Semitism* (Seabury Press, 1979).

4. THE SINAI COVENANT: OBLIGATIONS AND RESPONSIBILITIES

Worship. Use the following restatement of the Decalogue at the opening of the Sunday liturgy. After each verse the people may respond, "Lord, have mercy upon us, and incline our hearts to keep this law." Properly, it is followed by a general confession and absolution.

I. Only God has proven worthy of unreserved faith and unbounded trust. You shall not worship transitory gods, but shall serve only the living God.

II. You shall not enshrine any notion, ideology, or interest as God and allow yourself to be dominated by it.

III. You shall not lay exclusive claim to God's blessing, or call upon God to bless your selfish purposes.

IV. Show reverence for the land; regard those who labor with respect.

V. Treat older persons justly with deference for their wisdom.

VI. You shall not threaten the lives of others by aggressive behavior, or participate in death-dealing policies.

VII. You shall not threaten another person's marriage or family life, or indulge in sexual promiscuity.

VIII. You shall not deprive other people of their freedom or livelihood.

IX. You shall not cause other persons to be treated unjustly.

X. You shall not grasp what belongs to someone else or seek for yourself what belongs to all people.

—Adapted from Brian Haggerty, *Out of the House of Slavery* (Paulist Press, 1978), pp. 135–136

Nurture. Break up into ten small groups. Assign each group one of the Ten Commandments. Ask each group to compare and contrast the contemporary restatement of their commandment as found in the worship section, the version in Birch's commentary, and other Bible translations. On the basis of this conversation have them seek to grasp the intent of their commandment and its implication for human life. Then discuss how local, state, and national policies make it difficult for you and your congregation to keep this commandment.

Next have each group create a large drawing to represent their commandment. Place these drawings on the wall for everyone to see. Provide refreshments, and then go on a journey together to see each drawing. Discuss the drawing together and then give the group that created it a chance to express their understanding of its intent, the ways in which present laws (or the lack thereof) make it difficult to keep this commandment, and what might be done to remedy this situation.

Witness. In the light of your conclusions in the nurture section, write letters to your local, national, and state elected representatives. Either express your concern and ask them what they are doing, or, if you know of legislation you believe helpful or unhelpful, express your convictions. Issues related to the Ten Commandments include military spending, consumption, conservation, social security, welfare, housing, equal rights, racial discrimination, criminal justice, capital punishment, the aging, health care, and education.

Adult study. This Bible study might best be conducted with the members of all your church boards and committees. In preparation, have each group develop a list of all the actions initiated by them and performed by your congregation during the past year related to both

Christian service and social action. When you gather, share your list and ask persons to describe the God they believe is revealed to the world on the basis of your congregation's actions during the past year.

Next read the assigned lessons together and have someone report and comment upon the commentary by Bruce Birch. Now have persons describe the God indicated by the lessons. Share, compare, and contrast the two descriptions. Before you close have the group agree on some actions that might be taken beginning in Lent so as to be more faithful to the picture of God in the Scriptures.

5. BEYOND THE BREAKING POINT

Worship. At the Sunday liturgy, use the prayers for the church and the world written during the nurture session. Make sure your specific intercessions include all of the following: the church, its members and mission; all in authority, especially those who govern the nations of the world and administer international agencies; the welfare of the world and all peoples; concerns for the local community and for those who suffer neglect, oppression, or injustice; those who are in any trouble, need, sorrow, or sickness; the departed; future generations.

Nurture. Have a large supply of newspapers and news magazines available. Create a series of large bulletin boards using the headings found in the worship section. Direct the group to go through the newspapers and magazines and cut out stories and pictures that fit each of the categories and are of concern to your group.

Next have the group, using materials from the same newspapers and magazines, create a large mural representing the vision of the world they believe God desires and is acting to create. Discuss the differences between these two pictures of the world. Share your feelings about the world you experience today. And list the concerns you want to bring before God. Then write the prayers to be used in the liturgy. Last, identify organizations or voluntary associations that address these concerns and gather information about them.

Witness. On the day the prayers are used in the liturgy, have a series of booths in the parish hall. Let each booth represent a voluntary association or organization whose purpose is to effect change in the world or to minister to the needs of people denied God's vision. Have interpretive material on each group available to be handed out and have one or more persons in each booth to help explain the activities of their group and to solicit members and contributions.

Adult study. Join in neighborhood groups. Before you meet, read the assigned lessons and the commentary by Walter Brueggemann. Also have two or more persons read *Congregational Life-Style Change for the Lean Years* (ed. by Dieter Hessel; Program Agency,

United Presbyterian Church, 1981) so as to prepare a report on the book's content.

When you gather, review the assigned lessons and share your thoughts about Brueggemann's commentary. Discuss what it means to be faithful in a day when our social order is under judgment and a new social order is aching to be born. Then discuss the need for risk, for giving up control, and for the loss of security so that we might be vulnerable to God's will for our individual and corporate lives.

Next, have someone report on the book *Congregational Life-Style Change for the Lean Years.* Discuss ways your families and congregation might change the way they presently live in order to support and encourage a more just and abundant way of life and to be a sign and witness to the coming of God's new age.

6. ANTICIPATIONS

Worship. During the Eucharist, at the offering, invite each member of the congregation to come forward, bringing food for the church's food pantry and a special money offering for Bread for the World or CROP, along with the bread and wine.

Nurture. Show *Hunger,* a twelve-minute film that can be rented from the Learning Corporation of America, 1350 Avenue of the Americas, New York, N.Y. 10019. Give each group of five persons two dollars each and send them to a local store to try and buy a nutritional lunch. Return, eat your meal, and discuss your experience.

Discuss the Lord's Supper as a visionary banquet in which there are no strangers or estranged people and where everyone is well fed. Plan ways to make each Sunday Eucharist such a banquet. Also plan for this week; consider the suggestions in the worship section and learn the song.

Witness. Find out who the hungry are in your community. Attempt to discover the fundamental reasons for their hunger, such as low wages. Using the food offered at the Eucharist, see that the hungry are notified of its existence in the church's food pantry. Encourage them to come and use the food pantry.

Adult study. Suggest that every organization or group in your church engage in a common lectionary Bible study. When the members gather, split the group in half. Have one half create a dramatization of the biblical account of Lazarus; have the others create a contemporary version of the Lazarus story, revealing some group of persons in the world who are trapped by injustice. Present the dramatization. An alternative dramatization would focus on Jesus' cleansing of the Temple, which reveals the difference between prophetic faith-in-action and private, self-serving religion. An illuminating discussion of the difference is offered by Parker Palmer in *The Company of Strangers: Christians and the Renewal of America's Public Life* (Crossroad Publishing Co., 1981).

List on newsprint other groups throughout the world who are trapped by injustice. Reflect on the possible causes for their plight and list these on the newsprint. For example: poverty—lack of money, lack of opportunity for employment, low wages, lack of self-esteem or motivation to work, lack of political power, lack of choice, and so forth. Now, list as many local manifestations of this larger problem as you can. For example: low pay in local factories, high rates of unemployment among particular groups, inadequate housing, transportation, or day-care facilities.

Raise the question of how your group can help bring God's freeing power to those in need and to those whose hearts are hardened, so that at this Easter season they might have a sign of God's kingdom coming. Aim to develop concrete plans of action.

7. THE PASSION

Worship. Develop a dramatization of the passion narrative for use in the Sunday liturgy, using a narrator and spoken parts. Write a script that includes the congregation in acts such as waving palms and in speaking, such as the shouts "Crucify him!" at the trial. This dramatization can be elaborate with costumes and scenery or simply a play-reading without either. In developing your drama, strive not to perpetuate anti-Jewish attitudes; for example, in terms of Jesus' death, place the emphasis on the Roman government and not on the Jews. In developing your drama, see the texts for dramatizing the passion narrative in years A, B, and C that appear in *From Ashes to Fire: Services of Worship for the Seasons of Lent and Easter* (Abingdon Press, 1979).

Nurture. Using as many persons in the congregation as are interested, prepare for the Sunday drama. Read through the text. Then take each character (for example, Judas who betrays Jesus, Peter who denies Jesus, the disciples who ignore Jesus' needs, the false witnesses, the religious leaders who feel threatened, the crowd that encourages violence, and Pilate who is too weak to follow his conscience) and ask those present to close their eyes, identify with that character, and become that person in the story. At the close of each meditation give people an opportunity to express how they felt imagining themselves as that person or group.

Before you choose persons for parts and begin your rehearsal, remind the group that Jesus identified with poor, lonely, hungry, sick, hurt, trapped, oppressed, and dying persons, and with those who suffered from injustice. Discuss where and how the passion narrative is still lived out in our country.

Witness. As the Palm Sunday story begins with a demonstration on behalf of God's reign of justice and peace, equality and freedom, unity and the well-being of all people, decide what place or places in your community might be appropriate for a similar peaceful demonstration. Print fliers to be passed out which explain your position. Make posters to communicate what you are doing, and then form a group of all ages to join you in a modern Holy Week demonstration. Think ecumenically in planning this event. Hispanic communities have a tradition of public reenactment of the triumphal entry. Remember to notify the media so that your demonstration will receive coverage.

Adult study. In preparation for this session have the members of the group read the assigned texts and the commentary by Frederick Herzog. When you gather, begin the session with a foot-washing ceremony. In silence and candlelight, while Lenten music is played, wash each other's feet. When finished, share your experiences and reflect on them in the light of Herzog's commentary.

Present the following characteristics of Christian service: (1) It buys nothing; that is, it is not necessarily appreciated, nor do we necessarily get credit for doing it. (2) It is not tied closely to effectiveness; that is, it is not done necessarily so as to produce some measured result. (3) It means being with another in compassion; that is, being present to others by putting oneself in a position of sharing their vulnerability and of being vulnerable to them. (4) It involves suffering on our part; that is, it is not doing something with and for another in which we pay no price. (5) It involves commitment over the long haul; that is, it is not a momentary act.

Discuss these characteristics and what they imply for our personal lives and for the life of our congregation. Move the discussion to a guided meditation, using these steps:

1. Go back to the time in life when you experienced the grace of sacrificial love and relive it in your imagination.

2. Review the past week. Where have you observed persons who need sacrificial love?

3. Listen to learn what specific action of service God is calling you to, in regard to this awareness.

4. Give yourself to that act and in your imagination live it out.

5. Express gratitude to God for this new possibility of grace in your life. Let the group discuss their meditations and end with a prayer of commitment to these sacrificial acts of service on behalf of persons and/or groups.

IV. EASTER

Sunday or Festival	Year	First Lesson	Second Lesson	Gospel
Easter	A	Acts 10:34–43 or Jer. 31:1–6	Col. 3:1–4	John 20:1–18 or Matt. 28:1–10
	B	Isa. 25:6–9	I Cor. 15:1–11	Mark 16:1–8 or John 20:1–18
	C	Ex. 15:1–11 or Isa. 65:17–25	I Cor. 15:19–26	Luke 24:1–12 or John 20:1–18
2d Sunday of Easter	A	Acts 2:14a, 22–32	I Peter 1:3–9	John 20:19–31 or Matt. 28:11–20
	B	Acts 4:32–35	I John 1:1 to 2:2	Same as A
	C	Acts 5:12–16, 27–32	Rev. 1:4–8, 9–13, 17–19	Same as A
3d Sunday of Easter	A	Acts 2:14a, 36–41	I Peter 1:17–21	Luke 24:13–35
	B	Acts 3:12–19	I John 3:1–7	Luke 24:35–48
	C	Acts 9:1–20	Rev. 5:11–14	John 21:1–19
4th Sunday of Easter	A	Acts 2:42–47	I Peter 2:19–25	John 10:1–10
	B	Acts 4:8–12	I John 3:18–24	John 10:11–18
	C	Acts 13:15–16, 26–33 (44–52)	Rev. 7:9–17	John 10:22–30
5th Sunday of Easter	A	Acts 7:55–60 or Acts 6:1–7	I Peter 2:2–10	John 14:1–14
	B	Acts 8:26–40 or Acts 9:16–31	I John 4:7–12	John 15:1–8
	C	Acts 14:8–18	Rev. 21:1–5	John 13:31–35
6th Sunday of Easter	A	Acts 17:22–31 or Acts 8:4–8, 14–17	I Peter 3:13–22	John 14:15–21
	B	Acts 10:34–48	I John 5:1–6	John 15:9–17
	C	Acts 15:1–2, 22–29	Rev. 21:10–14, 22–27	John 14:23–29
Ascension Day		Acts 1:1–11	Eph. 1:15–23	Luke 24:46–53
7th Sunday of Easter	A	Acts 1:6–14	I Peter 4:12–14, 5:6–11	John 17:1–11
	B	Acts 1:15–17, 21–26	I John 5:9–13	John 17:11–19
	C	Acts 16:16–34	Rev. 22:12–14, 16–17, 20	John 17:20–26

(or readings for Ascension Day, if observed on Sunday)

The fifty days from Easter to Pentecost include Ascension Day to affirm that Jesus Christ is Lord of all times and places, principalities and powers.

A. THEMATIC ESSAYS

1

"AND THE LORD APPEARED FIRST TO MARY": SEXUAL POLITICS IN THE RESURRECTION WITNESS

Walter Wink

Resurrection	Jer. 31:1–6		
Appearances	Isa. 25:6–9;	Col. 3:1–11	John 20:1–18
	65:19–25	I Cor. 15	Mark 16:1–8
	Ex. 15:1–11		Luke 24:13–48
			Matt. 28:36–49
			John 20:19–31
			(21:1–19)
Ascension Day	Acts 1:1–11	Eph. 1:16–23	Luke 24:44–53

No part of the Christian message is more central, ineradicable and world-transcending than the resurrection of Jesus, and no part is more difficult to proclaim. It is an affront to our world view and our historically conditioned (and constantly changing) notions of what is possible. It is a riddle for the historian, defying all explanation. And it is a challenge to credulity, since it asserts that God really can be victorious over the injustices and wrongs perpetuated by the powers that be.

Biblical scholars have long noted that the *message* of the resurrection is earlier than the *stories* about it. The stories of the appearance of the risen Jesus are unique to each Gospel, were apparently not a part of the earliest traditions, certainly not linked to the passion narrative at an early time, and most likely developed in different church centers considerably after the fact. They are not so much historical reports as inferential narrations of the *meaning* the church had found in the indisputable fact of the risen Christ's presence with them, in the church and in their own lives. For them, then, the modern problem of historicity scarcely existed, since their own repeatedly reinforced experience of Christ's real presence was the only significant proof then—or ever—that the resurrection message was true.

The very vividness of their own experience of death and rebirth in Christ so relativized the issue of "what really happened" that hostile allegations of grave-robbing could be countered by simply making up a story to prove it wasn't so: Pilate stationed soldiers at the tomb (Matt. 27:62–66; 28:11–15).

But one aspect of the resurrection story *is* found in all four Gospels: the account of the empty tomb (Matt. 28:1–10; Mark 16:1–8; Luke 24:1–12; John 20:1–18). Here, despite a multitude of differences,[1] we find unanimity on a basic core: that Mary Magdalene and perhaps other women followers of Jesus came to the tomb on Easter morning and found it empty.

Since Paul mentions neither the empty tomb nor female witnesses to the resurrection in his list of witnesses in I Cor. 15:3–8, and since he attests to the antiquity of his tradition (which would make it prior to A.D. 55), most critical scholars until recently assumed that the empty-tomb story was a creation after the fact. Many reconstructed the sequence of events in this order: Peter, and later the rest of the disciples (following Paul's list) experienced Jesus as with them, as if alive. But if he is alive, he must have been resurrected by God. If he has been resurrected, his body must have been taken to heaven from the tomb. Hence the tomb must be empty. Hence the story of the empty tomb was created to fit experiential fact.

This chain of inference leaves several untidy problems, however. Why, if the early church *made up* the story of the empty tomb, did they choose *women* to be the first witnesses? For in Jewish society women had no standing as witnesses whatever. And why have them witness the tomb already empty, instead of seeing Jesus in the act of being raised, on distant analogy with Elijah in II Kings 2? Why would Mark speak of a "young man" in the tomb, rather than angels or an angel, as the other Gospels do? Why mention the tomb at all, since in the various narratives it of itself does not produce faith? (The one exception is the late editorial addition in John 20:8.) The story in fact *created* problems; now the charge of grave-robbing would have to be countered. The Fourth Evangelist, had he not felt bound by his tradition, would have been better off to omit it altogether, and have Jesus go straight to God from the cross, as Hebrews (ch. 9) seems to suggest. That would have fit much better his notion of the cross as exaltation.[2]

These difficulties suggest another possibility: that the story of the women at the empty tomb was quite early after all, and included an appearance of Jesus to Mary Magdalene and perhaps other women with her, and that this tradition was suppressed in a power struggle over the role of women as apostles and leaders in the early church.

It is striking that in all four Gospels, plus the longer ending of Mark, Mary Magdalene is mentioned first among the women; that in John's Gospel and in Matthew and the Marcan longer ending, Jesus appears first to Magdalene, even before appearing to Peter; that women are mentioned as present at the founding event of the church (Acts 1:14;

2:1) and were singled out as destined to receive the outpoured Holy Spirit coequally (Joel 2:28–32 cited at Acts 2:17–21). Is it possible then that Paul's list in I Corinthians 15 deliberately omits reference to women witnesses in order to gain standing as a credible report? It is significant that Paul does not say that Jesus appeared *first* to Peter; significant also that Paul cites this tradition to support his own claim to apostleship. The apostleship (which had included at least one woman for certain: Junia, Rom. 16:7)[3] is beginning to be limited to those *men* who had "seen" the risen Lord. Since the term used by Paul for seeing *(ōphthē)* suggests a vision, there seems no good reason why such visions should cease; indeed, we continue to hear such reports right down to our own day. So Paul's including himself and then closing the list seems arbitrary, to say the least. Apparently the problem of authority drove him to it. But such expedients must not any longer blind us to the price paid. For what we find him doing was beginning to happen throughout the church, as Jesus' radical new attitude toward women was gradually softened and then abandoned altogether by the burgeoning growth of hierarchical structures dominated by men.[4]

We can see this process developing right through the resurrection accounts. In John 20:1–18, for example, we find an extremely complex narrative built up from at least two, perhaps more, traditions.[5] *That* several sources are employed here seems indisputable; *how* is a matter of great disagreement. What does seem clear, at least, is that the footrace between Peter and "the beloved disciple"—itself evidently another sign of the political use of the resurrection stories, in this case to enhance the authority of the beloved disciple and his successors in the church—has been added (vs. 2–10). Mary, in v. 2, concludes that Jesus' body has been stolen or moved without even looking into the tomb—which she only does in v. 11. Peter and the other disciple do look in, and see only grave cloths (vs. 6–7), whereas she sees two angels (v. 12). The beloved disciple "believed" on seeing the empty tomb, whereas it only increased Mary's grief (v. 11). In v. 2 Mary departs to go tell the disciples; in v. 11 she is still standing outside the tomb, alone. Why, if the empty tomb already produced faith in the two male disciples (v. 8), is Mary sent to the disciples to witness to Jesus' resurrection (v. 17)? Why, if the disciples (or at least the beloved disciple) "believed" in v. 8, do they go back home (v. 10) instead of bearing witness themselves?

In short, vs. 2–10 appear to be an addition, intended as an antidote for the uncomfortable precedence accorded Mary by the original story.[6] Thus somewhat neutralized, the account can continue of Jesus' appearance to her and his commissioning of her to be the first apostle of the resurrection, the apostle to the disciples, the fountainhead of faith in the risen Jesus. For, stupendous as her role is, Peter and the other disciple have preempted it. *Her witness is superseded.* For the beloved disciple (even before Peter; cf. also 21:7) has believed in the risen One, having not seen him, and is therefore more "blessed" than she (20:29).

Remove vs. 2–10, however, and an altogether different picture emerges. None of the disciples had ever been healed by Jesus. According to Luke, Magdalene had. She is not the prostitute that tradition has associated her with (Luke 7:36–50), but a former demoniac (Luke 8:1–3; Mark 16:9). Perhaps she was not alone but, as in the Synoptic Gospels, was accompanied by at least one other woman ("we," John 20:2). How consistent, how characteristic, how very like God, to make the first appearance of Jesus be to an unfit witness, a member of the oppressed sex, someone outside the inner circle of Jesus' male disciples.

Matthew also reflects something of this same tradition, though he apparently draws on an independent source. Jesus appears to "Mary Magdalene and the other Mary" (Matt. 28:1), who grasp his feet (compare "don't cling to me" in John 20:17), and are commissioned by Jesus to "go and tell" the disciples (Matt. 28:9–10).

Now watch what happens to this tradition elsewhere. In Mark's longer ending, an independent piece of tradition not based on the canonical Gospels, Mary is explicitly named the "first" to whom Jesus appeared. When she tells the disciples, however, "they would not believe it" (Mark 16:9–11), rejecting her authority as a witness to the risen Lord.

In the Marcan version of the empty tomb account, the women are so terrified and awed by the presence of the "young man" that they disobey his command to tell "the disciples and Peter" (Mark 16:7). The sequence here is odd; has "and Peter" been added in the struggle over whose was the primacy in encountering the risen Jesus and, thus, whose would be the primacy of authority in the church?

Is it not strange that, despite the *assertion* that the Lord appeared first to Peter (found only in I Cor. 15:5 and Luke 24:34), there is not a single story, not even in the apocryphal Gospels, of such a first appearance? In any case, the women are to tell the men; only the men will know what to do with such news. This does not accord with the few but revealing indications we have that women not only converted in droves but headed house churches (Acts 12:12; 16:14–15, 40; Rom. 16:1–2 (?), 3, 5; I Cor. 16:19; Col. 4:15), opened new fields for evangelism (Phil. 4:2–3) and served as Paul's co-workers (Rom. 16:3, 6, 12; Acts 18:1–3, 18–19, 24–26; I Cor. 16:19; II Tim. 4:19–21), were persecuted and jailed just like the men (Acts 8:3; 9:1–2; 22:4–5; Rom. 16:7), were apostles (Rom. 16:7), disciples (Acts 9:36–42),[7] deacons (Luke 8:3; Mark 15:40f.; Matt. 27:55f.; Rom. 16:1–2; I Tim. 3:8–11), led churches (Philemon 1–2), and even, in one case, had authority over Paul himself (Rom. 16:1–2—"for she has been a ruler over many, indeed over me")![8] Likewise, Mary Magdalene showed no fear whatever in the John account, even though she went to the tomb alone while it was still dark. But in Mark and Luke the women are depicted as frightened, flighty, bearers of "idle tales" (Luke 24:11), and dependent on the men.[9]

The power struggle over who was an authorized witness to the resurrection continued for almost three centuries. The women did not so easily give up! And the battle continued to be fought, in large part, over who were the valid witnesses of the resurrection.

In the Epistula Apostolorum (early second century), the women are still depicted as the first to see Jesus. Moreover, additional stress is laid on their being sent to witness to the male disciples. So reluctant were the men that the risen Jesus had to send a second woman, and finally, when the men still did not believe, went along with all the women to convince the men himself.[10]

In the Gospel of Mani, a Gnostic Christian writing of the second or third century, Magdalene is commanded by the risen Christ to "do this service *(leitourgia):* be a messenger *(angelos)* for me to these wandering orphans. Make haste rejoicing, and go unto the Eleven." Here again their unbelief is anticipated. Mary is even made a "pastor" of Christ to the Eleven, sent to bring "the sheep to the shepherd."[11]

Hippolytus of Rome (end of the second century or beginning of the third) echoed the theme of Mary Magdalene and the other women as apostles and evangelists, a note carried over also in Gnostic literature as well. The apocryphal Gospel of Mary Magdalene actually reverses the usual sex-role stereotypes of the culture and depicts the men crying and helpless, and Mary as confident, strong, and encouraging. Her very success in consoling the disciples causes them to turn on her in jealousy—particularly Andrew and Peter, who attack her for thinking that she, a woman, might have better access to the truth of Christ than they, the men, did. Peter is made to admit, "We know that the Saviour loved you above all other women," but this also leads him to ask irritably, "Has he preferred her over against us?" But Levi chastizes him: "But if the Saviour hath made her worthy, who then art thou, that thou reject her? Certainly the Saviour knows her surely enough. Therefore did he love her more than us." Thus persuaded, they all went off to preach the gospel.[12]

The tide, however, had already turned. The vast majority of churches had long since come under male hierarchies, and women had been reduced to the roles of deaconesses and enrolled widows.

The repressive male views interpolated into Paul's letters (in I Cor. 14:33b–38) and views ascribed to him in letters not by him (Eph. 5:21–23; I Tim. 2:8–15; 5:3–16; Titus 2:3–5), or in other epistles (I Peter 3:1–6), became the accepted standard of the church. Women who exercised authority were marginalized, accused of heresy, or silenced. The infamous "Jezebel" of Rev. 2:20–23 sounds like nothing more than an ardent Paulinist who was simply repeating what Paul said about the freedom to eat food sacrificed to idols (compare I Cor. 8:1–13; 10:14–33). Women prophets, of whom the early church had quite a number (I Cor. 11:5; Acts 21:9; Rev. 2:20–23) were forced to turn to "heretical" Montanism or Gnosticism in order to exercise their divine gift. The victory of the males was virtually complete, except in one regard. They left untouched the traditions about Jesus' treatment of women. There we find not only the absence of any negative statement but a thoroughgoing revolution in the woman's role.

How ironic that the resurrection, that act of liberation by which the power of death was put to death and humanity liberated from the seduction of the powers, should have become the battleground on which men and women fought out the issue of male domination of the church. The lines were drawn: Peter vs. Mary, men vs. women. The liberating story of the risen Christ in time became the legitimating charter for male supremacy. The word that freed, enslaved.

We today can scarcely continue to read these accounts innocent of that costly struggle and its consequences. How fortunate for us that we today are blessed with the means to hear the story told again, thanks to the critical approach, in something of the way it was originally told: And the Lord appeared first to Mary Magdalene.

For this act of restitution in the reading of Scripture means that we today can achieve what the early church only began, and lost: complete parity and equality between women and men in every area of ministry and work.

Why else would the Lord have appeared first to Mary?

2

LIFE AT THE DAWN OF THE KINGDOM: THE READINGS FROM ACTS FOR THE EASTER SEASON

Justo and Catherine González

The Early Church (The Way)   Acts 2:22 through Acts 17
                                              (Plus pertinent references
                                              to the rest of Acts)

As we look at the lectionary readings for the Easter season, the first thing that impresses us is that there are no Old Testament lessons. Except for Years B and C, and then only on Easter itself, the book of Acts has been substituted for the Old Testament. This absence of the Old Testament in the Easter season is to be deplored for two reasons. First, it serves to reinforce the community-held view that the events of the New Testament have somehow obliterated the value of the Old. When we reach the highest point of the Gospel, the resurrection of Jesus Christ, we seem to be able to dispense with the Hebrew Scriptures.

Secondly, and more directly related to our theme, the absence of the Old Testament from our lessons for this season makes it very difficult to interpret correctly the readings from the book of Acts itself. Read alone, without its historical grounding on the experiences and the hopes of Israel, Acts is easily misinterpreted as a book on general religious principles, or on how religious people ought to behave, to organize their community, and to announce their beliefs to others.

But Acts is much more than that. Set within the entire scope of biblical history, the events of Acts take place at the dawning of the kingdom. They take place at the moment when the hopes of Israel are beginning to be fulfilled.[13] That is why, at the end of his Gospel, the author of Luke-Acts tells us that the resurrected Jesus connected the recent events in Jerusalem with the promises of Scripture (Luke 24:27, 44–48). Again, at the beginning of Acts, we are clearly told that the risen Lord appeared repeatedly to the disciples, "speaking of the kingdom of God" (Acts 1:3). But the disciples do not understand what this means, and at the very moment of the ascension are asking: "Will you at this time restore the kingdom to Israel?" (1:6). Jesus answers with the promise of the Holy Spirit. It is at the time of the fulfillment of this promise that Peter announces that the days of the kingdom have indeed begun: "This is what was spoken by the prophet Joel: 'And in the last days it shall be . . .' " (2:16–17). Much later, toward the end of the book, Paul declares that he is being persecuted for announcing the fulfillment of "the hope of Israel" (26:7; 28:20).

To try to understand Acts apart from this context is to turn it into a book about general religiosity. And to base our Easter season worship and preaching on such general religiosity is to miss the most important point of the season we are celebrating: that the community to which we belong is the postresurrection community. It is the community that believes that in the events of Easter the new order has conquered the old, difficult though it may be to believe this in the midst of injustice, faithlessness, and persecution. The church of the book of Acts—and the church today, when it is faithful to its calling —is a sign of the kingdom that has dawned. That church lives by the Holy Spirit, as the firstfruits, the seal, the down payment of the kingdom.

One of the common tendencies in the church today is to assume that the chief theme of Easter is life after death, specifically in the form of the resurrection of the dead. The book of Acts makes it very clear, however, that the Pharisees already had the belief in the resurrection of the dead. That was one of the things that differentiated them from the Sadducees. Easter is much more than a divine sign that the Pharisees are right and the Sadducees are wrong. What separated the Pharisees and the Christians was the fact that, while the Pharisees expected the resurrection of the dead at the end of history, the resurrection of Jesus had occurred within history. His resurrection was the sign that the kingdom, the end, had begun. What was surprising was that the kingdom dawned in such a hidden fashion in the midst of a world history that continued alongside it. The expectation had been that when the kingdom dawned, it would conclude history and therefore be an event that could not go unrecognized. Easter is the celebration of the resurrection of Jesus. It does tell us something about our own resurrection, but its central message is to tell us that the kingdom has begun in an unexpected way. It is for that reason that the post-Easter season stresses the character of the community that is formed as a witness to the kingdom itself.

What are the specific characteristics of this community that reflect the life of the kingdom?

1. First of all, there is the *inclusiveness* that it shows in its common life. Isaiah 56 is one of the clearest statements of the expectation that at the end, in the last days, the covenant would include those who were presently not a part of it. In that passage, the foreigner and the

eunuch are told that they will be made joyful in God's house of prayer that shall be for all peoples. The eunuch was excluded by the law from being added to Israel if born outside, and was therefore in a more difficult position than the foreigner. In Acts 8:26–39 we find the account of the Ethiopian eunuch. He is baptized and added to God's people. The promise of Isaiah is being fulfilled. The account of the conversion of Cornelius in Acts 10:24–35 shows the addition of a Gentile. Obviously, a central feature of the whole book of Acts is Paul's mission to the Gentiles. This inclusiveness is not to be seen as a liberal rejection of a mistaken exclusiveness on Israel's part, but rather as the sign of the dawning of the kingdom, to fulfill the expectation of Israel.

2. *Justice* and *abundance* are two other characteristics of the promised kingdom. Often in the prophets we find the imagery of a great banquet—an image taken up by the New Testament, as in the feast of the Lamb in Revelation. Justice does not mean simply that the good will be rewarded and the evil punished. It also means that things will be so ordered that all will have what they need. Read, for instance, Micah 4:4: "They shall sit every man under his vine and under his fig tree, and none shall make them afraid." What God intends, and what the faithless and unjust people thwart, is this abundance which is closely connected with justice. This is why Deut. 15:4–5 says: "But there will be no poor among you . . . , if only you will obey the voice of the LORD your God, being careful to do all this commandment which I command to you this day." This text (which ought to be remembered by those who misquote "the poor you have always with you") clearly shows that poverty and need are the result of unrighteousness, of injustice. And the way Scripture promises an end to need in the kingdom is not simply by increased production, but also and most particularly by better distribution.

In this context, two of the lectionary texts for the Easter season, Acts 2:42–47 and Acts 4:32–35, show how the early church understood itself as the firstfruits of the kingdom. When both of these texts tell us that the first Christians had everything in common, or that they sold what they had and gave the proceeds to the needy among them, they are not simply drawing a sentimental picture of the early church. They are telling us that, because the members of that church believed the kingdom had dawned, they began to live out the life of the kingdom. It was not simply a practical expediency. Nor was it simply that they loved each other so much. It was that, as those who believed in the resurrection of Jesus, they could no longer live as if the old order were still sovereign.

The episode of Ananias and Sapphira, so often used as proof that the system did not work, can only be used in that manner if the commonality of goods is seen as an expedience, or as an experiment in love in action. When, on the other hand, that commonality is seen in its eschatological context, the episode of Ananias and Sapphira shows that it *did* work. Since the church that had everything in common did so because it had the Spirit of God, to lie to such a church was to lie to God (Acts 5:4). When the church, by the manner in which it structures its life, does not live out of the kingdom which it proclaims, it is a lie before God.

In Acts 4:33 we are told that "with great power the apostles gave their testimony to the resurrection of the Lord Jesus, and great grace was upon them all." This statement appears in the middle of the passage on the commonality of goods, which is affirmed both before and after. In other words, we are told that there is a direct connection between the power of the witness and the living of that witness in the very life of the church. The same connection may be seen in the passage in Acts 2.

3 Another common theme in the biblical view of the kingdom is the *empowerment of the powerless*. And, once again, this is a constant theme in the life of the early church as Acts depicts it. Peter declares that Pentecost is the fulfillment of Joel's promise that the most unlikely people would be empowered by the Spirit: sons and daughters, young people and old people, menservants and maidservants. The humble and unschooled Galileans confront the prestigious and wise Sanhedrin. Stephen, at the very moment of dying as a blasphemer against God, sees the throne of that very God. Simon the magician, dubbed by his fellow citizens "that power of God which is called Great," is humiliated by Simon the fisherman. Paul the persecutor becomes Paul the persecuted, and in doing so gains in stature. All this happens because the Crucified has risen and has been exalted to the right hand of God. In the church of the risen and exalted Galilean carpenter, Galileans, carpenters, fisherfolk, eunuchs, and all those whom society puts down are exalted.

4. These are the positive characteristics of the community. But we must not forget that this church was set in the midst of a world that was indeed not the kingdom. Though the inner life of the community was marked by love and joy, by generosity and sharing, its life in the world was marked by *persecution*. Nor could anything else be expected. The community of the kingdom is a witness to God's will. A sinful world lives from values that run contrary to the will of God. Nothing other than conflict can therefore be expected. It is for good reason that the other lessons for these days after Easter will reflect the theme of persecution.

But what is clear from the book of Acts is that early church's strange response to the persecution that came upon it. Stephen, the first martyr, followed the model of the cross itself, and, at the point of death, prayed that God would forgive those who were killing him (Acts 7:59–60). Ananias, the Christian at Damascus, has every right to fear Saul, the persecutor of the church. Yet, when commanded by

God, he goes to Saul and heals his blindness, even calling him "brother" (Acts 9:10–19). The jailer in Philippi is saved from suicide by his prisoner, Paul (Acts 16:25–34). *Reconciliation* with persecutors abounds, even when it is one-sided, as in the case of Stephen.

5. The church is *growing rapidly* throughout the book of Acts. It grows in spite of persecution. It grows because of the attractiveness of the kingdom it represents. Acts does not deal with the problems in the various churches. The letters of Paul do that far more. Acts gives us the rapid outline of the expansion of a community that sufficiently represents the kingdom that it calls to itself those who yearn for such a life. The joyful exuberance of the young church is reflected in every chapter, sometimes in the ministry of one person, but often in the description of the little communities that are established.

Their ability in mission, their effectiveness in attracting others to the community, was directly related to the clarity with which they saw themselves as the beginning of the kingdom. To the degree that we have lost that sense of who we are as the church, we have lost also the sense of mission and the ease of carrying out mission. For the Christians that we see in Acts, mission happened, even when they were not planning to create churches. In our own day, mission seems to be a task that requires inordinate planning and organizing, and then has little effect on the society in which we live. Acts reminds us that mission flows easily from a sense of who we are as revealed in our common life together as disciples, and from our readiness to respond to others with the same peace. We cannot substitute programs of mission for actually living as witnesses to the kingdom.

6. One last characteristic of Acts needs to be mentioned. To be the community of the kingdom did not mean that Jesus had left them with this task, and they were on their own to do it. Obviously, *the power of the Holy Spirit* in their midst is a strong theme that is dealt with particularly at Pentecost. But it occurs also throughout Acts. The Holy Spirit sends Philip from one place to another (Acts 8:39). The Holy Spirit is poured out on Gentiles as the sign that they are to be added to the people (Acts 10:44–48). Barnabas and Saul are sent by the Spirit to Cyprus (Acts 13:4). The council at Jerusalem simply reports that "It seemed good to the Holy Spirit and to us" and responds to one of the most difficult questions facing the young church (Acts 15:28).

The presence of the risen Christ in their midst is also strong, though this is a more hidden theme. The crucified One appears to Saul on the road to Damascus, and his powerful presence has effect (Acts 9:1–9). Stephen at his death sees the ascended One (Acts 7:56). The community itself centers its common life on the meetings where they break bread together (Acts 2:42, 46; 20:7). This was usually on the first day of the week. We need to understand these words in order to see the full implication. To break bread together was not simply another way of saying they ate a meal. Very specifically, the words refer to Communion. For the church at that time, the Communion meal was most appropriate on the first day of the week, Sunday, because it was the day of the Lord's resurrection. The Lord's Supper was not a remembrance of the past as much as it was the celebration of the actual presence of the risen Christ at table with his disciples, and as such a foretaste of the heavenly banquet in which all shall be fed. Worship is the hidden center of the life of faith in Acts as in the whole New Testament. They were the kingdom community, because the King was in their midst. He had conquered death and sin, and therefore they did not need to be afraid of the persecution that came upon them.

The kingdom is not governed by an absentee king, but by a present and living Lord. If we do not feel ourselves to be indeed the community of the kingdom, we need to see whether or not our common worship gives us the reality of the King's presence among us. Worship and mission are not separate agendas for a local congregation. True worship prepares us for the joyful mission that we see in Acts.[14]

The book of Acts is almost two thousand years old. But still today it presents us with a clear choice, that posed by Easter: if the kingdom has dawned, either we are its citizens, and seek to obey and to proclaim its new order of peace and justice, or we have no part in it. Either we take the side of the Galileans, the eunuchs, the Gentiles, and other assorted social rejects, or we take the side of the old order and deny the resurrection which we affirm verbally. We either stand with the blasphemer Stephen, condemned by the civil religion of his time, forgiving them, and seeing the way open to the very throne of God, or we deny that other One who was crucified for His blasphemy, and whose resurrection we claim to celebrate in the Easter season. We either have the Spirit that empowers the powerless, or we do not have the Spirit of the risen Lord.

3

LIBERATION:
FROM WHAT, FOR WHAT?

Roy I. Sano

The Gift and Purpose of Life		John 10–17
The Shepherd Who Gives Life		10:1–30
Farewell Discourse Interpreting		
His Work		14:1–14, 15–29
Pattern of the Believer's Life	I John 1:1 to 2:6	15:1–17
	3:1–7, 18–24	13:31–35
	4:7–12	
	5:1–6, 9–13	
High-Priestly Prayer		17:1–26

For some, the exploration into the social meanings of the text may look like an alien question foisted on the text, or an extrapolation from the Bible's personal messages. Authoritative studies of the lections under consideration view the Fourth Gospel, for example, in a spectrum of religious and philosophical ideas unconsciously conceived on a horizontal axis, or on a chronological continuum depicted on an upward trajectory.[15] Liberation theologies, on the other hand, have emphasized the value of beginning our action and thinking "from below." This would suggest that a hierarchical perspective with a vertical axis may prove more helpful if we are to uncover neglected contextual messages within Scripture.[16]

Certain kinds of advanced training can catapult a pericope from its setting. Literary and historical considerations have instilled in us questions about the documentary sources behind the current text, as well as the preliterary or oral stages before them. Coupled with the dubious assumption that the earlier is always closer to the truth, we may be lured away from the fabric in which a passage appears currently as a clue to its meaning. Redaction criticism has come as a corrective. It has taught us to appreciate the constructive contribution made by the experiences and intentions of the writer of the document in the organization of the materials as we now have them.[17]

This study therefore will turn to the context of the lection for light on the meaning of the assigned passages. This approach will provide a fuller meaning of the cluster of readings in the setting of the whole

Gospel and the entire Epistle of John.

The impediments to a wholistic interpretation in these lections are considerable. The passages can be read primarily in individualistic and spiritualized fashion if they are read in isolation. The followers of Christ, for example, are called by name (John 10:3). The quest for selfish answers to prayers and for personal fulfillment can be sanctioned. "Ask whatever you will, and it shall be done for you" (15:7; cf. 14:14). Pictures of relationship with Jesus as the good shepherd (10:14, 27) or abiding in the true vine (15:4) can be reduced to cozy terms minimizing the ethical imperatives involved and the conflict with the world. Relationship with God becomes a "touchy, feely" game where people experience joy (15:11; 17:13). While all these individualistic and inward considerations have biblical foundations in these passages, we can skew them into chummy, unholy alliances.

Potent theological habits and cultural forces are at work. A "me generation" could be mentioned.[18] However, misdirected focus in salvation is also responsible. We live in a religious climate that is concerned about relationships, particularly manifested in a yearning for reconciliation with God and harmony with neighbor, while overlooking the *conditions* that make authentic relationships possible. We forget that redemption sets the stage for self-respecting reconciliation, as in the Exodus narrative, where the deliverance from bondage is the condition of the covenant with God and neighbor. Until we are out of the hands of lesser gods that manage and manipulate us, we cannot be freed for engaging relationship with God and others. This consideration helps us introduce into our interpretation of these passages a discussion of what it is that Jesus saves us from, what he saves us for.

I. DELIVERANCE FROM DEATH AND LIES

Deliverance from death. Believers are those who are no longer owned by the world with its powers and perspectives, according to these lections. "They are not of the world" (John 17:16). They are people *of* God as Jesus is *of* God (I John 3:1; 4:2–3, 15; 5:1). "Of God" has to do with origins and ownership—where Christians came from and what "possesses" them. Christians are no longer living under the destructive operations of this world, and thus are not subject to death. Even if they suffer signs of decay, it will be reversed decisively. By yielding to the life that works through Jesus, their persons bear witness to his claim: "I am the resurrection and the life; anyone who believes in me, though dead, yet shall live, and whoever lives and believes in me shall never die" (John 11:25–26, adapted). This applies to capacities of mind, choices of will, emotions that are astir within us as persons, as well as the reversal of both decay from environmental pollutions and corrosions of rich cultural traditions in many societies inundated with distorting forces.

Deliverance from lies. Besides being liberated from the powers of death and its destructive works, believers are also delivered from falsehood. The concern for life is coupled with concern for truth. "In him was life, and the life was the light for humankind" (John 1:4, adapted). The truth that becomes prominent in several places is the recognition that God is at work in Jesus. The word we are to have within us is that the divine presence is operative within Jesus and his works (John 5:16–18; 8:42; 10:38; 11:27; 14:10; 17:8; I John 5:1). It is worth rehearsing the works that prompted the controversy as to the forces operating in Jesus, whether divine or demonic (John 8:48).

Jesus participated in festive occasions such as the wedding in Cana by turning water into wine (John 2). He claimed that rulers of the dominant religious establishment were outside the reign of God, but could be reborn into it (John 3). He proclaimed good news to the Samaritans, people of mixed blood (John 4). He healed the lame at Bethesda (John 5). He fed the hungry (John 6), restored sight to the blind (John 9), and raised the dead (John 11).

The problems emerged because this work broke sacrosanct laws. He contradicted the restrictive pictures of the scope of God's work. He brought salvation to untouchables—mixed blood and heretical Samaritans, and women of ill repute. He demonstrated that the healing powers of God operated on days set aside for rest (John 5:9–16; 7:23; 9:1–40). His saving work was a sacrilege; his claim to be in touch with God while challenging the established understanding of the holy amounted to blasphemy. He threatened to discredit the sacred tenets of their ethos. Such an invalidation would invite changes in policies of Roman occupation forces that would terminate their protections of those who *lived under* them. "If we let him go on this way, everyone will believe in him, and the Romans will come and destroy both our holy place and our nation" (11:48).

Those who believe the divine presence is operating in Jesus are freed from the domination of half-truths, if not outright lies. Whereas God may have worked through that high form of Judaism at one point in history, for a particular people, God in Christ was releasing that same life through other forms. Old bounds were surpassed. Sacrosanct doctrines were contradicted. Even if this could threaten the termination of privileged protections, the divine work coursing through Jesus was releasing new life which prevailed over death in these precarious circumstances. Those who yielded to this force, who entrusted their life to this medium of divine operation, had freed themselves from constricting pictures of divine work. They were freed from safe protection to live confidently in the open. Indeed, this was the truth that shall make us free (8:32).

Beginning from below. In our day the doctrines of development, national security, and domestic tranquillity have become sacrosanct ideologies, comparable to the religious ethos we find Christ battling. We depict these doctrines in romantic terms and exaggerate the goodness of their achievements. Their application in the present has turned what truth they may have contained into false promises. Technological changes, the resurgence of neglected sectors of the human family, and the climate of intense international rivalries have made them into sentences of death for vast reaches of the human family. The doctrines of national security and development may have been pertinent for a particular people, but they have become a curse.

If Christian salvation means anything, it must deliver this earth from the domination of the destruction and false hopes these doctrines and their agencies now perpetuate. If Jesus is the good shepherd who "came that [we] may have life, and have it abundantly" (John 10:10), surely he will deliver us from the "thieves" of this day who come "only to steal and kill and destroy" (10:10). If God is still God, surely that divine reality will be revealed in doing battle against the "devil" who "was a murderer from the beginning and has nothing to do with the truth" (8:44).

Speaking of salvation as deliverance from such domination is to suggest that our starting point is *below* the reign of the hosts of lords; we begin *from below* the reign of principalities and powers which produce exploitation of cheap labor, the violation of human rights, the indulgent use of resources, and the corrosion of rich spiritual and cultural heritages. The twin interests in life against death and destruction, and in truth versus falsehood, make sense to us in these terms.

II. FREE FOR SOLIDARITY IN MISSION

Freedom for mission in the world. If faith in Jesus means yielding to the divine presence that was at work in him, then it means we will continue the work of Jesus (John 14:12). He released new life which subverted death produced by evils; he made the truth demonstrably cogent and promised the Spirit of truth (14:17; 16:13). We were invited to an even greater work (14:12). Those who are productive will be made more productive by paring away what is excessive and unproductive (15:2–3).

Those who are liberated from the false claims made in ancient truth which time has made uncouth, and who work to free others from the hold that the half-truths and outright lies of this culture have over them, will be doing the work of Christ. This will mean doing battle against the reigning ideologies of development and national security, while challenging the neglect of human welfare, emptying prisons of creative persons held in check, reversing the pollution of our fragile planet, overturning the repression of budding forms of life in emerging societies and neglected groups, to show how the liberated life prevails over destructive forces.

Any work of this kind will be challenged by the "world." Just as they had opposed and hated Jesus who challenged the reign of principalities and powers, the entrenched interests of this day will abuse those who pursue the ends Jesus sought (John 15:19–20). There is no escaping this resistance, because we were sent into the world (17:18). The abuse will not come out of evil intent. Persecutors will think they are doing good. "Whoever kills you will think he is offering service to God" (16:2).

The alienation from the world should be linked with the occasional references to the absence of Christ (John 14:3, 28; 16:7, 17, 28; 17:11). We have made too much of the presence of Christ, particularly in that holy moment, the Lord's Supper. While the affirmation has solid biblical grounds, so does his absence. Jesus is the Coming One, and thus presently absent. The divine presence we now experience is known as the Holy Spirit, the Counselor or Advocate (John 14:15–17; 16:7–16). We are assured that "he who is in you is greater than he who is in the world" (I John 4:4). That is the present fact, based on the past. "In the world you have tribulation; but be of good cheer, I have overcome the world" (John 16:33). We taste some of that reality now. "This is the victory that overcomes the world, our faith" (I John 5:4). As we are reminded in that setting, this faith believes God has acted in Jesus (I John 5:5; see also I John 4:3, 14–15). These realities give grounds for peace, "not as the world gives," but the peace associated with yielding to that God who worked in Jesus and continues working in us through the Spirit.

Solidarity in mission. Following Jesus will bring opposition, but also brings with it grounds for inward composure, the "peace which passes all understanding." These emphases should be highlighted in any consideration of our relationships with God and neighbor. Otherwise, we will reduce the images of close relationships into cheap, self-indulgent, cozy "fuzzies." Such pictures of the Christian life are highly marketable, but they represent distortions adapted to unregenerate hankerings.

Those who experience persecution will have the grounds to appreciate the emphasis on collaboration and coalition which are suggested in these lections when they speak of loving one another (John 15:9) and humbly serving co-believers (13:34–35, related to foot-washing in 13:1–20). The unity one experiences and promotes is not an isolated value or end in itself as it can become in our obsessive concern for reconciliation. That unity is tied to faithfulness in a difficult mission (17:11, 21, 22), even laying down our lives for each other (15:12–17). Notice how this closeness or friendship involves costly service and *solidarity in mission.* Those who have tasted some measure of that deliverance from the powers of death and the grip of false consciousness are freed to work with God in the same mission Jesus had, reflecting the divine presence. These are substantive grounds for peace and joy (14:27; 15:11). Thanks be to God for the fullness of our salvation and the wholeness of our mission! Praises be to this God! Amen.

4

POSTURE OF THE PERSECUTED
Edward M. Huenemann

Posture of the Persecuted

I Peter 1:3–9, 17–21
2:1–10, 19–25
3:13–22
4:12–19; 5:6–11

Rev. 1:9–13, 17–19
5:11–14
7:9–17
21:1–5, 10–14, 22–23
22:12–14, 16–17, 20

The understanding of power determines life-style for individuals and societies. Life is shaped by it. Lust for power[19] corrupts life's nature and purpose. The power of love sustains it and fulfills its promise. The conflict between the lust for power and the power of love is the central focus of the biblical story. Its dramatic conclusion is the resounding "hallelujah" of those who believe that Jesus the Christ (the power of love) "shall reign for ever and ever." This eschatological vision of the believer is poetically projected in Rev. 5:11–14.

I

This vision of sovereignty—of meaningful order—so central to John's reading of history is a poetic projection that asserts a truth not readily confirmed by the apparent logic of history. The everyday experience of Christians in John's time would not have confirmed such an expectation. They were persecuted. What confirmed the expectation was the *worthiness* of "the Lamb who was slain." It was the drawing power of love in the sacrifice of the "Lamb" which required this poetic projection of its sovereignty. The reality of its power was known to John, as it is to us, by faith. Life is not simply or merely what it seems. Life has dimension, meaning, and purpose. Life *is* poetry—or, in religious terms, life is worship. It is known and experienced in the light of ultimate commitment. That is why the cross is its center—the contradiction in which historic logic is conquered by meaning. Who or what one worships determines the order, the sovereignty under which one lives. Poetic projection is therefore not idle dreaming or idol worship, it is the expression of what faith knows to be true even when the prosaic experience of history seems to contradict it. "Worthy is the Lamb who was slain!"—Worthy to be the sovereign of the universe! Love has power! True power is exercised in love.

This "dogmatic" base of Christianity makes the persecution of Christians as inevitable as the cross of Christ. The perversion of a proper regard for power, from the *love of* power to the *lust for* power, makes the clash unavoidable. Lust for power is the desire for self-aggrandizement by robbing others of the power that is legitimately theirs. Love of power is a proper appreciation of and regard for the power given to each to function creatively in relation to all. The issue in the conflict is that of justice, which is the exercise of power in the context of love. The conflict is therefore a political struggle—or a struggle for creative and compassionate order—in our life together, i.e., the political arena.

This vision of the sovereignty of love projected in the passages from The Revelation to John represents the eschatological perspective of the early church. It is important to note that the perspective does not merely deal with otherworldly matters or only with the future. It is the *present* which is determined by the eschatological hope here expressed. John saw the "new Jerusalem, coming down out of heaven from God" (Rev. 21:2, 10). The issue is the impact of the sovereignty of Christ on the new order, the new city, *now!* Impacting and re-creating all "life together." It is not a vision of merely private, personal salvation but a social vision of true sovereignty in the political order. The Lamb is the light of this new city. "By its light shall the *nations* walk; and the *kings* of the earth shall bring their glory into it, and its gates shall never be shut by day—and there shall be no night there; they shall bring into it the glory and the honor of the nations" (Rev. 21:24–26). It is this essentially sociopolitical vision of the sovereignty of Christ which determines the believer's hope and present dilemma.

II

How shall Christians live in a world that does not share this vision and does not live by the same eschatological expectation? This is the question addressed in the passages selected for the lectionary from I Peter. Their point is to share Christ's suffering and glory. The end is union with, or life in, Christ, not escape from the struggle.

"Beloved, do not be surprised at the fiery ordeal which comes upon you to prove you, as though something strange were happening to you. But rejoice in so far as you share Christ's sufferings, that you may also rejoice and be glad when his glory is revealed. . . . For the time has come for judgment to begin with the household of God" (I Peter 4:12–13, 17).

Christians live at the beginning of the judgment of the nations. The focus of this beginning is on the community of believers, "the household of God." Christians need to know both the time and the place in which they live if they are to understand their own appropriate posture in life. Why should they be among the persecuted? Why not among the winners, the successful and comfortable? What is going on here?

What is going on is an ultimate power struggle, the impact of which is most immediately felt in "the household of God." The struggle has to do with authority, with sovereignty, with governance, with politics, with the exercise of power. The seismic shift in perspective is caused by Jesus as the Christ whose worthiness subjects every exercise of power to a new and radical judgment. A total shift in the understanding of how *human* community is possible is required. This demand for total shift is first known in "the household of God," and therefore the community of believers becomes the center of the most intense struggle. The politics of life is not only to be revolutionized, it is to be transfigured.[20] Not only do power positions have to change, but the very perception and practice of rule and what it means have to change. The whole nature of the power game has to change and players with new skills must appear. Everything depends on the birth of a radical new community born out of a vision of the "worthiness" of Jesus Christ—the new humanity.

III

The strategy of life in this new community is faithfulness—i.e., trust in and loyalty to Jesus as the Christ. It is adherence to an ultimate sovereignty of grace. It is a new political stance. All ultimate judgment is referred to the humanity made known in the sovereignty of Jesus as the Christ.[21] To this center the new community is committed; in fact it exists only in relation to this center.

It is this faithfulness to this newly recognized sovereignty which makes lesser sovereigns nervous but gives the believing community its confidence and dynamic. The community's posture is clearly expressed in the introductory section of the first chapter (I Peter 1:3–9). The purpose and goal of the community's existence is "the revelation of Jesus Christ" (1:7). But this revelation will occur not simply beyond the struggle but through the struggle of the believing community. "For a little while you may have to suffer various trials" (1:6). The faith by which this community lives is to be tested to prove its genuineness

(1:7). The worthiness of Jesus Christ and the genuineness of his community both come to light through suffering. The community is to be sprinkled with his blood (1:2).[22]

The believing community must become aware of the Christian realism of I Peter if the illusion of "cheap grace" is to be avoided and if the salvation of souls is to become real (I Peter 1:9). The exercise of faith and trust does change human beings in community. It makes them whole with an integrity, through unity with the humanity in Jesus Christ and communion with each other, which is a gift afforded only in and through struggle.

IV

So radical and passionate a commitment to the sovereign humanity of Jesus Christ by a believing community is inevitably a subversive disturbance in any body politic. Radical obedience to Jesus Christ could be understood as ground for disobedience to and rejection of any and every human institution in the name of piety. Peter obviously anticipated this possibility and therefore insists that the necessary correlate to obedience to Christ is *voluntary* submission to the proper authority of every human institution (I Peter 2:13–16). The imperfection of human institutions is ground, not for either ignoring or destroying them, but for serving them. Peter is not, however, suggesting any compromise of the believers' freedom under the sovereignty of Christ. They are to "live as servants of God" (2:16) who serve human institutions and people functioning in them, not as their slaves but as volunteer servants. As believers who are "mindful of God" (2:19), they will inevitably encounter unjustified suffering. Peter is not suggesting that in the service of human institutions believers offer to them what belongs to God alone, i.e., uncritical and final devotion. Believers give to Caesar only "what is Caesar's," even when the master is "overbearing." Believers give what is due to every institution and those who exercise authority in it, but not uncritically! They do not pay what is not due![23]

It is this free and critical, though not hostile, stance which distinguishes authentic from inauthentic piety in the political arena of life. But it is precisely this critical stance which invites persecution from those who overreach their proper authority. In a power-hungry world, resistance by Christians—particularly when they form an alternative level of community—will inevitably be persecuted. Insecure lust for power will view such new, emergent life-together as conspiracy. That is the real situation which Christians have to deal with.

Yet sooner or later every authority shall learn what this service and resistance by believers means. It is precisely through this conflict that Christ is revealed. The struggle is part of the coming revelation of Jesus as the Christ, at whose appearance every "authority" will learn what his or her gift of power was for. Not lust for power, but the power of love will make the final decision and will fulfill humanity.

The persecuted already know this when they read their own history in the light of the transfigured Christ, who "suffered under Pontius Pilate" but whose power of love cannot be won by lusting after it but only by patiently serving it in a community which resists all unworthy authority. The persecuted know why "the Lamb who was slain" is "worthy" and what "sprinkling with his blood" means. The pursuit of justice in the service of love is costly. Its price is a cross, and no one knows its promise better than the persecuted. By their suffering they both know and proclaim what is worth living for—the sovereignty and community of Jesus as the Christ—the new humanity.

V

This glimpse into the life and thought of the early church exposes a perspective almost totally foreign to the American scene. The expectation of power, profit, and success in our society rests on an anthropological vision of the strong man as the fulfillment of humanity. Yet this lust for power and its correlative feeling of powerlessness are not unchallenged in our society. The "man for others" and the power of love are sufficiently known to make critique possible.

The problem is that the strong man has become the model for political life and the man-for-others the model for religious life. Pragmatism and political realism are dictating that these distinct models of humanity be assigned to separate spheres. Religion and politics should not mix; unless, of course, religion can be used to serve the strong.

This restricted view of the possibility of human survival, and primarily *American* survival, has its Achilles' heel. Those who suffer neglect and injustice in this mad rush for the concentration of power begin to hunger and thirst for another option. The man-for-others begins to make more sense to them as they begin to experience the reality of being "despised and rejected by men," people "of sorrows and acquainted with grief." When their cry for justice is suppressed as unworthy of political attention and not significant in the race for survival, the question of the nature of that humanity which expects to survive *without* others becomes explicit.

In this conflict between the two visions of what it means to be human, the church—like the prophetic tradition in the Bible and like its Lord—must understand and find its solidarity with the poor and persecuted. It has no other choice if the heavenly vision of The Revelation to John and the understanding of sovereignty in I Peter are useful at all in focusing its option.

Knowing its prophetic option, the church participates in the "transfiguration of politics," not merely as another power play, but as a gift of the grace of our Lord Jesus Christ, in whose sovereignty the church believes and whose will for life together it serves. Believers persist in "breaking bread together" as, and with, the persecuted of the kingdom where life with and for others is fullness of joy.

—Is such "poetic projection" still possible on the American scene?
—How can such secular responsibility be assumed by institutional churches?
—What knowledge of the gospel defines the posture of the persecuted, as distinct from the signs sought by security seekers?
—How can the "preaching of the word" revise the logic of history?
—Give examples of unsilenced voices of the persecuted, as faithful persons expect and work for justice, in resisting unjust government *and* in the compassionate exercise of government power.
—Where, if not with the church, shall critical judgment and responsible action begin?

BIBLIOGRAPHY

Boesak, Allan. *Farewell to Innocence.* Orbis Books, 1978.
Calvin, John. *Commentaries on the Catholic Epistles.* Tr. and ed. by John Owen. Edinburgh, 1855.
Hall, Douglas John. *Lighten Our Darkness.* Westminster Press, 1976.
Haroutunian, Joseph. *God with Us.* Westminster Press, 1965.
Herzog, Frederick. *Justice Church.* Orbis Books, 1981.
Huenemann, Edward M. "Hope and Order—Studies in the First Letter of Peter." *Enquiry: Studies for Christian Laity,* Dec. 1969–Jan. 1970.
Lehmann, Paul. *The Transfiguration of Politics.* Harper & Row, 1975.

B. A WHOLE APPROACH

EASTER

Scott I. Paradise

Easter occupies a place so central in the Christian tradition that neither millions of chocolate bunnies nor tons of Easter eggs can entirely obscure its origins in the resurrection of Jesus Christ. But American churches have almost entirely individualized its significance. With relief they put the gloomy rigors of Lent behind and amid banks of lilies celebrate the return of spring, the rebirth of life, and the vindication of Jesus' goodness. With assurance they grasp at the hope of personal immortality beyond the grave or individual resurrection on the last day.

EASTER AS A POLITICAL EVENT

Yet the church was never meant to be a loosely knit collection of individuals who believe in the resurrection. It is the community of the resurrection. Through the life and teaching and impact of this community, the resurrection proved to be more than a religious and privately personal happening, or even a celebration of God's power to save believers. Easter is a social, economic, and political event, as the readings for the Easter season make abundantly clear. Although in the assigned readings the themes treated overlap, they present a consistent picture with complementary emphases. In this picture, the poor, the oppressed, the outcast, and those of no account find new dignity and power. Thus they offer a radical reversal of perspective to that of the powers of this world. They offer a view of a kingdom not of this world, but in it now and standing as a growing challenge to the world.

As Paul Lehmann comments on Phil. 3:10–11:

> The power of Christ's resurrection is the power to live in this life prepared for death and free from the fear of death. It is the power to live in this life without taking this life for granted, or making any of the values and achievements of this life the measure of its meaning and purpose. The power of Christ's resurrection is the power to live in this life with a lively and liberating confidence that God's new world is the

warrant for and confirmation of hope, and is already under way in all those struggles in which we are called to share his sufferings in conformity with his death. To share Christ's sufferings is to stand with and for all in this life who are without opportunity, without power, and without hope, and to make their cause and claims one's own. This succinct summary of the politics of Easter is apostolically warranted and calls for the celebration of Easter as a political feast.[24]

The familiar story begins three days after the crucifixion when women intending to embalm the corpse find the tomb empty and then their Lord alive. During the great half-hundred days following, the risen Christ appears repeatedly to groups of disciples until his ascension and the coming of the Holy Spirit at Pentecost. The Gospel readings for this season begin with the resurrection narratives and continue with passages from John giving Christ's encouragement and instruction to the disciples in their mission. But within a week after Easter the main story in the lectionary readings begins to shift to the book of Acts, where they afford glimpses of the birthing of the apostolic church. The readings from I Peter and the book of Revelation offer support and advice to Christians experiencing persecution.

EASTER SEASON THEMES AND EVENTS FOR THE AMERICAN CHURCH

To bridge the nineteen centuries between the early witnesses to the resurrection and the experience of American churches during the Easter season is our task. Insofar as they recover the New Testament sense of the presence of the risen Lord and the faith that eternal life in the kingdom has already begun for the baptized, American Christians can escape the dread many feel in the face of death. But the recovery of such things comes hard when the quality of church life violates so blatantly the marks of the kingdom. For early Christians the presence of the kingdom impelled full sharing in a thoroughly inclusive community of believers. For us, eleven o'clock Sunday morning is the most segregated hour of the week, not only racially but also economically.

A Sunday visit to a wealthy suburban church drives this point home. Nearly everyone is white. Everyone is also attractive, prosperous, respectable, fashionably dressed, and meticulously turned out. Seldom in sight are minorities, the poor, the crippled, the retarded, the convicts. In that fellowship it becomes easy to imagine that the whole world consists of beautiful, successful, and powerful people. With everyone so wealthy, sharing among the congregation in the apostolic mode would be hugely complicated and relatively meaningless. The economic segregation of neighborhoods, the residential base of many churches, and the ethnic origins of many denominations and congregations undermine aspirations toward inclusiveness. In churches in prosperous neighborhoods the widening gap between the rich and the poor can be easily disregarded, the poor can be blamed for their poverty, and the cry for justice can sound very faint. Churches in this situation tend to drift a long way from the spirit of the New Testament community of the resurrection. They seem to have come to this pass less from malevolence than from forgetfulness. If only larger-than-life-sized photographs of Appalachian poor, late-night city subway riders, prisoners in the county jails, or the hungry in Somalia could hang on the walls of prosperous churches as reminders!

Most American congregations know even less about persecution than about diversity. Yet news reports abound with reports of Cambodians, Haitians, Argentines, Philipinos, South Africans, Poles, or Salvadorans who are persecuted, tortured, detained, or who disappear or are driven from their homes through no fault of their own. A few reports describe the experience of those who suffer because, for Christ's or justice's sake, they oppose a government action. So privatized has the understanding of Easter become that many American Christians are only vaguely aware of a religious mandate to oppose government actions that betray the cause of the poor and the oppressed.

These general themes, of eternal life now, of inclusive Christian community, and of the link between faithfulness and persecution, can be appropriately celebrated throughout the Easter season. The seven-week season sandwiched between Easter Day and the Feast of Pentecost is punctuated, however, by several special days observed by churches and/or society at large. May Day may be the first. As a celebration of the rites of spring, its focus parallels the secularized Easter of daffodils and baby chicks. And when spring comes we need to rejoice. Perhaps with a more intentional celebration of May Day, Easter would experience less distraction from the theme of the resurrection. In Europe May Day has also become a celebration of labor, not a nod to working people in general as has Labor Day in this country, but a feast honoring workers movements and the movements struggling for justice for the workers. Such a feast dovetails neatly with such Easter themes as inclusiveness, justice, and sharing abundance at the common table.

Mother's Day comes shortly after. The Easter emphasis recommended here offers an opportunity to make Mother's Day more than a bouquet and some sentimental words for an exploited nonperson. The pews of many churches are lined with older women who have sacrificed their own growth for their menfolk, as well as angry mothers of a younger generation who balked at the pyre of such sacrifice and have been abandoned by their spouses. Perhaps mothers do not need words of praise as much as some help, an opportunity to grow, a chance to wield power. In how many churches do mothers preach the sermon on Mother's Day?

If Easter comes late, Memorial Day falls within the Easter season.

This can be a day of remembrance for departed loved ones, particularly victims of war. At this time traditional Christian words of Easter can comfort those who mourn. To remember those who laid down their lives for their friends affirms the spirit of Easter. To allow Memorial Day to become an occasion for glorifying American foreign policy and castigating its critics betrays it.

Ascension Day always precedes Pentecost by ten days. It marks the departure of the risen Lord into heaven to be seated at the right hand of God. Traditionally some churches have stressed that Christ's place in heaven signaled an acknowledgment of his Lordship over all the powers of this world. This point might prove equally appropriate on the Feast of Christ the King in the fall. Others have stressed the words of the angels in Acts 1:11 that Christ will come again from heaven and that his followers ought not just stand there gaping. They have a big job to do to establish a community.

PARISH LIFE FOCUSED ON EACH THEME

The four preceding essays on the Easter season lectionary and themes reveal the social implications of the resurrection so clearly that only the blinders of our cultural conditioning could have hidden them from us. Although, in the second of these, Justo and Catherine González properly deplore the shortage of Old Testament readings in the Easter season, one reading included in the lectionary (Ex. 15:1–11) packs enough social import to compensate for the paucity of Old Testament companions. (Note also the corporate meaning of resurrection in Ezekiel 37.)

In the exodus story the parallel between the rescue of Israel from Egyptian slavery at the Red Sea and the release of humanity from slavery to the powers of this world at the empty tomb rings familiar chords in the ears of the most individualistic congregation. But the Red Sea crossing was a corporate event. There God rescued a whole people and created a free nation from a band of slaves. Likewise at Easter, God did not merely save a collection of individuals. God created a community whose membership was open to all humanity.

As they proceed to discuss the readings from the book of Acts, the Gonzálezes stress that the community of the resurrection, whose birth it describes, maintains the traditions of community in its common meals and the sharing of possessions[25] while constantly increasing the diversity of the community. Acts records the falling of barrier after barrier that had divided people for centuries as women, Greeks, Romans, Samaritans, Ethiopians, and assorted outcasts received baptism and the Spirit and became part of the new community. Although parish suppers remain, the book of Acts challenges American congregations with their loss of other marks of the new age.

Sano's essay points to the social meanings of the texts from John's

Gospel and his first Epistle. They reveal the liberation given by the truth Jesus taught and his resurrection. Jesus' ministry taught the power of love, which the risen Christ proved is more powerful than death. The powers of this world would have us believe that power comes from wealth and from the barrel of a gun. These readings challenge American congregations to discern the lies about social and political life by which they are taken in. Their lies usually take the form of false ideology and social myths. When they believe them, Christians frequently accept and collude with evil rather than resist it. When their lies fail to convince, the powers of this world try to intimidate by coercive power, which is ultimately the power to kill. American congregations need to discuss the ways they feel coerced and threatened by the powers of this world and how by Christ's resurrection they become free of their coercive power.[26]

The readings from John for the Easter season do not include the Gospel's most explicit references to persecution (John 15:18–24, for instance). But the texts from Revelation and I Peter addressed by Huenemann deal with it directly. Even though they see the powers of this world as corrupt and under judgment, the authors of these texts do not counsel members of the resurrection community to disobey human institutions. Rather, I Peter urges that believers give them voluntary and critical service even though persecution is the likely result. In such persecution Peter says believers ought to rejoice, because they share the sufferings of Christ. American congregations rarely address the difficult choice here presented between slavery to the powers of this world and suffering with Christ in persecution. But some see through the lies of the powers of this world and do suffer because they speak the truth and act with freedom. They have earned the right to be heard by Christians in the United States and around the world.

Wink's essay on the resurrection stories gives a striking example of a successful attempt of the early church to obscure the liberating power of the resurrection in the case of women, and of the church's failure to erase the evidence of that liberating power from Scripture. Wink's textual analysis suggests that Mary Magdalene saw the risen Lord first. By that priority women won status and authority in the community's earliest days. They lost this position, however, as the church became so hierarchical that women were neither considered authorized witnesses to the resurrection nor even allowed to preach. Wink's analysis stands as an act of restitution in the reading of Scripture which makes imperative complete parity and equality between women and men in every area of ministry and work. As part of the act of restitution, the sermon on Easter should often be preached by women, and surely leadership roles in worship should feature women!

Easter is the time to reexamine the profile and styles of leadership in each congregation and church body, all the more so in denominational assemblies. Easter is also the time to tell the story of women and racial minorities in the church, and of their emergence from second-class membership and subordinate ministry to shared leadership, so today we say, "Never again!"

A WHOLISTIC EASTER PROGRAM

The coalescence of these themes suggest a wholistic program to explore social and political implications of the life of the community of the resurrection. In its early years this community—unlike many segregated, exclusive, ethnic congregations in America—welcomed all comers and exalted those whom society put down. Through this Easter program congregations might come to know and understand the oppressed and the outcasts of the world, who come in many categories:

1. *Women.* They are hardly outcasts in this country but even after the gains of the last decade, the path to equality is still blocked by old prejudices and structural sexism.

2. *The poor.* The aged, the uneducated, the ill, the disabled, the unemployed often fall into this category. In many American communities they are rendered invisible.

3. *Minorities and refugees.* These include Hispanics, blacks, Haitians, Cambodians. Many Americans never see such people, let alone meet them as people and hear them tell their story.

4. *Convicts.* To visit prisons is hardly a popular church activity. Neither do convicts often visit churches.

5. *Political martyrs.* Saints of the New Testament knew well the insides of prisons. Their modern counterparts abound abroad. Americans rediscovered this genre during the civil rights movement.

6. *The institutionalized.* VA hospitals, mental hospitals, nursing homes contain large numbers of forgotten people whom society happily forgets.

7. *Untouchables.* Alcoholics, gays, the disabled, drug addicts, prostitutes are often regarded with distaste if not held in contempt by the respectable.

The many-sided challenge for a congregation to begin to know and embrace and honor and empower the outcasts or downcasts in these categories requires an organizing committee of the parish's worship, hospitality, education, and social action committees meeting jointly. A most energetic congregation might organize a series of activities with a different category each week of those whom society puts down. A minimally ambitious congregation might focus on only one of the categories, but one perhaps more broadly defined. In this case the joint committee might organize the same kinds of activities but fewer in number and spread through the seven weeks of Easter.

PRISONERS: AN EXAMPLE

Consider prisoners as one category of the oppressed that a congregation might begin to know in an Easter program. They come in three sorts: *convicts,* who have been found guilty of committing criminal acts; *victims,* or those imprisoned because of who they are, or their condition; and *martyrs,* or those imprisoned because of their witness to their faith. Most Americans need to know more about all three.

More than 6,500 penal institutions (jails, detention centers, and prisons of all security levels for adults and juveniles), locking up more than half a million people on any given day, are operated in the United States. More than half of the five million imprisoned each year are not convicted of crimes, but await trial, and many of these are too poor to make bail. Others end up in jail because of truancy, drunkenness, or mental illness. Meanwhile, convicts are experiencing longer sentences and more overcrowded conditions. The overcrowding in state prisons has backed up in local jails.

First the congregation's joint committee, with the help of the chaplain, organizes a visit to a jail, prison, or detention center in the area. This should include a visit to two prisons if there is a women's prison within reach. Several members of the congregation of different ages make up the group. They tour those parts of the prison accessible to special groups and have discussions with prison officials, guards, inmates, chaplains, and groups advocating prison reform to learn what life in prison is like and how the corrections system functions. The next Sunday they report back to the congregation either in a general gathering—during coffee hour after church or in their various parish groups in smaller meetings. They discuss the reasons for the class, racial, and ethnic mix in the prison, the effectiveness of the corrections system. They also note the relationship of women to the corrections system, and the responsibilities of the churches. Although the visit and discussion ostensibly plays an educational role, an expression of interest and concern by the church serves as a witness and has an impact on the situation.

The joint committee then invites people with experience in corrections to a common meal with the congregation. Former convicts (Luke 14:13), parole officers, or prison chaplains are the honored guests. They come prepared to speak about their experience and discuss its meaning with the congregation. Above all, the committee needs to invite former prisoners who have served time because of their witness to their faith. Such persons are not restricted to the book of Acts or past centuries; they can be found today. Some were imprisoned in the civil rights movement, some for their opposition to the Vietnam War or to military service, some challenged the arms race or demonstrated against nuclear power. Some were released from prisons of foreign regimes and found asylum in this country. Close listening to what these say may give essential hints to the meaning of the resurrection for today's church. So important is their testimony that they deserve a special occasion to speak.

The joint committee also organizes opportunities for members of the congregation to reflect on the themes of resurrection and release to prisoners with a Bible study planned for six sessions, once a week through the Easter season:

First week. Recollect biblical heroes who were imprisoned and the circumstances of their imprisonment. Joseph, Samson, Jeremiah, John the Baptist, Peter, and Paul belong on the list. Jeremiah 32:1–5, 37, and Acts, chs. 5; 12; 16; and 21:17ff. deserve special attention.

Second week. Consider modern Christians who have suffered imprisonment, exile, and even martyrdom. Discuss the circumstances of their arrests. Dietrich Bonhoeffer,[27] Martin Luther King,[28] Rosa Parks,[29] and Daniel Berrigan[30] stand out among the more famous of these.

Third week. Review the promises and acts of God to bring liberation to slaves, captives, and prisoners of all stripes. Exodus 14 claims attention here. Look also at Isa. 42:6–9; 49:8–9; 61:1–4; and Lev. 25. According to I Peter 3:19, Jesus upon his resurrection even went to release the souls imprisoned in hell. Consider also the liberation promised in the Easter season readings in John's Gospel.

Fourth week. Read Matt. 25:31–46 and discuss Jesus' warning that his followers are to visit prisoners. How does this parable relate to the resurrection? to us?

Fifth week. Ponder the suggestion in Luke 21:12, and in the Acts passages mentioned above, that the faithful run the risk of imprisonment. Discuss the meaning of I Peter 4:12–19 and Phil. 1:29 to 2:13 (an Epistle itself written in prison) for Christians in this century. What has happened to the connection between faithfulness and suffering with the risen Christ?

Sixth week. Discuss and agree on action to which members of the congregation might commit themselves. Of the many possibilities that present themselves, consider at least forming a parish group to visit inmates, working for the release of political prisoners through Amnesty International (parish membership chapters might be appropriate), creating a support group for controversial witnesses protesting government actions that seem to betray the cause of human liberation. The Bible study groups might try to agree on some follow-up action in the light of their Bible study and present their suggestion to the congregation for discussion and, if possible, decision.

Curiously, almost no published American services of worship exist which address the Easter social themes of freeing the prisoners and facing political martyrdom in this century. Most of those that do exist focus on very specific themes. Perhaps the most appropriate service for a congregation undertaking this program is not Christian—but a Freedom Seder written in 1968 for Jewish observance but used in ecumenical gatherings.[31] Traditionally the seder, a Jewish family Passover ceremony, celebrates the rescue of Israel from slavery at the Red Sea as recorded in Exodus 14–15. In the seder, Jews remember their redemption from former servitude and their obligation to have pity toward the oppressed. In this new Freedom Seder particular forms of oppression of our time are addressed, as are particular opportunities to redress them. It needs to be amended for use in the 1980s. Though seders are usually family events, they can be observed with a whole congregation. The Freedom Seder makes most sense early in the Easter season.

The Quixote Center has produced a powerful Vigil Service for El Salvador.[32] (The format of this service can be adapted for vigils that focus on other situations of oppression and martyrdom.) It takes place in semidarkness with lighted candles symbolizing the martyrs and with their photographs displayed on a screen. As the circumstances of the death of each martyr are described, a candle is snuffed out. Toward the end of the service the congregation makes a series of commitments to work for peace and justice. With each act of commitment a candle is relit, signifying the rebirth of the spirit of the martyred in the lives of the worshipers. This service can be modified according to each parish's particular program. The congregation may find this most powerful toward the end of the Easter season when political martyrdom has been discussed.

V. PENTECOST

READINGS

Sunday or Festival	Year	First Lesson	Second Lesson	Gospel
Pentecost	A	Acts 2:1–21 or Isa. 44:1–8	I Cor. 12:3b–13	John 20:19–23 or John 7:37–39
	B	Joel 2:28–32 or Ezek. 37:1–14	Rom. 8:22–27 or Acts 2:1–21	John 15:26–27 or John 16:4b–15
	C	Isa. 65:17–25 or Gen. 11:1–9	Rom. 8:14–17 or Acts 2:1–21	John 14:8–17, 25–27 or John 14:15–26
1st Sunday After Pentecost (Trinity)	A	Deut. 4:32–40	II Cor. 13:5–14	Matt. 28:16–20
	B	Isa. 6:1–8	Rom. 8:12–17	John 3:1–8 (12–17)
	C	Prov. 8:22–31	Rom. 5:1–5 or I Peter 1:1–9	John 16:12–15 or John 20:19–23
2d Sunday After Pentecost	A	Gen. 12:1–9	Rom. 3:21–28	Matt. 7:21–29
	B	I Sam. 16:1–13	II Cor. 4:5–12	Mark 2:23 to 3:6
	C	I Kings 8:22–23, 41–43	Gal. 1:1–10	Luke 7:1–10
3d Sunday After Pentecost	A	Gen. 22:1–18	Rom. 4:13–18	Matt. 9:9–13
	B	I Sam. 16:14–23	II Cor. 4:13 to 5:1	Mark 3:20–35
	C	I Kings 17:17–24	Gal. 1:11–24	Luke 7:11–17
4th Sunday After Pentecost	A	Gen. 25:19–34	Rom. 5:6–11	Matt. 9:35 to 10:3
	B	II Sam. 1:1, 17–27	II Cor. 5:6–10, 14–17	Mark 4:26–34
	C	I Kings 19:1–8	Gal. 2:15–21	Luke 7:36 to 8:3
5th Sunday After Pentecost	A	Gen. 28:10–17	Rom. 5:12–19	Matt. 10:24–33
	B	II Sam. 5:1–12	II Cor. 5:18 to 6:2	Mark 4:35–41
	C	I Kings 19:9–14	Gal. 3:23–29	Luke 9:18–24
6th Sunday After Pentecost	A	Gen. 32:22–32	Rom. 6:3–11	Matt. 10:34–42
	B	II Sam. 6:1–15	II Cor. 8:7–15	Mark 5:21–43
	C	I Kings 19:15–21	Gal. 5:1, 13–25	Luke 9:51–62
7th Sunday After Pentecost	A	Ex. 1:6–14, 22; 2:1–10	Rom. 7:14–25a	Matt. 11:25–30
	B	II Sam. 7:1–17	II Cor. 12:1–10	Mark 6:1–6
	C	I Kings 21:1–3, 17–21	Gal. 6:7–18	Luke 10:1–12, 17–20

Sunday or Festival	Year	First Lesson	Second Lesson	Gospel
8th Sunday After Pentecost	A	Ex. 2:11–22	Rom. 8:9–17	Matt. 13:1–9, 18–23
	B	II Sam. 7:18–29	Eph. 1:1–10	Mark 6:7–13
	C	II Kings 2:1, 6–14	Col. 1:1–14	Luke 10:25–37
9th Sunday After Pentecost	A	Ex. 3:1–12	Rom. 8:18–25	Matt. 13:24–30, 36–43
	B	II Sam. 11:1–15	Eph. 2:11–22	Mark 6:30–34
	C	II Kings 4:8–17	Col. 1:15–20, 28	Luke 10:38–42
10th Sunday After Pentecost	A	Ex. 3:13–20	Rom. 8:26–30	Matt. 13:44–52
	B	II Sam. 12:1–14	Eph. 3:14–21	John 6:1–15
	C	II Kings 5:1–15ab	Col. 2:6–15	Luke 11:1–13
11th Sunday After Pentecost	A	Ex. 12:1–14	Rom. 8:31–39	Matt. 14:13–21
	B	II Sam. 12:15b–24	Eph. 4:1–6	John 6:24–35
	C	II Kings 13:14–20a	Col. 3:1–11	Luke 12:13–21
12th Sunday After Pentecost	A	Ex. 14:19–31	Rom. 9:1–5	Matt. 14:22–33
	B	II Sam. 18:1, 5, 9–15	Eph. 4:25 to 5:2	John 6:35, 41–51
	C	Jer. 18:1–11	Heb. 11:1–3, 8–19	Luke 12:32–40
13th Sunday After Pentecost	A	Ex. 16:2–15	Rom. 11:13–16, 29–32	Matt. 15:21–28
	B	II Sam. 18:24–33	Eph. 5:15–20	John 6:51–58
	C	Jer. 20:7–13	Heb. 12:1–2, 12–17	Luke 12:49–56
14th Sunday After Pentecost	A	Ex. 17:1–7	Rom. 11:33–36	Matt. 16:13–20
	B	II Sam. 23:1–7	Eph. 5:21–33	John 6:55–69
	C	Jer. 28:1–9	Heb. 12:18–29	Luke 13:22–30
15th Sunday After Pentecost	A	Ex. 19:1–9	Rom. 12:1–13	Matt. 16:21–28
	B	I Kings 2:1–4, 10–12	Eph. 6:10–20	Mark 7:1–8, 14–15, 21–23
	C	Ezek. 18:1–9, 25–29	Heb. 13:1–8	Luke 14:1, 7–14
16th Sunday After Pentecost	A	Ex. 19:16–24	Rom. 13:1–10	Matt. 18:15–20
	B	Ecclus. 5:8–15 or Prov. 2:1–8	James 1:17–27	Mark 7:31–37
	C	Ezek. 33:1–11	Philemon 1–20	Luke 14:25–33
17th Sunday After Pentecost	A	Ex. 20:1–20	Rom. 14:5–12	Matt. 18:21–35
	B	Prov. 22:1–2, 8–9	James 2:1–5, 8–10, 14–18	Mark 8:27–38
	C	Hosea 4:1–3; 5:15 to 6:6	I Tim. 1:12–17	Luke 15:1–10

Sunday or Festival	Year	First Lesson	Second Lesson	Gospel
18th Sunday After Pentecost	A	Ex. 32:1–14	Phil. 1:21–27	Matt. 20:1–16
	B	Job 28:20–28	James 3:13–18	Mark 9:30–37
	C	Hos. 11:1–11	I Tim. 2:1–7	Luke 16:1–13
19th Sunday After Pentecost	A	Ex. 33:12–23	Phil. 2:1–13	Matt. 21:28–32
	B	Job 42:1–6	James 4:13–17, 5:7–11	Mark 9:38–50
	C	Joel 2:23–30	I Tim. 6:6–19	Luke 16:19–31
20th Sunday After Pentecost	A	Num. 27:12–23	Phil. 3:12–21	Matt. 21:33–43
	B	Gen. 2:18–24	Heb. 1:1–4; 2:9–11	Mark 10:2–16
	C	Amos 5:6–7, 10–15	II Tim. 1:1–14	Luke 17:5–10
21st Sunday After Pentecost	A	Deut. 34:1–12	Phil. 4:1–9	Matt. 22:1–14
	B	Gen. 3:8–19	Heb. 4:1–3, 9–13	Mark 10:17–30
	C	Amos 7:12–17 or Micah 1:2; 2:1–10	II Tim. 2:8–15	Luke 17:11–19
22d Sunday After Pentecost	A	Ruth 1:1–19a	I Thess. 1:1–10	Matt. 22:15–22
	B	Isa. 53:7–12	Heb. 4:14–16	Mark 10:35–45
	C	Amos 8:4–8 or Hab. 1:1–3; 2:1–4	II Tim. 3:14 to 4:5	Luke 18:1–8
23d Sunday After Pentecost	A	Ruth 2:1–13	I Thess. 2:1–8	Matt. 22:34–46
	B	Jer. 31:7–9	Heb. 5:1–6	Mark 10:46–52
	C	Zeph. 3:1–9	II Tim. 4:6–8, 16–18	Luke 18:9–14
24th Sunday After Pentecost	A	Ruth 4:7–17	I Thess. 2:9–13, 17–20	Matt. 23:1–12
	B	Deut. 6:1–9	Heb. 7:23–28	Mark 12:28–34
	C	Hag. 2:1–9	II Thess. 1:5–12	Luke 19:1–10
25th Sunday After Pentecost	A	Amos 5:18–24	I Thess. 4:13–18	Matt. 25:1–13
	B	I Kings 17:8–16	Heb. 9:24–28	Mark 12:38–44
	C	Zech. 7:1–10	II Thess. 2:13 to 3:5	Luke 20:27–38
26th Sunday After Pentecost	A	Zeph. 1:7, 12–18	I Thess. 5:1–11	Matt. 25:14–30
	B	Dan. 7:9–14	Heb. 10:11–18	Mark 13:24–32
	C	Mal. 4:1–6 (3:19–24 in Heb.)	II Thess. 3:6–13	Luke 21:5–19
27th Sunday After Pentecost (Christ the King)	A	Ezek. 34:11–16, 20–24	I Cor. 15:20–28	Matt. 25:31–46
	B	Jer. 23:1–6	Rev. 1:4b–8	John 18:33–37
	C	II Sam. 5:1–5	Col. 1:11–20	John 12:9–19

Sunday or Festival	Year	First Lesson	Second Lesson	Gospel
All Saints, Nov. 1*	A	Rev. 7:9–17	I John 3:1–3	Matt. 5:1–12
	B	Rev. 21:1–6a	Col. 1:9–14	John 11:32–44
	C	Dan. 7:1–3, 15–18	Eph. 1:11–23	Luke 6:20–36
Thanksgiving Day**	A	Deut. 8:7–18	II Cor. 9:6–15	Luke 17:11–19
	B	Joel 2:21–27	I Tim. 2:1–7	Matt. 6:25–33
	C	Deut. 26:1–11	Phil. 4:4–9	John 6:25–35

*or on first Sunday in November
**lections ad libitum, not tied to A, B, or C

Pentecost celebrates the gift of the Holy Spirit to the church. It begins an extended season of semicontinuous readings of Old Testament, Epistle, and Gospel. A few themes not emphasized in other seasons are highlighted here.

A. THEMATIC ESSAYS

1

THE FESTIVAL OF PENTECOST
AND TRINITY SUNDAY

Esther C. Stine

Day of Pentecost	I Cor. 12:4–13	Acts 2:1–21	John 14:8–27
	Joel 2:28–32		John 16:5–15
	Isa. 65:17–25		John 14:25–31
Trinity Sunday	Ezek. 37:1–4	II Cor. 13:5–14	Matt. 28:16–20
	(Isa. 6:1–8)	Rom. 5:1–15;	John 3:1–8
	(Prov. 8:22–31)	8:12–17	John 20:19–23
		I Peter 1:1–9	

I. THE AMERICAN EXPERIENCE OF PLURALISM

Although the word "pluralism" is used quite frequently by contemporary Americans, we are not always clear either about the meaning of the word or the experiences toward which it points. Like all words, "pluralism" takes a specific coloring and content from the contexts in which it is used. In turn, contexts have histories. These constitute our experiences of the word and its meaning. Clarification of meaning through understanding contexts and their histories is crucial if we are to hear, speak, and enact God's Word for our time.

The word "pluralism" first came into existence in Western culture in the philosophical works of Christian Wolff (A.D. 1720), who used it to describe certain beliefs about the basic structure of reality. The prevailing belief at that time, called "monism," held that despite all the evidence of appearances, reality was simply one all-pervasive substance. Wolff opposed this view. In contrast to monism, he asserted that appearances in all their diversity are real, and thus reality itself is composed of many substances. He called this view pluralism.

Wolff's successor, the great Immanuel Kant, accepted pluralism as the most accurate belief about reality, and he extended the meaning of the word in two directions: in the fields of psychology and politics. In psychology he juxtaposed pluralism and egoism. The latter was a way of perceiving the world as if it were simply an extension of oneself (today's "narcissism"). The former was a way of seeing the world in its own right, with modesty and for the sake of fellowship.

214

In the field of politics, Kant expressed a form of political pluralism: the king was to avail himself of a council of many voices before he made decisions or acted.

The philosophical and political context for the word remained the primary base for its meaning. In 1915 Harold J. Laski underscored the political nature of pluralism. Laski lived in a state which was a war machine, demanding strict obedience and the worship of the nation. He was horrified to see how people were killing other people by the millions simply because the state said they should. In opposition to such monolithic nationalism, Laski called for the construction of a political order composed of many different factions. The document he cited to illustrate such a pluralistic political order was *The Federalist Papers,* written by James Madison and others. The United States is the example *par excellence* of pluralism in politics.

Thus, the American experience of pluralism is first of all and most basically political. Its roots lie in our Revolution, and the meaning of the Revolution gave pluralism its meaning. Unlike the French Revolution, to which it is often compared, however, the American struggle was not first and foremost an attack upon privilege. Nor was the notion of pluralism it engendered rooted in any way in a universal doctrine of the rights of man. Quite the contrary. The experience of the American Revolution was the attempt of English persons and British subjects to secure the rights belonging to them as citizens. The Revolution was typified in Patrick Henry's call, "Give me liberty or give me death." It was for the sake of "liberty" that pluralism was built into the fabric of American political life. And, as subsequent history has revealed, "liberty" is perfectly consistent with the preservation of privilege.

It is very important to underscore this relationship between political pluralism and liberty if we are to understand the potentiality for contradiction within our society. The authors of our constitution believed that if liberty were going to be at all possible, we must guard against the construction of a monolithic political system. What is important, therefore, is that we build a pluralism of flourishing human associations. It was believed that the sin in any one such association would temper the sin in other such factions. Liberty also meant that propertied people should be free to join any group that they preferred. But blacks could not vote and women could not join companies as fully accepted workers. So the liberty that was experienced through political pluralism was secured at the expense of individuals and groups in the country—and it still is!

Early in American history we began to experience power in terms of a power elite. William Greenbaum, in an article entitled "America in Search of a New Ideal," defines this power elite as "old-stock Americans (deriving from pre-1790 families), the upper class (defined by military, industrial, political, and professional status), Episcopalians, and Presbyterians."[1] This power elite maintained its position of power by building structures of "distance." By this is meant that it kept other individuals and groups from full participation in those associations which really constituted the "pluralism" of power guaranteed by our political theory. For example, in the arena of economics, the power elite built structures (and the mythologies to support them) that tolerated the inequitable distribution of goods and that treated persons as commodities.

The immigrations that took place between the end of the Civil War and the turn of the century began to put incredible strain on the pluralism that ensured "liberty" for the privileged. At this time the rubric "the melting pot" emerged as the way in which structures of power could continue to exist with the guise of a plurality of human association without recognizing equality within diversity. Members of racial, cultural, and ethnic groups could fit into the structure of power only as individual citizens somehow managed to leave behind them all their cultural, racial, and ethnic differences. Yet, to leave these differences behind and to participate in the larger society depended primarily on economic and political power itself. So even the "melting pot" carried in it the contradiction of the very pluralism it supposedly sought to ensure. Today we still experience structural disenfranchisement of large segments of our racial and ethnic populations in the processes of governmental policies concerning education, health, and welfare programs.

Pluralism functioning simply as the playmate of liberty denied pluralism in the sense of equality. The struggles of the 1960s, 1970s, and now the 1980s are efforts to place pluralism in the context of the desire for equality. Whereas the call for liberty implied that "as citizens" individuals were free to pursue their own interests, liberty was conceived of strictly in this individualist sense. Thus large groups of the population, by virtue of that which made them a "group," found opportunities closed to them. The call for equality is the demand for a social structure that will, in fact, provide the same opportunities for all members of a group and for all groups, while at the same time affirming their differences. We will misunderstand the existence of national and global pluralism today if we do not recognize that it now affirms this claim of equality.

It is in the midst of this struggle to put pluralism together with equality that the Word of God must be heard and spoken.

II. The Rootedness of the Church in Pluralism and Equality

When we speak of pluralism coming together with equality we are speaking about a new experience of power. It is precisely this experience which the church claims for its beginning. The experience of the early church on the day of Pentecost reveals the movement toward the empowerment of pluralistic communities and the affirmation of their diversity within their unity.

The Pentecost event features two groups of people that already know pluralism. One of these communities is that of the believers in Christ. Its pluralistic nature (which is a hint of what is to take place) contains the disciples, the brothers of Jesus, about one hundred and twenty "brethren," plus the women and the mother of Jesus (Acts 1:13–15). Luke was writing at a time when the church was struggling to maintain itself in a patriarchal culture. Therefore, his account subtly disenfranchises the women from positions of leadership in the church with the saying that only males who accompanied Jesus are considered eligible to be apostles (in contradistinction to the Pauline condition that anyone who has seen the resurrected Lord is eligible: I Cor. 9:1). Yet, the fact that Luke adds them explicitly to his list indicates the actual prominence that women held in the earliest communities of the church.

Elisabeth Fiorenza makes the point that the earliest Jesus traditions expect a transformation of all social conditions because of God's intervention in Jesus Christ. "Therefore, the Jesus movement can accept all those who, according to contemporary societal standards, are marginal people and who are, according to the Torah, 'unclean'—the poor, exploited, public sinners, publicans, Samaritans, the maimed and sick, and last but not least, the women."[2] This is reflected in the Lucan account of the community of believers.

The second pluralistic community present on the day of Pentecost is "devout men from every nation under heaven" (2:5). The text mentions at least thirteen different countries of origin with all that is implied in that for differences and distinctness culturally and socially.

Out of these two pluralistic communities the event of Pentecost makes, at least for that time and place, one community. The believers speak and the devout hear. In the event of speaking and hearing God's Word, they are united into one community. All the differences that are in their midst, at least for this one event of God's Word, affirm rather than impede the reality of the community formed by the event. The text says, "We hear them telling *in our own tongues* the mighty works of God" (2:11).

The climax of the event comes in the mocking words located in v. 13: "They are filled with new wine." As with so much mockery, this is a hidden statement of truth. New wine is fermenting wine. It is filled with new power, which, as Luke has already pointed out, is always ready to burst old wineskins (Luke 5:37). The new pluralistic community of Pentecost has raised up an egalitarian model of human community. The claim is being made: pluralism and equality go together

III. Related Affirmations of Egalitarian, Pluralistic Community

John 14:15–26 gives further depth and meaning to the event of Pentecost. The new egalitarian pluralistic community in Acts is the work of the Holy Spirit. In the discourse in John, Jesus promises the Holy Spirit to those disciples "who keep [his] word." Faithfulness becomes the context within which the empowering gift of the Spirit is given. A new community is promised. This new community is one in which love of neighbor and love of God are the unifying elements as well as the only requirements for belonging (vs. 20, 23).

And finally, Isaiah 65 deepens the vision of this new community as egalitarian and pluralistic. The passage raises up certain kinds of differences that are to be overcome in the new community. One of these is the difference constituted by the vulnerability and weakness of age: the infant who lives but a few days and the old man who does not fill out his days. These are but symbols for all who find themselves in fragile circumstances, unable to fulfill the promise that God's creation holds out to them. The second difference has to do with work that fulfills the promise of God. Here the difference expressed is openly and blatantly a matter of justice. People build but someone else inhabits, they plant and someone else eats. In this most vital aspect of human life, people are not in control of their own destinies. They are oppressed.

The Isaiah passage holds out the vision that in "the new heaven and the new earth" (the time of new wine!) those who have been unable to have control over their own destinies will have been liberated. Natural—as distinct from imposed—differences will be accepted in the new community. The wolf and the lamb will feed together, the lion will eat straw along with the ox, and "they shall not hurt or destroy in all my holy mountain" (v. 25). Acceptance of differences shall undergird equality. The liberation promised in Isa. 65: 17–25 is the enactment of a pluralistic community built around the reality of equality.

IV. The Rootedness of Empowerment in the Doctrine of the Triune God

The vision of an egalitarian pluralistic community based on the liberation of the weak and powerless is a theme central to the biblical witness. Yet elements of that witness have given rise to great problems in our time for persons who are down under. Not the least of these people have been blacks and women, both of whom have found the basic images of God offered to them by Western Christianity to be not only problematic for their faith but also part of the mechanisms of oppression. Sabelo Ntwana, a South African theologian who suffered under house arrest for five years in his country because of his activities on behalf of the biblical vision of community, has written at length on the traditional Trinitarian doctrine of God.[3] For him and for his South African sisters and brothers, God the Father, Son, and Holy Spirit—as understood through the witness of the West—has become, in their situations, God the white male tyrant. (How true this is in the experience of pluralism in American society!) If the doctrine of God is basically a doctrine about power, then that power is acted out by the churches according to their grasp of what God is doing. For black South Africans (and other marginated people) the prevailing doctrine of the Trinity carries with it all the dehumanizing authority patterns that have excluded them from making the basic decisions about where they live, where they are to work, and how they will organize their lives with others. Not only are these decisions made for all these people, but they are actually made in favor of others, namely, the elite power structure. But the oppressed see God working quite differently—from the underside.

It is important, therefore, that we who are the church look at our understanding of the Triune God, recognizing that it has become a tool of oppression, and asking what is crucial about that doctrine to our life of witness in a world seeking equality for many groups. The way into such a discussion is through the understanding of the Spirit.

Ntwana says that the doctrine of the Triune God must be reinterpreted in terms of "the spaces between people," where humanity exists—i.e., "in the relationships that bind them together, that are mutually affirming, that are liberating and that create a wholeness."[4]

Isn't this precisely how we are to understand the Spirit? Joseph Haroutunian writes, "The Spirit interdwells my brother [and sister] and myself for our communion with God and with one another in Christ Jesus."[5] It is the Spirit of God which fills the spaces between people, bringing them into creative relation with one another, creating community where there was once only oppression. In this sense, the Spirit always powerfully directs us toward the Other (Jesus and the neighbor), rather than toward itself. In this kenotic role it takes on the characteristics of the feminine.[6]

The experience of the prophet Ezekiel is the experience of the power of the Spirit to put together that which has been put asunder. The dry bones of the people of Israel, representing the brokenness of human community, can be made whole again by the power of the Spirit (Ezek. 37:1–14). What has been two (v. 17) may become one (vs. 17, 22).

But just as Ezekiel sees this oneness as a sign of faithfulness to God so also Paul in Romans 8 speaks of our being led by the Spirit to become children of God. Such assumption of the role of God's children, however, is possible only as we suffer with Christ, the Liberator. The empowerment of the Spirit is that it ties us to Christ, and tying us to Messiah Jesus it ties us to all the marginated weak groups in our society who are calling for equality and not conformity.

The doctrine of the Triune God ensures social equality as the central value of community. The Spirit that binds us to Christ and makes us the children of God is "of the same substance" as God the Creator and the Word which became flesh in Jesus. The Spirit's being of the same substance with God means that the community which is formed by God, Word, and Spirit is a creative community of equality. The act of creating human community which is the work of this Spirit is a creation "in the image of God." Such an act of creation ensures that community always takes precedence over individualism and that privatization of the goods necessary to community is impossible. This act of creation also radically relativizes all earthly powers and distinctions (Gal. 3:28), rendering all creatures in community equal before God. This same act of creation which is communal, nonprivatizing, and relativizing also identifies where God is indeed present with godly power in the world, namely with those who are weak and powerless.

The Spirit empowers in our social life the creation of a community of many groups where each is equal and uniquely separate yet bound to the other in the common task of keeping society humane. It is the work of the Triune God—of the Creator, who made us for such community (Isaiah 65); of the Word become flesh, who was crucified, dead, and buried, and who rose again for the sake of the poor, the captive, the blind, and the oppressed (Luke 4:18); and of the Spirit, which breaks down all barriers unjustly separating group from group (Rom. 8:5-6) by uniting us in suffering and in peace with Jesus Christ.

The doctrine of the Triune God is the safeguard against the privatized and individualistic conception of empowerment reigning in our world. The reality of the Spirit as God means that the Spirit is not a ghost that grants prosperity to those who labor hardest, or the author of ecstatic experiences that lift us out of the suffering life toward some divine haven. The Spirit which is God is the "new wine" which creates community, the power or union filling with love our distance from God, and with justice the spaces between persons.

V. IMPLICATIONS FOR PLURALISM IN AMERICA

The cry for equality can only be stifled by some form of authoritarian or fascist social structure that will maintain present power relationships. If the church is to be the "new wine" in our pluralistic society, it will begin to examine the value contradictions in our American experience. For example, it will address the contradictions between our beliefs in justice and private property; between individualism and conformity; between privatization and community; between family, social, occupational, and residential mobility; between self-reliance and ravenous materialism; between dominance of nature and harmony with nature. Second, it will begin to develop a life-style which reveals that justice calls for interdependence and that equality breeds mutuality. Third, it will open itself to the powerlessness and weakness of the marginated groups of our society and become a channel by which power is redistributed among all the people. Fourth, it will search for ways to show the world that differences of race, culture, and sex are the sources of creativity and new life for us all when persons of these differences are fully equal decision-making partners in the ebb and flow of life. Finally, it will search for creative ways in which, in a pluralistic world based on equality, it can show forth that "the creation itself will be set free from its bondage of decay and obtain the glorious freedom of the children of God" (Rom. 8:21).

2

A STRATEGY FOR PREACHING
FROM THE SYNOPTICS IN PENTECOST

Neill Q. Hamilton

The lectionary lessons in Pentecost provide for almost continuous reading of the central chapters of each of the Synoptic Gospels. This lack of selectivity implies that the controlling lessons for this season will be the Epistles, where the church is intensely conscious of itself as a post-Pentecostal community engaged in mission in the power and presence of the Holy Spirit, and that the Old Testament lessons will keep to the fore the full prophetic responsibility of the people of God for history and creation.

Still, the figure of Jesus has a crucial connection to the believer's and the community's life in the Spirit. Each of the Synoptics contains the promise to believers of baptism in the Spirit (Matt. 3:11; Mark 1:8; Luke 3:16), but, with one exception (testimony before courts of persecution), they never display what that experience looks like. Instead we see Jesus only receiving the Spirit at his baptism. But that is enough, for his being led by the Spirit immediately into the wilderness of temptation stands for the assumption that Jesus' whole ministry is carried out in the power of the Spirit. That is tantamount to saying that if the church and believers wish to see what baptism in the Spirit looks like, they must look to Jesus as its norm.

We see then the wisdom of the continuous reading of the lessons of Jesus' ministry during the Pentecost season. The experience of the Spirit is by itself highly subjective. It needs to borrow content from the other members of the Godhead to prevent it from being prostituted to God-contrary ends. The claim of a Corinthian that the Spirit made him curse Jesus, probably to avoid persecution for confessing Jesus as Lord, was only the first of a long line of such abuses that reaches to our day (I Cor. 12:3).

The primary function of the Gospel lessons in the Pentecost season should be to control the subjectivity of persons and congregations who give spiritual reasons for avoiding responsibility for the whole will of God as displayed in Jesus—sent by the Father and led by the Spirit. More particularly the lessons need to show how that whole will of God includes responsibility for social justice. It is no secret

222

that there tends to be a great gulf fixed between those among us with a deep sense of social responsibility and those who claim to interpret mission in a more spiritual sense. The figure of Christ in the Gospels acting in the power of the Holy Spirit is meant to bridge that gulf. So the strategy of Pentecost should be to cut to the Synoptic lesson for the sermon on those Sundays when the preacher-liturgist judges that the lesson could correct some spiritual misconception of a particular congregation. The Gospel lessons in Pentecost are a safety net strung under a church tempted to displays of spiritual gymnastics.

I. Eschatological Consciousness

Actually that puts our strategy too negatively; it is also a positive strategy in that Jesus, as archetype of life and ministry in the Spirit, grounds the social mission of the church. The Gospel lessons are a safety net whose presence encourages the church to take the risks appropriate to the call to mission. The first lesson the Jesus of the Pentecost teaches us is that all social action must be grounded in eschatological consciousness. By eschatological consciousness I mean the sure and steady hope that God will one day restore the structures of creation and society to their intended function: e.g., Rom. 8:18–25 (9th Sunday, Year A). This is the social significance of the event portrayed in Mark 13:24–32 (26th Sunday, Year B). All the church's mission efforts for justice must be carried on in the confidence they borrow from God's triumph at the End. This hope has several corollaries.

A typical failing of the American churches has been to take up crusades for social causes with the expectation that in the End the final solution will be an American one. Indeed from Jonathan Edwards on we have usually supposed that America will soon be the scene of the final coming of the kingdom of God. The coming of the Son of Man on clouds stands in judgment on all such Camelot expectations, just as when we first meet that symbol it stands in judgment on Israel's dreams.

Mark first presented a picture of the coming of the Son of Man to fend off Judaism's expectation that the End would come as a national triumph through a holy war of national liberation. Judaism had begun such a war against Rome in A.D. 66. Mark's Gospel arose in part as an explanation of why that Christian community could not participate in this nationalist project. It was this picture of the coming of the Son of Man to the whole earth simultaneously as much as any other element in the early church's theology that turned the followers of Jesus from a Jewish sect, ethnic and nationalist in scope, into a world religion transcending the claims of race or political units.

The immediate effect of eschatological consciousness is to separate social concerns from the parochial self-interest of nation or ethnic group. So the first corollary of eschatological consciousness is that our concerns for social justice must be global in scope.

A second corollary is that justice will finally be a divine gift rather than a human achievement. The Son of Man comes down to us; we do not rise up to him. What a relief! Far from discouraging us in our efforts to be agents of divine justice, this End encourages us to do our best without needing to win out, to triumph, to overcome. It is enough that we are faithful to the constant struggle whether we win or lose at any particular turn. And when we do find ourselves effective agents of reconciliation we know at heart that the result was a secret gift of God's providence pointing on to the final gift.

Eschatological consciousness paces us for the long haul; it teaches patience, endurance, steadfastness. This is the final note of Luke's lesson (Luke 21:5–19) on the 26th Sunday, Year C: "By your endurance you will gain your lives."

Another aspect of this same corollary is that no one can calculate the time when efforts for justice will pay off, just as no one can predict the day or hour of the coming of the Son of Man. The grace of justice comes in God's own time. That is the final note of the Marcan lesson on the 26th Sunday, but it was Luke's distinctive contribution to warn the church against too hasty an expectation of the End. In this Luke corrects even Mark by adding that misleading prophets say "The time is at hand" (Luke 21:8), for in Luke's day disciples were being distracted from mission by wondering if the risen Christ would *"at this time* restore the kingdom to Israel" (Acts 1:6). Eschatological consciousness, as Luke especially developed it, is the best protection against Type A behavior in mission for social justice.

One final corollary of what we are calling eschatological consciousness unfolds in the pericope on "Paying Taxes to Caesar," Matt. 22:15–22 (22d Sunday, Year A). Its context is the continuing attempt of Matthew's opponents at Jamnia to present Christianity as subversive to the Roman Empire. Jesus rejected the revolutionary stand of refusing to pay taxes—but to the astonishment of all, he also refused to take a merely loyalist stand that would have made the Roman government the providential equivalent of the kingdom of God. The point of this New Testament lesson then and now is that although earthly governments deserve respect for the measure of justice they bring, Caesar's things and God's things are never the same thing.

In summary, eschatological consciousness draws attention to the structural change called for in the coming reign of God, cautions us against expecting too much too soon from our efforts for justice, all the while encouraging us to hope in God for final vindication of the oppressed and for grace to receive preliminary vindications along the way, and finally warning us off of every prevailing political arrangement's claim that to trust in it is to trust in God. But eschatological consciousness by itself only sets the formal context for God's demand that we engage in mission for justice. The content and drive of that demand is love.

II. LOVE, THE WELLSPRING OF JUSTICE

Along with eschatological consciousness, love is the other essential element in the New Testament's grounding of mission for social justice. If there are any Sundays in the Pentecost season when the Gospel lesson deserves priority, they arise each year when the love commandment is the Gospel lesson—Year A, 23d Sunday (Matt. 22: 34–40); Year B, 24th Sunday (Mark 12:28–34); Year C, 8th Sunday (Luke 10:25–37). Love of God mandates love of neighbor. To love one's neighbor is to respond to that neighbor's need whenever and wherever that need arises, as the parable of the good Samaritan in Luke explains. It was a willingness to live in this spirit of love to neighbor that accounts more than any other single factor for the early church's winning the Western world away from its rival religions. The emperor Julian complained:

> Why do we not observe that it is their benevolence to strangers, their care for the graves of the dead, and the pretended holiness of their lives that have done the most to increase atheism [Christianity]? It is disgraceful that when no Jew has to beg, and the impious Galileans [Christians] support not only their own poor but ours as well, all men see that our people lack aid from us.[7]

It is a short step from support of the poor to systemic change in the service of justice, but that step had to wait for modern consciousness. When one begins to see social systems not as fateful impositions of divine providence but as the creations of those who inhabit them, a new dimension of love for neighbor comes to light. Much of the misery of our neighbor comes from the way social systems distribute well-being. Once love realizes that, it is discontent with meeting a neighbor's need merely on an ad hoc basis. Love sees that if a public water system were installed, it would be a much more effective way of slaking thirst than sloshing cups of water from house to house.

Eschatological consciousness always knew that social systems were one of God's concerns, but until the dawn of modern consciousness, we supposed we could do nothing about them. Now eschatological consciousness driven by love is bound to unfold in the mission to love our neighbors by reform and re-creation of social systems for the enhanced good of our neighbors. It is one of the signs that the Spirit continues to guide the church that love finds these new ways to express itself. The charismatic movement in the Third World demonstrates that when the experience of the Spirit matures, it comes to include mission for justice.[8]

Every Gospel mandate to care for some particular need of our neighbor includes the mandate to address that same need through social systems as well as through individual relief. For example, Matthew's vision of the criteria for the final judgment asks us (countries, churches, citizens) not only to feed the hungry and thirsty but also to remove the sources of hunger and drought; not only to clothe the naked but also to make it possible for all to buy the clothes they need; not only to visit the sick but also to remove causes of illness through systems of public health and to devise health systems that make that care available to all; not only to visit the imprisoned but also to ask if they would be there in the first place if they had had adequate legal aid (27th Sunday, Year A, Matt. 25:31–46). Love maturing in the Spirit follows every human need of our neighbors to its systemic roots.

Luke's highlighting of the importance of women to Jesus' ministry (Luke 8:1–3) and his famous story of Mary and Martha (9th Sunday, Year C, Luke 10:38–42) that puts the theological education of women above the good housekeeping seal of approval can now be seen to be the grounds for a Christian feminist movement. [I can only take it as a hint of sexist prejudice on the part of the compilers of the lectionary that the story of the woman who anointed Jesus for his burial was omitted, even though this is the only story in the whole Synoptic tradition that includes a promise of Jesus that it would be told in her memory wherever the gospel is preached in the whole world! (Matt. 26:13; Mark 14:9.) True, Luke's version is scheduled for 4th Sunday, Year C (Luke 7:36–50), but there she' has become a symbol of the fallen woman who needs to be forgiven much. Perhaps the answer is to use the 4th Sunday to preach on one of the parallels.]

Luke's featuring of the Samaritans (6th Sunday, Year C, Luke 9:51–62; and 8th Sunday, Year C, Luke 10:25–37) becomes a mandate for promoting the rights of religious minorities with unorthodox theology and worship. Other lessons orient the mission to champion the sanctity of marriage and the rights of children (20th Sunday, Year B, Mark 10:2–16) and reinforce ethnic inclusiveness (13th Sunday, Year A, Matt. 15:21–28). You get the point. In each of the cases of Gospel sympathy for the outcast, oppressed, poor, and needy, the history of Western culture will show that these texts have been the occasions for the rise of movements for justice on their behalf.

III. Maturing for Mission

One last theme deserves attention in the continuous reading of the Synoptic Gospel lessons. It is the theme of maturing in discipleship to the point where the rank and file of clergy and laity in the churches are ready and willing to engage in the mission for justice that so many Pentecost texts ground.

It is no secret that perhaps a majority of church members are relatively indifferent to the justice implications of Jesus' teaching and example, compared to their endorsement of evangelism and charity as the proper work of the churches. It is a comfort to realize that the first disciples came to the eschatological consciousness and radical love that Jesus taught only after a process of growth. Instead of eschatological consciousness, the disciples began with the nationalist, ethnocentric expectation that Jesus came to fulfill the dreams of a parochial and militant Judaism. Only in connection with the disastrous war that ended in A.D. 70 did the church finally identify itself as transcending nation and tribe.

Only an extended process of maturing enabled the early church to shake itself free of attachment to the Jewish status quo. We need to arrange a similar process of maturing for our parishioners, so that they may shake off their attachment to the status quo to which late Protestantism is largely committed. We may contribute to that process of maturing by tracing the development of the disciples in the lessons of Pentecost and offering their experience as a model for our own maturing.

When the four fishermen responded to Jesus' call they did so because they hoped for cabinet posts in the new government which the Messiah would set up after Israel was liberated from Roman domination. That is the point of the request by James and John (22d Sunday, Year B, Mark 10:35–45). Later James was so strong an opponent of merely Jewish dreams that Herod pleased the Jews by making him the first martyr among the Twelve (Acts 12:1-2). In Luke the same John who at an immature stage had suggested calling fire down on the Samaritan village (6th Sunday, Year C, Luke 9:51–56) later accompanied Peter in bringing the baptism of the Holy Spirit to Samaria (Acts 8:14–17).

A major theme of all three Gospels is the inability of the Twelve to understand the cost of discipleship while they were with Jesus, for example, rejecting out of hand the ideas of the cross and poverty (15th Sunday, Year A, Matt. 16:22-23; and 21st Sunday, Year B, Mark 10:26). After the resurrection they embraced both for the sake of the mission.

To summarize: The sweep of lessons in Pentecost provides a safety net under the church that keeps the adventure of mission for justice from falling to the ground of parochial consciousness and limited love by holding out a larger eschatological consciousness and radical love —which with time can mature into readiness to take the risks and pay the price of a discipleship engaged in mission for justice.

IV. INTERPRETING FREQUENTLY ABUSED TEXTS

It so happens that the two texts most frequently quoted to abort responsibility for social mission are found within the sections of the Synoptic Gospels assigned to the Pentecost season. They are: "The kingdom of God is within you" (Luke 17:21, KJV and RSV margin) and "You always have the poor with you" (Mark 14:7; Matt. 26:11). The problem is that neither of these texts is included in a lectionary lesson, but they are so often misused that we need to find a way within the spirit of lectionary loyalty to address them lest they continue to be used to undo all the positive force of the lessons that the lectionary did choose.

The text about the poor is accessible through the alternate form of the story found in Luke 7:36–50 (4th Sunday, Year C), as we noted in connection with neglect of the woman whose story is mandated "wherever the gospel is preached in the whole world." I would recommend bringing in the Marcan parallel (Mark 14:3–9) that Sunday to make clear that the continuing presence of the poor in no way lessens the church's obligation to minister to them and to modify a system that perpetuates their number, as though to say "the sick we always have with us" would lessen our obligation to work for healing and better public health. Obviously, the use of this text to avoid the missions of charity and justice is gross bad faith, since both versions assume the practice of giving to the poor and the Marcan version has Jesus specifically endorse the practice with "whenever you will, you can do good to them"[9] Actually, the conflict of ministering to Jesus *or* to the poor can never arise now that Jesus has risen. Indeed, according to Matthew, to minister to the needs of the poor, now, is to minister to the risen Christ who meets us in them incognito (Matt. 25:40).

Luke 17:21 is misused to collapse the kingdom of God down to a private, inner religious experience. The saying occurs as a partial answer to the Pharisees' question about when the kingdom of God is coming. Mark answers the same question in the lesson about the coming of the Son of Man (26th Sunday, Year B, Mark 13:24–32). Indeed, Luke follows the saying with a version of the coming of the Son of Man. So Luke parallels the Marcan lectionary lesson both by addressing the question of when and by referring to the coming of the Son of Man. These two parallels make it natural to allude to Luke when dealing with the Marcan lesson.

Two points need to be made: (1) Luke could not possibly have intended that the kingdom of God was an inner, religious experience, since the "you" it would be "within" were the Pharisees whom Jesus was addressing. (2) The only senses in which Luke claims the kingdom to be in the midst of this world are (*a*) in the graceful, charitable, and justice-promoting ministry of Jesus ("If it is by the finger of God that I cast out demons, then the kingdom of God has come upon you," Luke 11:20); and (*b*) in the disciples' ministry insofar as it replicates the pattern of Jesus' ministry ("Whenever you enter a town and they receive you, eat what is set before you; heal the sick in it and say to them, 'The kingdom of God has come near to you,' " Luke 10:8-9). By the same token the kingdom of God only "draws near to us" and is "in our midst" when we faithfully continue the full justice-promoting ministry that Jesus modeled and commissioned.

3

PENTECOST ECONOMICS

Larry L. Rasmussen

How does life in the power of the Spirit intersect the realities of economic life? That depends in part upon the meaning given "economics." The everyday sense of the word refers to the production of goods and services in society, minimally for survival and maximally for widespread material well-being. There is another, theological, use of the word. "Economy" has a rich heritage, especially in Eastern Christianity, and it will be used here to draw together the "economy" of God, manifest in the Spirit, and the everyday economics of the believing community.

Eastern Christianity distinguishes two subjects for Christian reflection—*theologia* and *oikonomia* (theology and the divine economy). The subject of theological reflection is the mystery of God's triune reality, the Godhead "in itself," as distinguished from reflection upon "the divine economy." The divine economy designates the relation of the Godhead to the earthly drama of redemption. It explores the relationship of the Triune God to the world so that "all things" *(ta panta)* might be set in right relationship and God might be "all in all." The drama of redemption centers in "the economy which Christ carried out when he suffered for us in the flesh."[10] What was this economy and what was its connection to the Pentecost church?

I

The rather startling account of the voluntary communism of the Pentecost church in Acts 4:32, 34 was not without ties to popular Greco-Roman culture. "Possessions are sin" is an expression that occurs in both Plato and Josephus.[11] "The love of money is the homeland of all evils" occurs in the writings of Democritus and Diogenes as well as in I Timothy (6:10).[12] Scythians of the time were well known for sharing possessions.[13]

Yet to locate the economics of the early church in the stream of Greek culture is to err badly. It misses deeper channels that reach far back into Hebrew tradition. "And no one said that any of the things which he possessed was his own" (Acts 4:32) echoes the Mosaic covenant. In that covenant it is a fundamental notion that the earth and all things in it belong to Yahweh, and that serving Yahweh entails the just distribution of community resources according to need. "There was not a needy person among them" (Acts 4:34) indicates the fulfilling of what was in fact a covenantal obligation that there should "be no poor among you" (Deut. 15:4). Indeed, the litmus test of covenant-keeping faithfulness was its treatment of those who were not well placed to pursue their own interests and address their own needs—the poor, the hungry, the widow and orphan, the stranger.[14]

It is this kind of economics that Isa. 58:6–14 reflects. Both covenantal obligation and covenantal blessing are bound up with the practice of such economics (vs. 6–7).

Covenantal economics was practiced by the Acts community. Theirs was a common purse in the sense of sharing wealth and making community resources accessible on the basis of need. The economics were those of mutual aid in which members shared hardships and successes, and each member was expected to think in terms of the welfare of the whole group. No one would go without the necessities of life. Through the community, God would provide. (Work, too, was held "in common" in that those able to work had to contribute if they expected also to receive.)

Yet the communism of the Pentecost church is not wholly explained even by the strong echoes of the tradition as remembered through the prophets. The middle verse of the Acts 4 text (v. 33) is critical to the account. It is not simply a passing report inserted into what is otherwise a narrative account of that community's extraordinary material arrangements. Rather, it links "the economy which Christ carried out" to the economics carried out by the community: "And with great power the apostles gave their testimony to the resurrection of the Lord Jesus, and great grace was upon them all."

Among other things, "the resurrection of the Lord Jesus" is a dramatic signature to the trustworthiness of Jesus and his ministry. What he had announced in word and deed, the advent of the kingdom, had been shown with compelling power in his own body, the community which participates ecstatically in the event itself. It is a participation that ramifies into their economic life together. Those caught up in the Spirit, which ratifies the resurrection in their very midst, "had to" practice new-age economics. The ultimate future, begun in the triumph of the crucified Messiah, had become the norm for the everyday life of the community itself. The eagerly awaited eschatological prospect need wait no longer, indeed *could* wait no longer, now that "great grace was upon them all" in the reality of the resurrection and

the giving of the Spirit. The community's treatment of its own possessions had to reflect the new reality which they grasped and which
grasped them.

II

It was not difficult to know what to do. The long tradition of the
covenant informed them, remembered in such as the Isaiah text. But
there was the more immediate and decisive experience of the community with its Lord. Here the signs were clear, given the events of
Easter and Pentecost. This included the appearances of Jesus to the
post-Easter community, which in turn meant a vivid remembering of
the days with Jesus before. In that the community discerned the
shape of its corporate life.

What was that remembered experience, passed on by the apostles
in their teaching? The appointed Gospel text from John 6 is about two
episodes. The first is the feeding of the multitude with the five barley
loaves and two fish of a child. The second is the controversy around
Jesus that issues from his claim to be "the bread of life," the true
bread "which came down from heaven." It is not bread "such as the
fathers ate" (and died in the wilderness), but bread the eating of
which means "eternal life." It is Jesus' own life: "The bread which I
shall give for the life of the world is my flesh" (John 6:51). It means
a taste of the kingdom for those who feast on it.

The disciples hear this as "a hard saying" and Jesus, sensing their
offense, asks if they too wish to leave his ranks, and Peter replies:
"Lord, to whom shall we go? You have the words of eternal life; and
we have believed, and have come to know, that you are the Holy One
of God" (John 6:68–69).

The church has interpreted this Johannine narrative eucharisti-
cally. That is entirely proper and in keeping with the Gospel writer's
own account (see John 6:51–58). The eucharistic meaning is underscored by the postresurrection appearances. The same recognition of
who Jesus is and the life he bears occurs most often in the breaking
of bread (see Luke 24; John 21). It occurs at mealtime, or in accounts
where the talk is of the fellowship of eating and drinking together.

This may seem coincidental. It is not. A certain *table fellowship*
distinguished the community around Jesus. It made clear its character. And in retrospect, i.e., following the resurrection, it also made
clear to the gathered community the shape and character of their
community as the community of the new age. That table fellowship
is mentioned in Acts 2:44–47.

What is behind table fellowship and what apparantly is a link to
holding "all things in common"?

Jesus became head of a new family that shared a common life
together. Its members broke with the customary basis in kin and

nation. Jesus even called people away from burying their father's corpse, and in so doing called people to commit a sacrilege.[15] The disciples are to "leave the dead to bury their own dead" (Matt. 8:22; see also Mark 1:20; Luke 9:59–62) and forsake all to follow Jesus. Jesus himself identifies his mother and brothers as those "who do the will of my Father." He does not even celebrate Passover with his "natural" family, as required by Scripture, but with his new community of disciples.

Such conduct was offensive enough. But what resides at the heart of the gospel that doubled the offense was table fellowship *as the inclusion of the excluded.* Eating with public sinners such as tax collectors and prostitutes, extending the intimacy of a common table to Samaritans and women, blessing those otherwise despised and without hope or help—the crippled, the blemished, the marginated; all this was the kind of hospitality that distinguished the community around Jesus from the multitudinous sects of a religiously florid day. It was the hospitality of the kingdom filled with the Spirit, hosted by Jesus who was himself filled with the power of the Spirit (see Luke 4:14ff.) The Pentecost community came to see itself in that light, as participants in the eschatological reality of the kingdom coming. From the *ethnē* (the peoples or the nations) Jesus was drawing together a new community where social barriers were being broken down in favor of holding all things in common.

Joining the community meant a clear decision of cost. It meant taking up the cross, even to the point of sacrifice. And it meant renouncing material goods in favor of the poor—the "fasting" of the Isaiah reading. Breaking bread together "in their homes" (Acts 2:46) is the Pentecost community's continuation of the drama that came to expression in the table fellowship with Jesus, "the bread of life" (John 6:35).

III

Differently said, "the economy which Christ carried out when he suffered for us in the flesh" has a vivid focus in all that table fellowship signified, including a discipleship community of sharing that remembered Jesus through the apostles and that was caught up in the power of the Spirit after the resurrection.

Later eucharistic development gave expression to this as a central sacrament of the church and the climactic point of worship. But the clear connection with the economic life of the community was severed. A common table was not seen as mandating a common purse, as it was for the church at the point of its origins. Gustave Martelet writes:

To involve human food and drink symbolically in a meal of love implies at the very least that in real life we have done nothing to deprive others of them; and, even further, that we are doing or have done ... everything that is humanly and Christianly necessary and possible to ensure that these elementary supplies are produced in sufficient quantity and shared equitably. If this were not done, to take the bread and wine and offer them to the Lord would become intolerably false, since we would be seeking to give God with one hand what we were unjustly withholding from men with the other.[16]

Economics in Christian perspective has, then, a certain frame of reference. Its point of departure is not some economic theory or analysis, though both are vital for Christian ethics. Its point of departure isn't even in general observation of the human condition or of common human conduct in economic life. Its point of departure is "the divine economy." The beginning point is confession, confession such as Paul's:

When anyone is united to Christ, there is a new world; the old order has gone, and a new order has already begun. From first to last this has been the work of God. He has reconciled us ... to himself through Christ, and he has enlisted us in this service of reconciliation. What I mean is, that God was in Christ reconciling the world to himself. (II Cor. 5:17–19a, NEB)

In the Pentecost church, those "enlisted in this service of reconciliation" shared a common table and a common purse. Indeed, economic sharing becomes *part of* the redemption in Jesus, *part of* the divine economy, redemption that continues in the power of the Spirit.

Economic life is only a portion of the life of the community, of course. But it belongs to early Christian understandings that have cosmic reach. In the end, the matter is God's *oikonomia* by which justice is done and all creation flourishes ("a new world"). The economics of the community reflects the Eucharist, is part of its detail and a vivid symbol of the inclusive and costly table fellowship with Jesus.[17]

IV

What are the implications for the church's economic life today? Our hermeneutical method should be contextual and ecclesiological in character. The basic posture is that of the Scripture reader's identification with a present-day community that struggles with current issues in the light of Christian faith and looks for illumination from other communities engaged in similar struggles. The biblical communities of faith hold a special place here, since theirs is the privileged place of origins and the source of the normative faith claim that

God's reality, and the world's, is seen with compelling clarity in the story of Israel and Jesus.

Space does not permit a review of the complexities involved in moving from biblical materials to current economic realities. But we offer the following guidelines as in keeping with the moral trajectory of the texts:

1. *Equality is the presumption.* The testimony of the early church and of church renewal movements over the centuries is to press economic sharing in the direction of equality. There is a presumption in favor of an equal sharing of economic benefits and burdens. If economic inequalities are to be justified, they are justified only if it is reasonably expected that such inequalities will serve the common good (and not lodge with private interests and select groups only).

2. *Enough is best.* A consistent witness of biblical traditions is that the truly abundant life is one of self-discipline and a restraint upon the multiplication of material desires. Material indulgence corrupts rather than liberates. "Enough is best" rather than "More is better" is the maxim.

3. *The poor are the test.* An economy that has the resources to meet basic needs—food, shelter, clothing, health care, work, and festivity —and does not meet them, fails the test of justice. Material sufficiency for all is the first economic goal. "The daily distribution" (Acts 6:1) is on the basis of fundamental needs. This makes treatment of the poor the test of any economic arrangement, actual or contemplated. Will the excluded now be included? How are the walls dismantled so that "table fellowship" is extended to ever-widening circles?

4. *The mute and the weak are to be heard.* Some neighbors have no voice and cannot attain their own due. Someone else must speak for unborn generations and the requirements for their material well-being. Someone must also speak for that part of creation which is nonhuman nature, the environment, upon which all life is utterly dependent.

5. *The oikoumenē is the context.* "The whole inhabited world" has supplanted the nation as the major domain of economic life and policy. Normatively this has always been the case for Christians, since "neighbor" is universalized. But there is in our time a new opportunity to take seriously the *oikoumenē* in economic life.

4

PRAISE THE CREATOR—
CARE FOR CREATION

William E. Gibson

"Creator" is not one of the names of God. The biblical writers do not bid us, "Praise the Creator"; they continually cry, "Praise Yahweh!" The Lord God *is* the Creator, and praise of God is *always* praise of the Creator. "Happy is [the one] . . . whose hope is in the LORD his God, who made heaven and earth, the sea, and all that is in them; who . . . executes justice for the oppressed" (Ps. 146:5–7a). The psalmist praises God for care of creation and for liberation of the oppressed. "The LORD upholds all who are falling, and raises up all who are bowed down. The eyes of all look to thee, and thou givest them their food in due season. Thou openest thy hand, thou satisfiest the desire of every living thing" (Ps. 145:14–16).

God's judging and renewing work today serves the same end. And if in our time the earth must be numbered conspicuously among "the oppressed," the care of creation becomes a matter of liberation, played out upon the field of the totality of grace.

I. CREATION, DELIVERANCE, AND CARE

The biblical writers took God's identity as Creator-Redeemer for granted.

God's work as Creator and Liberator is at the center of liturgy, as in the traditional kiddush—the ancient prayer sanctifying the Sabbath rest:

> Praised art Thou, Eternal God, King of the Universe, Creator of the fruit of the vine. Praised art Thou, Eternal God, who hast sanctified us with Thy commandments, and hast bestowed upon us the precious gift of the Sabbath as our loving inheritance, a reminder of the work of creation, the first among our sacred days recalling our liberation from Egypt . . .

The prophets and the apostles were remarkably explicit in saying that the God who creates is the One who delivers. Thus in Second Isaiah it is the God "who spread forth the earth and what comes from it" who gives Israel "as a covenant to the people, . . . to bring out the prisoners from the dungeon" (Isa. 42:5–7). And the writer to the Colossians hails the incarnate Son as the One in whom all things were created and reconciled (Col. 1:16, 19–20).

In biblical literature the Creator delights in the creation and rules it not only to order it but to care for it. "The LORD is good to all, and his compassion is over all that he has made" (Ps. 145:9). The Lord asks the human creatures, made in God's image, to share in God's "dominion" (Gen. 1:26) in such a way as to be agents of God's care. The creation is not given away to human beings but entrusted to their caretaking. It still belongs to God, who continues to remind them, "The world and all that is in it is mine" (Ps. 50:12b). Men and women are expected to draw on the sustenance of earth, as do the other creatures, but in so doing they are "to till it and keep it" (Gen. 2:15). By working they are to make respectful cultivation and use of creation for human need, and at the same time to participate in God's work of caring for the whole habitat, human and nonhuman, and of preserving its wholeness. Human dominion, as the unique privilege and responsibility of participating in God's compassionate rule and continuing care of creation, has to be in keeping with God's intention to be good to all.

This, of course, is a statement of the biblical theme of stewardship or trusteeship. It is not capsulized in any one text, nor labeled "stewardship." The theme, however, is inescapable—"a concept of stewardship that is everywhere present in biblical thought," whereby humankind is understood to be "responsible before God for the use of the created world, the social health of the people, and the maximal development of each person's abilities for the up-building of the community."[18]

To praise the Creator, in biblical speech and spirit, is necessarily to be involved in the care of creation. Characteristically, the language of praise stays in the indicative, reciting the manifold works of God. (Ps. 146:6–7, 9; 104:27f.) If this is what God is doing, and this is what we praise God for, it is what we as God's people must also be involved in doing. The liturgical indicative contains a profound ethical imperative.

To care for creation today becomes necessarily a response to a new realization concerning the impact upon nature of the whole modern age of science, technology, and industrial expansion. The material benefits of modernity have been based upon exploitation of nature. Quite abruptly, within the last few decades, we have been caught up short by massive evidence that the use of nature in Western civilization far exceeds the bounds of any proper "dominion." Conquest has displaced care as the predominant human intention toward the natural world.

The earth, with its numberless creatures and intricate support system, is imperiled. The care of creation has been bungled. The operative concept of stewardship has been grossly inadequate. To reassert care in our time is to seek to set creation free.

II. THE EARTH AS VICTIM

Thanks to eloquent and prophetic spokespersons for the earth and the poor in the decade of the 1970s, we have no excuse for not realizing that the rise and spread of modern industrial civilization, for all its actual and potential benefits, has constituted a massive assault on God's good creation. One of those spokespersons, E. F. Schumacher, identifies "the roots of the life-and-death problems of industrial society," including "the roots out of which the [nuclear] bomb has grown" as "a violent attitude toward God's handiwork instead of a reverent one."[19] So to identify the roots is to locate the problems "deep, in the heart and soul of every one of us."[20] At the same time, *"speaking from a worldly point of view,"* Schumacher holds that "industrial society, unless radically reformed, must come to a bad end"—an end which "now that it has adopted cumulative growth as its principal aim . . . cannot be far off."[21]

Schumacher lists five reasons why failure must issue from the spectacular successes of our society: (1) the disruption of certain organic relationships so that world population grows beyond the means of subsistence; (2) the disruption of other organic relationships so that the means of subsistence themselves are threatened, as industrial poisons spread and food is adulterated; (3) the rapid depletion of nonrenewable fuels and metals; (4) the degrading of human moral and intellectual qualities (through such phenomena as the debasement of the quality of work and the incessant appeals to greed and envy to stimulate consumption); and (5) the breeding of "a violence against nature which at any moment can turn into violence against one's fellow men, when there are weapons around which make nonviolence a condition of survival."[22]

Like the recurring biblical mandate to do justice to the poor, the mandate to care for the creation comes to us now in a moment of extraordinary crisis. On the one hand, the terrible gap between the rich and the poor persists and widens, not because the earth's bounty is basically too small to go around, but because the human family does not share with any kind of equity the good things of God's creation. On the other hand, the unprecedented ecological situation means that resources and ecosystems have already been so strained that they cannot bear much longer the continuing extension of the violent patterns of development deplored by Schumacher. The demands of justice and of stewardship come together in the imperative of new economic and political arrangements, within and among nations, to foster sufficient sharing in sustainable harmony with nature.

The biblical theme of redemption/deliverance/liberation requires

—now—a conception in Christian thought large enough to embrace the whole created order, organic and inorganic. The earth itself has become co-victim with the oppressed poor. The work of God, and the people of God, is to protect and restore the earth and the poor. The Greek word *oikonomia* (household management or stewardship), from which we derive the words ecology, economics, ecosystem, and ecumenical, suggests the scope of our task.

In the Hebrew story the land occupies a central place in God's promise to the covenant people and remains essential to their continuing well-being. It suffers the consequences of sin and injustice, participates in the pain associated with judgment, and shares in the hope of restoration. The Lord's controversy is "with the inhabitants of the land"; and when there is "no faithfulness or kindness and no knowledge of God in the land," the consequence is that "the land mourns and all who dwell in it languish," including "the beasts of the field, and the birds of the air; and even the fish of the sea" (Hos. 4:1, 3).

Jeremiah depicts the earth as victim, suffering the awful judgment of God upon the foolish, faithless people—a devastation and desolation so total that it returns the earth to its primeval condition (Jer. 4:23–26). Not even the most cataclysmic military sweep could have inflicted such total horror in Jeremiah's time, but we know that our technology and our weaponry can.

In a very different vein, Psalm 96 has the whole earth rejoicing at the coming of the Lord, who will judge the peoples with righteousness, equity, and truth. Once again we may feel that the vision of the biblical writer surpassed the imaginative reach for which the ancient situation could account, and that the poem is uniquely applicable to the present crisis. "Let the heavens be glad" if the coming judgment and deliverance bring an end to the atmospheric buildup of carbon dioxide from fossil fuel consumption (with potential for warming the earth, melting the polar ice caps, and flooding the coastal cities). "Let the sea roar" with joy when the rivers cease to carry into it the waste and poison that now threaten to exceed its capacity to absorb them. "Let the field exult" when prime agricultural land no longer falls victim to soil erosion, salinization, chemical contamination, and urbanization. "Let all the trees of the wood sing for joy" when the demand for wood products is brought into balance with the replenishment of the forests.

At the beginning of the 1980s, *The Global 2000 Report to the President* provides new, official detail, from governmental modeling, on the victimization of air, water, field, and forest. They, together with the world's poor, are the projected victims of present trends which, if allowed to continue, will make the world in 2000 "more crowded, more polluted, less stable ecologically, and more vulnerable to disruption than the world we live in now."[23]

The earth mourns. Will the judgment instrumental to deliverance, the "new things" that God declares (Isa. 42:9) in the global crisis of this extraordinary historic moment, issue in a new covenant of faithfulness (Hos. 2:18–20) that can yet turn the mourning into joy?

III. NATURE AND GRACE

Facts alone will not establish the new covenant of faithfulness. As Joseph Sittler has observed, human beings "are quite capable of marching steadily into disaster fully equipped with the facts." Indeed, he continues, "pride, comfort, and idolatrous and brutal hardness of heart have for several generations permitted the American nation to stare straight into the face of poverty, injustice, and the calcified privilege of the powerful—and leave national priorities unchallenged."[24] The biblical story, however, can engender a fundamental change of heart as it connects the knowledge of God with the facts about limits, perils, and systemic injustice (cf. Hos. 4:1–6; 6:6; and 2:18–20). That change of heart is a response to grace. The "care" sufficiently motivated to bear the cost of involvement with God in protecting and restoring the earth and the poor arises most authentically from the realization that the whole creation is the arena of God's grace. The whole web of relationships and processes by which we are and in which we live serves the purposes of God's giving and disclosing.

Nature is not to be excluded from a contemporary understanding of God's giving and disclosing, writes Sittler in *Essays on Nature and Grace.* A human being "lives in a nexus of human relations and nature relations" and is in the contemporary world as "a creature who, for the first time, has the structures and powers of the natural world sufficiently and growingly within his manipulative grasp to form it toward an order for human life of dreamlike potentialities, or to utilize his knowledge-power toward an unimaginable hell."[25]

Nature, no less than fellow selves, is constitutive of a human self. It sustains human life and provides the basis and the material for human work, human achievement, and human community. Nature suffers from human cruelty, greed, and carelessness. Like the offended neighbor, nature thus violated is an entity with which a right relationship must be restored. Conviction of one's violation of nature becomes an essential component of the knowledge of one's need of God's forgiveness. Nature becomes an instrument of God's judgment, as the limits to the human freedom to manipulate nature with impunity assert themselves. And nature participates in the redemption for the sake of which Jesus Christ came into the world. It shares in deliverance and will be integral to the eschatologically consummated kingdom of God.

"We know," Paul writes to the Romans, "that the whole creation has been groaning in travail together until now" (Rom. 8:22). More-over, having been "subjected to futility," the creation is waiting "with eager longing for the revealing of the sons of God." In God's consum-mation "the creation itself will be set free from its bondage to decay and obtain the glorious liberty of the children of God" (Rom. 8:19–21).

We may not understand entirely what Paul's words mean, and perhaps he did not either. But we may understand better than he the meaning of the "futility" and "bondage" inflicted upon the earth. In a time of headlong rush to ecological disaster, we can begin to see that our own liberation cannot be accomplished apart from the liber-ation of nature.

In the letter to the Colossians we find a remarkable linkage of the creating and redeeming work of God in Jesus Christ. The incarnate Son is identified not only as "the image of the invisible God" but as the preexistent One in whom "all things were created, in heaven and on earth, visible and invisible." In him "all things hold together." In him "all the fulness of God was pleased to dwell, and through him to reconcile to himself all things" (Col. 1:15–20). In a similar passage in Ephesians (1:3–10), the uniting of all things in Christ is hailed as God's "plan for the fulness of time" (1:10). The repetition of "all things" in these passages constitutes the divine charter of solidarity and harmony, embracing not only the whole human family (beginning with the *oikeioi* or household of God described in Eph. 2:19–20) but everything else in all creation, past, present, and future.

Under that charter, stewardship takes on a new dimension as the celebration and preservation of created unity and ecological har-mony. To care for the earth becomes truly an act of praise of the one in whom all things hold together. The expectation that in Christ all things will be reconciled and united forbids that anything or anyone should be violated, abused, heedlessly or wantonly destroyed along the way to such a consummation. Meanwhile, in the historical crisis of the present time, ecological fact belongs ineluctably to the context of faithfulness. The liberation of the oppressed people will be no liberation if it destroys, whether through warfare or development, the capacity of earth to nourish their lives and those of their posterity. The production and distribution of goods and the preservation of many species of God's creation must be sufficient for all and sustain-able for all to come. Such are the requirements of ecumenical and intergenerational justice.

Sittler concludes his discussion of nature and grace with what he calls the "nonarguable datum" of "the necessity for the organization of life toward continuation, care, and enhancement *if life is to be at all.*"[26] This goes far beyond utilitarianism. It means to care for nature "under the rubric of grace," with "due regard for [the] given structure and need" of natural things. If things cannot continue *to be* without that due regard, this supplies to faith a sufficient verification of "an

intrinsic 'good' in things that are."[27] If love must transcend enlight-
ened selfishness and even self-conscious mutuality in order to meet
the needs of creatures, and to protect and restore the integrity and
wholeness of the creation, then the persons and the things that claim
our love can be recognized, not only as beings of value, but as occasions of God's grace.

"The creation itself will be set free" (Rom. 8:21). "Let the heavens
be glad, and let the earth rejoice" (Ps. 96:11). The work of judgment
and liberation is God's, but the consummation is not in sight. The
outcome of the present crisis is far from clear. People who are nurtured by the biblical story, and who respond in faithfulness to God's
grace in the arena of all that is occurring, may discern their present
tasks in relation to the new activity of the God who steadfastly
upholds the earth and the poor.

BIBLIOGRAPHY

Brown, Lester R. *The Twenty-ninth Day: Accommodating Human Needs and
    Numbers to the Earth's Resources.* W. W. Norton & Co., 1978.
The Global 2000 Report to the President: Entering the Twenty-first Century.
    3 vols. U.S. Government Printing Office, 1980.
Jegen, Mary Evelyn, and Manno, Bruno V., eds. *The Earth Is the Lord's:
    Essays on Stewardship.* Paulist Press, 1978.
Schumacher, E. F. *Good Work.* Harper & Row, 1979.
Sittler, Joseph. *Essays on Nature and Grace.* Fortress Press, 1972.
Wilkinson, Loren, ed. *Earthkeeping: Christian Stewardship of Natural Re-
    sources.* 2d ed. Wm. B. Eerdmans Publishing Co., 1980.

B. A WHOLE APPROACH

PENTECOST

James and Margaret Adams

Pentecost is the season of the Holy Spirit and of the church, created by the Spirit. At Pentecost the Spirit gave birth to a new community with an alternative consciousness. For this reason the coming of the Spirit was not welcomed by the powers and principalities. They preferred the situation as it was; for as long as there are no empowered people with clear visions of a better future, the powers of the world maintain control.

The coming of the Spirit has commonly been perceived as an ecstatic religious event. But it is also a major public event with political significance. It reminded the secular authorities that their world was vulnerable. The events following Pentecost confirmed this. Before the crucifixion Peter was frightened by authorities, soldiers, and even house servants. After Pentecost he stood before the Sanhedrin and denied their authority over him. The political/social situation was exposed as relative and changeable rather than being absolute and static.

The Old Testament prototype of Pentecost is the experience of Moses at the burning bush. Before that event Moses lived in a world typified by the claim that the king was God. The confrontation with Pharaoh grew out of an alternative consciousness that God is King Israel then began the task of living in that new consciousness. For thi reason the Old Testament is the church's book. It is our earlier histor of living in the world with an unworldly awareness. Thus, the lectionary preacher would do well to pay particular attention to the Old Testament lessons in the season of Pentecost. The Old Testament is the book of the church in the season of the church.

There are at least five characteristics of an alternative consciousness found in the lectionary lessons. The first is an awareness of the wholeness of life—what is today called global awareness. This is the thrust of Gal. 3:23–29 (5th Sunday, Year C) and Isa. 55:10–13. In the former, Paul says our human distinctions are broken down so that we might live in the community of the Spirit. In the latter, the fertility of the earth is linked to the word of God, and nature will respond joyfully to the return from the exile. Isaiah described the renewal of the whole created order. William Gibson's essay links creation, deliverance, and care in one section; in a second section he links nature and grace.

A second characteristic of an alternative consciousness is the appreciation of gifts rather than the assignment of roles. This is the thrust of I Cor. 12:3b–13 (Pentecost, Year A) and Amos 7:12–17 (21st Sunday, Year C). The former passage speaks of the gifts of the Spirit given for the growth and nurture of the church. It says nothing about persons in the church maintaining an assigned role. The latter passage is the answer of Amos given to Amaziah. Amaziah wanted Amos to return to his place—to continue as a shepherd. Amos' answer was that he intended to exercise his gift as God called. Esther Stine's article on pluralism in the nation and the church amplifies this theme.

A third characteristic of an alternative consciousness is the hope of transformed social arrangements. This theme is found, for example, in Dan. 7:13–14 (26th Sunday, Year B) and Hab. 1:1–3; 2:1–4 (22d Sunday, Year C). In the first, Daniel reports a vision of a kingdom *to come* which shall have no end. This implies the limits of every other kingdom. In the second, Habakkuk cries out against a social order that depended on violence. Later he reports a vision confirming life for the righteous rather than the violent. All of the following essays touch on this theme, with a special emphasis given by Neill Hamilton when he writes of eschatological consciousness.

A fourth characteristic of an alternative consciousness is to acknowledge the rule of God rather than of the powers and principalities. This theme is found in Ezek. 37:1–14 (Pentecost, Year B) and II Kings 17:33–40. Ezekiel views the nation as created (and recreated) by God and its life as a gift to be lived in obedience. The latter passage describes the Northern Kingdom (Israel) after that nation's exile by Assyria. The issue described is the confusion of a people who try to worship and obey both Yahweh and the gods of the prevailing political system (Assyria). Rasmussen's article shows that characteristics of this obedience are justice and harmony.

The fifth characteristic of an alternative consciousness is the awareness that the Bible is to be read "from beneath" rather than "from above." The oppressed, who are God's special children, take more seriously the passages about the end of prevailing social systems, the vision of a new kingdom, and the reversal of rich and poor (e.g., the Beatitudes). Representative passages are Amos 8:4–8 and Isa. 5:1–7. Proponents of the prevailing social arrangements will exegete these passages historically, linguistically, and literally. The oppressed will read them as promises still valid today in which God promises judgment on the rich and the oppressor.

These five characteristics are representative, though not an exhaustive description, of the alternative consciousness that comes with life in the Spirit. The lectionary passages for Pentecost are filled with these and similar themes that can receive concentrated attention in adult Bible study organized by theme or by book(s) of Scripture.

The half year of Sundays from Pentecost to Advent is a time where there is maximum flexibility to take up sections of the Bible or to develop exegetical-expository themes that the ecumenical lectionary would otherwise slight. The preceding essays on readings in this season illustrate only a few of the possibilities. They do suggest as a basic organizing principle that theological-ethical themes of Pentecost Sundays ought to encompass God's *triune* activity! What follows is a discussion of selected themes for congregational praxis.

The Festival of Pentecost and Trinity Sunday

Esther Stinc proposes that Luke gives a picture of two pluralistic communities which, at the Pentecost event, become one. The first community is the community of believers whom Jesus has gathered around himself—the poor, exploited, sinners, sick, women, etc. The second is the community gathered in Jerusalem for Pentecost, representing thirteen nations (Acts 2:5ff.). In the event of speaking and hearing the word of God these two are united into a model of an egalitarian human community that is also pluralistic. The unifying character, as well as the only requirement for belonging to the community, is love of neighbor and love of God.

Stine centers on a second, related theme—the need for a new understanding of the Triune God that breaks out of masculine images so that all might experience equality as the central value of community.

Worship. The symbolic act suggested is twofold: first, worshipers are invited to come forward to tie a red ribbon (tongue of fire) to a bare branch. This act is a public affirmation of the worshiper's intent to share the fire of Pentecost with those who have been left on the margins of our society. After tying the red ribbon to the bare branches, the worshiper receives either a "live coal" from a campfire (presupposing that worship can take place, at least for its conclusion in an outdoor area) *or* a symbolic coal/fire. The pluralism of the congregation and of the ecumenical church is emphasized by a worship leader: all participants can be fire carriers—young, old, male, female, handicapped, robust, native to the geographic area, immigrant, rich, and poor.

Nurture. The story of Pentecost as recorded in Acts is experienced in the following way: the group is divided into small groups representing various people who were a part of the Pentecost celebration—followers of Jesus, apostles of Jesus, Jews from other parts of the world, Roman soldiers, priests and Levites, Pharisees and Sadducees. Each group has the same list of questions to discuss before the Acts account is read: Why are you in Jerusalem today? What are your expectations of the day? How do you feel about the other people who are in the city? What effect has Jesus' resurrection had on your life? Are there any others in this mix of people with whom you can identify and to whom you would turn for support?

After discussing these questions, allow each group to report to the total group what conclusions they reach. Then have the Acts account of Pentecost read.

Talk in twos or threes about the following ideas:

1. The Spirit of God came to the believers and brought together a diverse group of persons, empowering them to "be on fire" with love, and to distribute love through acts of justice.

2. Each of us can, with the gift of the Spirit's fire, offer a breath of fresh love to persons in need near and far. We can offer sight, food, shelter, education, health, promise of life, good work, friendship, forgiveness, companionship, caring.

Witness. Persons need to have an opportunity, on a sheet of paper or index card, to make a short list under each of the following categories:

> Places where wind/fire are present in our world.
> Places where wind/fire are needed in our world.
> People who bring wind/fire into our world.
> People who need wind/fire from us.

On the back of this sheet or index card, persons would then be encouraged to struggle with questions such as:

> What persons or groups in our society do not have control over their own destiny?
> How could we help bring liberation and share power with them?
> Where have the fires of pluralism and egalitarianism gone out?
> What can we do to fan the spark and make it glow again?
> To what do I commit myself in this regard?
> How can the community of faith support and uphold me in this commitment?

What are the implications of Stine's essay for the church's worship, education, and witness on the national holiday weekends of Independence Day and Labor Day?

For helpful theological observations on pluralistic worship that takes ethnic minorities seriously, see Justo and Catherine González, *In Accord: Let Us Worship* (Friendship Press, 1981), Chs. I–III.

Nurture. In a large room create the environment that visualizes a variety of symbolic ways that the Trinity has traditionally been imaged. This means using flat pictures, banners, mosaics, any representation of a symbol of the Trinity that can be found or made. As persons arrive for the nurture experience, encourage them to touch, reflect, observe, share what they already know about the Triune God.

Divide the participants into groups of three. Ask each triad to try to image a new way of explaining God as *God/Jesus Christ/Holy Spirit* without using masculine images (i.e., Creator/Word/Comforter; Rock/Redeemer/Sustainer; Way/Truth/Life; Wisdom/Liberator/Empowerer; etc.). Now create a banner, song, poem, litany, or other expression of this image that can be shared.

Worship. Focus on the Doxology. Sing:

> Praise God from whom all blessings flow;
> Praise God, all creatures here below;
> Praise God above, ye heavenly host:
> [Here each triad substitutes its image of the Trinity.]

Have the triads share some message to, for, or from God in the light of their new understanding of the Triune God. Speak particularly about how this changed understanding of God enables a new vision of humanity's role in bringing about a community that is pluralistic and egalitarian. Let this be a shared sermon time.

Witness. Covenant with one another in the local congregation to strengthen the triads that have been formed in nurture and worship. Spend time during this season enlarging on this new way of viewing the Trinity. Keep a log individually of how you are able to act with regard to others because of growing insights into the nature of the Spirit of God, in particular.

JESUS' DEEDS AND WORDS
(SELECTIONS FROM THE SYNOPTIC GOSPELS)

One of the most useful themes in Neill Hamilton's essay deals with the process of tracing the disciples' maturing in the lessons of Pentecost. Leaving behind their misguided expectations of cabinet posts in a new government that would overthrow the oppressor, they became leaders in a persecuted church. We are asked to observe the way the apostles matured in their understanding of mission and their ability to be in mission. This, Hamilton contends, should serve as a model for our own maturation.

Worship. Many congregations confirm youth and adults either during Holy Week or in late spring at Pentecost. If we can see confirmation as a rite of Christian maturing which might be celebrated more than once in a person's adult life, then we have a handle on understanding and marking the maturing process of life in the Spirit.

Designing a confirmation renewal ceremony would be extremely appropriate. As a part of this ceremony persons are invited to put on a stole, symbolizing a yoke. Taking on the yoke acknowledges a call to vocation, marks a personal decision for mission, celebrates a commitment to witness in the world, and symbolizes personal strengthening for Christian service in the world. Not everyone in the congregation is expected to take on a stole/yoke. Only those who want to mark a significant change in their own personal faith-pilgrimage would take such a symbolic action.

Others in the congregation could be invited to become "yoke partners" with those who accept stoles. By becoming a partner one covenants to support, pray for, encourage, and join a stole/yoke wearer in his or her Pentecost pilgrimage. A concluding act might be for the confirmands to sign a covenant of Pentecostal discipleship in front of the whole congregation, sealed with the witness of their "yoke partners."

Nurture. A sign reads: CARPENTER SHOP—YOKES A SPECIALTY. The area for nurture has several learning centers:

RESEARCH AREA: Here participants read, listen, and observe to find out why yokes are a symbol of discipleship. Using a concordance, look up all of the passages that tell about yokes, especially those where Jesus speaks about yokes. See if any information can be found about Jesus and Joseph and their carpenter shop and what they might have made there. Look for information about why ministers today wear stoles.

DESIGN AREA: In this area participants are invited to make a pattern for a stole for themselves. Several patterns might be provided for the basic stole. Persons should then be encouraged to think about how to personalize their stoles with a design, perhaps one relating to Pentecost and the meaning of discipleship. Symbol patterns to be put on the basic stoles are made in this area.

MANUFACTURING AREA: Scissors, glue, thread and needles, sewing machines (?), a variety of red fabric (the color of the festival of Pentecost) and green background fabric (the color of Sundays after Pentecost), solid-color felt scraps, etc., are available for those who intend to put their design into an actual stole/yoke.

AGREEMENT AREA: Here is an opportunity for those who are intending to "take a yoke upon themselves" to write out a covenant agreement, which is then signed, sealed, and witnessed during worship. The covenant contains that to which the disciple intends to be confirmed and commissioned. A list of possible commissionings is an important resource in this area.

Witness. To continue the idea of yoking, persons might be encouraged to yoke themselves with someone in the community who needs love, care, and support: someone who is outcast, a prisoner, hungry, or lonely. A reminder needs to be given—that yokes were used to enable two to work together toward some common goal. The Christian's yoking to a person in the community might have as its goal to work for specific societal change, e.g., better working conditions, increased employment opportunities, equitable distribution of governmental resources, improved housing situations. To avoid fragmenting the congregation's social concern into many small and perhaps discouraging individual efforts, it is important to anticipate and reinforce a few mission priorities, and to specify particular responsibilities that can be picked up by the confirmed.

A variation of this approach is to form *base communities* of twelve to twenty persons who seek to unite biblical-theological reflection with social analysis leading to action in the world focused on a major social concern or sector of society. The members of each base community are confirmed in their mission of service and advocacy, and in their ministry of care for one another.

ECONOMIC RESPONSIBILITY IN CHRISTIAN PERSPECTIVE

Rasmussen links justice and creation. The litmus test of covenant-keeping faithfulness, he says, is how the human community deals with those who cannot attain their own flourishing. God's economy is the relationship of a Triune God to the world so that "all things" might be set in a right relationship so that God might be "all in all."

A basic theme to be considered is how Jesus' resurrection is witnessed to both at table fellowship (in the communal breaking of bread) and in the daily distribution of resources according to need. Rasmussen reminds us of the connection of table and purse in God's economy. We are also reminded that Jesus includes the excluded at the table fellowship: tax collectors, sinners, Samaritans, women. Rasmussen suggests five affirmations which are an impetus for creating "anticipatory communities" that demonstrate in a contagious way how Christians can act responsibly in their economic life: (1) Equality is the presumption with regard to economic benefits and burdens. (2) Enough is best. (3) The poor are the test: "Material sufficiency for all is the first economic goal." (4) The mute and the weak who lack a voice and cannot attain their due are to be heard. (5) *Oikoumenē* is the context: The whole inhabited world is our neighborhood.

Worship. We suggest that worship reflecting this theme be enacted on World Communion Sunday. It has the potential to enable us to experience in a new way a primordial truth. The suggestion is to celebrate the Lord's Supper without actually using the elements of bread and the fruit of the vine. The idea comes from a story that John Westerhoff tells. John had been in Paraguay. While he was there, an escaped political prisoner told of a forbidden celebration of Easter Eucharist in prison several days before. The celebrant, also a prisoner, began:

This meal in which we are part, reminds us of the prison, the torture, the death, and the final victory and resurrection of Jesus Christ. He asked us to remember him by repeating this action in the spirit of fellowship. The bread which we do not have today, but which is present in the spirit of Jesus Christ, is the body which he gave for humanity. The fact that we have none represents very well the lack of bread and the hunger of so many millions of human beings. When Christ distributed bread among his disciples, and when he fed the people, he revealed the will of God that we should all have bread. The wine which we do not have today is his blood present in the light of our faith. Christ poured it out for us to move us toward freedom in the long march for justice. God made all persons of one blood: The blood of Christ represents our dream of a unified humanity, of a just society without difference of race or class. . . . This communion is not only a communion between us here, but a communion with all our brothers and sisters in the church or outside, not only those who are alive, but those who have already died. Still more, it is a communion with those who will come after us and who will be faithful to Jesus Christ. (John Westerhoff and Gwen Neville, *Learning Through Liturgy,* pp. 130–131; Seabury Press, 1978)

In your eucharistic celebration, we suggest that worshipers come forward, hold out their empty hands as the pastor places his or her hands over theirs, and that together they say, "Take, eat, this is Christ's body which is given for you, do this in remembrance of him. Take, drink, this is the blood of Christ which was shed to seal the new covenant of God with humanity. Let us give thanks, sure that Christ is here with us, strengthening us." Then hands would be raised to mouths, receiving body and blood of Christ. A kiss of peace would be shared when all have had opportunity to come forward.

Nurture. A number of persons might bring to small "house church" gatherings case studies of local situations where injustice prevails against people and nature. After discussion of the case studies, using denominational and ecumenical resources, they could spend a second part of their time together answering the question, "What would happen if we (both individually and corporately) take the following action(s) . . . ?" After making as exhaustive a list as possible, it would be appropriate to move to a final third phase. Some specific designing of "alternative action covenants" might be made for specific time periods, with sufficient guidelines, allowance for flexibility, and inclusion of ways in which children, youth, and adults can all be involved. Opportunity for "house church" groups to share with each other would be an important next step.

Witness. Take care to invite to the World Communion Service someone who might otherwise feel excluded from "table fellowship" with those who would be gathering for this celebration.

Take time to conscientiously work through the following exercise: On a sheet of paper answer the following questions: Who in our community or in the world does not have bread or wine right now? Who is a prisoner now? What kinds of prisons exist here? What can I do about this? What can our congregation do about this? What will I do about this? What can I propose to the congregation that we do about this?

Enter into some deliberate participation in an "anticipatory community" that has chosen some specific ways of supporting one another in the business of making Rasmussen's five points viable in actual life experience.

PRAISE THE CREATOR: CARE FOR CREATION

William Gibson proposes that to be involved in praise of God the Creator is necessarily to be involved in human care of creation. Stewardship or trusteeship of creation involves both care for the earth and the maximum development of a person's abilities for the upbuilding of community. Gibson specifically identifies a variety of ways that the earth has become the victim of humanity's irresponsibility: world overpopulation, disruption of organic relationships, depletion of nonrenewable goods, degradation of moral and intellectual standards, and the breeding of violence. The theme of organizing life toward continuation, care, and enhancement abounds in Scripture, especially in the linking of human liberation and the liberation of nature.

Worship. Plan for a service of worship in a graveyard. Include an honoring of the collective community with an emphasis on nature and sacred places. Outdoor services, particularly those held in cemeteries, have historically been connected with the sanctification of hallowed ground by battles "for freedom" or "against oppression." Activities that could also be included in this time are: rubbings of gravestones, particularly those that have some epitaph that speaks of Christian witness; write one's own epitaph; talk about "communion with the saints"; sing "For All the Saints" or "I Sing a Song of the Saints of God."

An additional dimension to this service could include the building of a Succoth booth in the near vicinity. This would be a visible symbol of thankfulness for the gifts of the earth and the community of faith's concern for the hungry. Traditionally, when services were held in graveyards, there was also a community feast. Why not have that feast in the Succoth booth?

Nurture. Preparation will be needed for the graveyard service. This would include researching the history of such services, providing information about the symbolism of such an event, digging up data about "Covenanters," knowing something about "hallowed ground." Participants might also like to have opportunity to think about, write about, and reflect upon personal heroes and heroines who have "gone on," including some way of sharing about their importance in faith development. Materials for the service need to be collected, and arrangements made for food preparation. Symbolic food might be included, especially if a Succoth booth is to be used.

Witness. Bring in local community people to eat, drink, and worship with you in the graveyard/Succoth booth.

Make public intentions to extend the influence of an ancestor who stood for justice, worked for equality, preserved the environment, knew how to be in mission; identify the specific ways this might be carried out.

Opportunity should be provided for individuals and the congregation to make commitment to specific ways of caring for creation, especially with regard to nonrenewable resources, violence, moral or intellectual degradation, population control, disruption of organic relationships.

Thanksgiving Day celebration should note the special knowledge of land, crops, and the life cycle that Native Americans shared with English colonists, only to experience a fate worse than the Israelites dealt the native Canaanites from whom they learned Succoth.[28]

NOTE: Care needs to be given to providing information about the Succoth celebration, instructions for building a booth, etc.

Leviticus 23:39–44 describes Succoth, or the week-long Festival of Booths, also called the Feast of Tabernacles (II Chron. 8:13). It celebrates both the cyclical renewal of the covenant (Ex. 24; Josh. 24; and II Kings 22–23) and the autumn festival of ingathering (Ex. 23:16; 34:22). The festival begins five days after Yom Kippur, the Day of Atonement (climaxing ten days of penitence), and eight days before Simhath Torah, the Joy of the Law (concluding the annual cycle of Synagogue readings from the Pentateuch).

On this delightful intergenerational occasion, "celebrants collected branches of myrtle, willow, and palm, and wove them together into a *succah,* a small booth or hut in which they slept and ate for eight days. These booths were fragilely constructed to remind the people that their salvation does not rely on temporary and material goods but on the steadfast and eternal God. So the roofs of the booths were left partly open, with only a few branches on top. This allowed the people to look at the stars—symbols of God's omniscience. Each succah was also hung with colorful fall fruits and vegetables as a visible reminder of the harvest which God provides. Leviticus 23:40 contains a command for the people to weave similar branches together to make a festive plume, a *lulab.* This plume of branches was finished by attaching a citron—a lemon-like fruit of the Holy Land. The lulab was a symbol of rejoicing and was waved in all directions during parts of the service to show that God is everywhere."[29]

Traditional readings of the festival highlight the theme of ecojustice and covenant renewal. Thus Ps. 118:1–9, 21–29 invites the congregational response, "O Give Thanks"; and after Ps. 121, the people raise their lulabs and cry, "Save us, we beseech Thee, O Lord." The service may conclude with children reading such covenant passages as Josh. 24:13–27 and Ex. 20:1–11.

PART TWO

LECTIONARY CRITIQUE

A. Reform and Use

1

CANON AND CALENDAR:
AN ALTERNATIVE LECTIONARY PROPOSAL

James A. Sanders

This essay is intended to be both critical and constructive. In it, I welcome the lectionary idea as a way to relate scriptural canon with community of faith. But I see real problems in the way Christian lectionaries have been traditionally conceived. Therefore, after reviewing the advantages and disadvantages of using a lectionary, I shall make a rather radical proposal to transform the lectionary vehicle.

I

The *advantages* of using a lectionary are numerous and compelling in large measure. They can cause the interpreter or preacher to read unfamiliar passages and move outside one's own canon-within-the-canon of favorite passages. The challenges to one's thinking about what is really in the Bible can be considerable if a lectionary is used. When I assign students seminary exegesis papers, I advise them to use one of two rules in selecting a passage to work on: they are either (1) to choose a passage they do not know, or (2) to choose one they do not "like." Lectionaries often provide just such passages for preaching and study! The interpreter learns more than otherwise about the Bible and perhaps more about himself or herself. James Barr advises professional or experienced biblical interpreters *not* to read the Bible only for others—to prepare that sermon or write that lecture or teach that class—but to read it first for themselves.[1] Use of a lectionary can induce such reading over against the practice of looking for the passage that says just what the preacher wants it to say to the congregation. Use of a lectionary can also help prevent the practice of conceiving of a sermon and then looking ad hoc for biblical passages to support it.

In many traditions the pastor is the congregation's teaching elder, and a lectionary can take some of the burden off him or her in the task of presenting the Bible truthfully to the faithful. The lectionary provides authoritative help from the larger church on how to "cover" the

Bible adequately. A great advantage of a Christian lectionary is that it correlates the Christian year and the Bible.

The two distinguishing, identifying factors in any religion or denomination are its canon and its calendar. Each is inherited from the earliest generations of the faithful when the crucial shaping of that particular group took place. Several religious calendars are operative in a country like ours. American Protestants can easily be deceived into thinking there is only one calendar used in this country because our particular cult most shaped our particular culture. But Roman Catholics have a slightly different calendar, the Orthodox a considerably different one, and the Jews a radically different one. Muslims and others in this country also have their calendars.

So there can be no doubt of the importance, for identity, of the calendar used in a particular religion. Of more importance is that religion's canon—its inherited scriptures also shaped by the earliest generations of the faithful. The function of a canon of scripture is to tell its adherents who they are and what they should do with their lives. A lectionary correlates canon and calendar: it is an ordered scheme of reading scripture adjusted to the religious calendar.

II

The advantages of using a lectionary are impressive, but the *disadvantages* are also clear. And the greatest of them all is that every lectionary I have seen, no matter how reformed and reforming, subordinates the canon to the calendar.

1. Actually I am inclined to put it more strongly: the calendar tyrannizes the canon in the lectionary format as traditionally conceived. And most of the festivals in the Christian calendar are but ancient agricultural and fertility-cult seasonal celebrations, barely Christianized. Christmas comes when it does out of the need early on to Christianize the winter solstice festival of lights; Easter was shaped by the need early on to tame the fertility rites of spring; and Pentecost comes when it does because of the Jewish Festival of Weeks, which was itself a Judaized spring harvest festival. So the canon is cut up into bits and pieces to serve the calendar.[2]

2. There is growing recognition and concern by lectionary builders today that the Old Testament especially is subordinated in Christian lectionaries to at best a supporting role to the New Testament passages chosen. Its main function in most lectionaries is to serve the Christian view of promise and fulfillment in which the Old Testament is seen as promise and the New as fulfillment. The Old Testament is usually gutted and sacrificed on the altar of the Christian need to believe it has superseded Judaism. But even the New Testament is reshaped by most lectionaries because of the dominant position of the calendar.

3. All the lectionaries I have seen perpetuate a Christocentric reading of the Bible as a whole. Some prevent any possibility of a theocentric reading of the Bible, even the New Testament. Lectionaries support the Christian bias that Christ revealed God. While it is true that sometimes an Old Testament passage in a Christian lectionary selection may cause some doubt about the viability of the self-serving denominational idea that its founder revealed God to the world, for the most part that dogma remains unchallenged.[3] A theocentric reading of the Bible makes it clear that in due season and in the fullness of time God revealed Christ and worked through him to bring God's story both to a climax and to the whole world, but such a reading also makes it clear that the gospel begins in Genesis, and that God cannot be co-opted to serve Christian needs.

4. Lectionaries as usually conceived destroy the Bible as Godspell, or God's story. God is the principal actor throughout the Bible, but Christian lectionaries leave the impression for the most part that the whole truth is told in the New Testament and that the Old Testament merely points to it. As a biblical scholar, I must emphasize that New Testament writers never intended to tell the whole truth. They presupposed that its readers knew their scripture, which was solely Old Testament, or most of what we call the Old Testament. They had no intention of going over all that ground again, but they rooted everything they reported of what God was doing in Christ and in the early church in their scripture, that is, in the story of what God had done before—precisely to try to show that God had been at it again, but this time climactically. Lectionaries as we know them do not present the canonical witness to God's power and work even in Christ and the early church. They tend to leave us to think that Jesus did it all, whereas *all* of what Jesus said and did pointed to God.

5. Finally, preaching or studying only by lectionary does not allow for one of the great Protestant traditions in preaching, that of moving apace through a whole book. Often in continuous study of a biblical book, the teaching elder is most responsible. This does perhaps better what a lectionary intends, namely, to compel the preacher or interpreter to work on passages he or she might otherwise never study. And it does something lectionaries largely hinder, i.e., studying biblical passages in their full context. Lectionaries by their form and by their nature of serving the Christian calendar seldom sponsor a full contextual reading of biblical passages.

Hence we see that there is both good news and bad news about lectionaries, and this is not even to address the whole set of other problems when one turns to the passages actually selected for lectionary reading. Sometimes one can see what was in mind when the various selections were made, but often one sees no clear relationship between them nor sees what theological sense the combination

makes. But this problem is really beside the point for our critique or
for our proposal.

III

Our proposal is that a responsible group work out a lectionary
system and sequence of readings that would honor the canon as
God's story and ours, as believing communities today. The model
would be the continuing practice in our mother faith, Judaism, where
the Torah is read through from beginning to end in a year's time. The
parashot or passages read in the week-long (actually eight- or nine-
day) Festival of Tabernacles in the fall complete the readings in
Deuteronomy and start again in Genesis. During the course of each
year the whole Torah is read, and in Orthodox synagogues that
means every word. In Reform congregations often a short passage is
selected in each sequential *parashah,* but even in many Conservative
congregations all of each section is read so that each year the faithful
hear the whole of the Torah story. Each year they go through the
narrative from creation to Moses' death on Pisgah's lofty height, and
start back to hear it and the laws all over again. In the reading the
faithful identify with their ancestors and go through the tension-filled
story of promise and precarious fulfillment.

The Torah, as canon *par excellence,* functions in two ways for the
people: it reminds them over and over again in their own ever-chang-
ing lives and contexts who they are and how they should shape their
lives.[4] Conjoined with the Torah reading is the recitation of many
psalms and the reading of a portion from the *haftarah,* or prophets.
They are traditional selections, though there have been many different groupings of readings from the prophets adjoined to the set Torah
portion. And they are related in one way or another so that the theme
in the Torah reading is reflected in the *haftarah* selection.

It has been our contention for some time that the canon as a whole
functions in the same way as the Torah if read so that it can do so,
i.e., as a continuous story.[5] The story that begins in Genesis with
creation and the call of Abraham and Sarah does not end with Moses'
death, but continues through the prophetic literature and into some
of the *hagiographa,* or Writings. The various ordering of books in the
major Septuagint manuscripts indicates efforts to present unfolding
history. God is the principal subject of the verbs of that history, and
most of it deals, episode after episode, with the integral relationship
between judgment and hope as it is demonstrated time and again in
that history.[6]

Biblical history is realistic, and it provides a mirror for the later
generations of readers to see themselves in it and affirm their identity
as the heirs of those who struggled with the tough issues of life and
death, sin, pride, suffering, and pain. They are the same struggles as

people have today: the same human tendency to confuse the Giver and the gift, to confuse our government with God's, and the constant temptation to think that God is weak or even dead.

It is both story and *his* tory, but the major characteristic of biblical history is its utter realism. It tells it like it is. It shows human cupidity and human generosity, human arrogance and humility, human sin and obedience, human suffering and joy, human inhumanity and hu maneness in the light of God's undying desire to have a community of witnesses who can see what really goes on in the real world, under the sovereignty of God.

If the full story is read with the very hermeneutics indicated in the biblical texts themselves, that is, theocentrically and not anthropocentrically or even Christocentrically, one does not yield to the temptation to try to make our faith-ancestors into models of morality. Rather one can celebrate the dominant theme of the whole of the canon—God's unyielding ability to work in and through human limits and sin to redeem all the situations we offer up out of our human free will.[7] The point is that if God could manage with us back there, God can manage with us today, for the human condition remains the same. *Errore hominum providentia divina:* God's grace works in and through human sinfulness. And that is the clarion note of hope the Bible strikes first in the Old Testament and persistently rings in the New.

If we Christians can grasp that point, then we will have our eyes opened to the New Testament's assertion that God was at it again in the first century, this time not in Israel under Egypt, or Israel under Assyria, or Israel under Babylonia or Persia or the Hellenistic powers, but in Israel through Christ under Rome in the last years before Israel was scattered throughout the world. The God who had called Abraham and Sarah with a plan, who had sojourned in the huts and hovels of the slaves in Egypt and had gone with God's people into the POW camps in Babylonia, was this time crouching in a cradle in Bethlehem in a Jew baby whose life was threatened by Herod's sword. So what's new? The New Testament is also biblical.[8] That was the belief of the Christians who wrote it. They did not budge without rooting in their scripture, the Old Testament, their report of God's work in Christ and in the early church. That is how convinced they were of the truth of their report.

What was new was their conviction that a new chapter was being added to the Torah story—not just to the Writings, but to the extended Torah story that continues through the Prophets, and that it was the climactic chapter, the one that completed the story as the true paradigm for seeing how God has continued and will continue to work till the eschaton, or until this real history is completed and consummated. The New Testament is mainly about God's work as redeemer in Christ, but this cannot be understood aright apart from

God's work as creator, sustainer, and judge of all peoples and as redeemer of God's whole creation.

Read alone or in conjunction with only bits and pieces of the Old Testament, the New Testament can be seriously misleading. No writer or contributor to it thought for a moment that we would abuse it by severing it from its own moorings and presuppositions as perceived in the New Testament. It was not until after A.D. 150, with Marcion and his efforts to sever the New Testament from the Old, that the question arose whether the Old Testament was canonical. All the New Testament writers assumed that, and referred to it constantly to make their case. Their question was whether the New Testament was biblical—not the other way around. They answered it enthusiastically in the affirmative!

Can such a whole story-line lectionary be devised? Yes. In fact, the basic work has been done by a task force on which I served at the request of the Youth Program of the Program Agency of the United Presbyterian Church, and it can be picked up again. In this proposal the weekend readings of the Gospel were the same as in the current ecumenical lectionary, but the weekday readings began in Genesis and followed the story line of the Bible right on through the Old Testament and the New. For example, in Year C, September through November (Sundays after Pentecost), we proposed the following schema to begin the parish program year:

Weekend Readings	*Daily Readings*
Luke 14–16	from Genesis 12–50
Luke 17–18	from Exodus, Numbers, Deuteronomy
Luke 19–23	from Joshua, Judges, I Samuel

It was exciting to see now often the weekend readings, governed by the calendar, were a good theological complement to the weekday readings of the Bible as story. So it can be done, and I think it should be done, if only as an available option.

IV

I have already rung the changes on the principal advantages of a whole story-line lectionary, but I would like to list the advantages, as I see them, in cursory fashion so that perhaps some dialogue can begin.

1. It would introduce a theocentric perspective in the churches so that God's work in Israel, in Christ, and in the early church can be seen as continuing today.

2. It would revive for the faithful God's continuing work as creator of all peoples as well as God's work as redeemer in Israel and in Christ.

3. It would challenge the Christian tendency toward a self-serving reading of the Bible, especially of the New Testament, with the tendency to feel that Christ somehow tamed God for us in the incarnation.

4. It would seriously challenge Christianity's continuing anti-Semitism and permit us, in reading the New Testament, to identify with our just counterparts, the good religious folk who rejected Christ.

5. It would put the New Testament back into the Bible and give it the perspective the New Testament writers themselves had.

6. It would underscore our need to pursue social ethics and it would put New Testament personal ethics in a larger canonical perspective.

7. It would put New Testament eschatology in the perspective of God's original work as creator, and God's continuing work as re-creator.

8. It would engender a reading of the whole Bible by the hermeneutic of the freedom of the God of grace, and it would challenge Christian tendencies to box God into our doctrines. We might learn how annoyingly free God's grace really is, even for those we *know* do not deserve it (like those who work only one hour in the cool of the day, yet earn as much as we).

9. It would show clearly that God revealed Christ as the climax of God's creation and would put a hold on our tendency to think that *our* Christ revealed God.

10. It would at least make a start on the absolutely necessary task of challenging our tendency to read the New Testament by a self-serving hermeneutic that distorts the doctrines of election and the church and permits us to think that to be "saved" is to get extra rewards rather than to serve as eyewitnesses to what God is doing in the real world today.

Let's give it a try. It is still not too late for the churches to become true servants of the Word, especially if they learn to read the Bible on its own terms.

2

USING THE CONSENSUS LECTIONARY: A RESPONSE

Horace T. Allen, Jr.

The widespread ecumenical use of the three-year Roman lectionary in North America is one of the more significant ecclesiological developments of our time. It is evidence of a new seriousness about the liturgical use of the Word of God, by both Protestants and Roman Catholics. As Vatican II's *Constitution on the Sacred Liturgy* directed, "The treasures of the Bible are to be opened up more lavishly so that a richer fare may be provided for the faithful at the table of God's word" (para. 51). A three-year lectionary was subsequently produced to implement that mandate and now, somewhat to the surprise of Roman Catholic authorities, it has rapidly become an important vehicle of extensive local ecumenicity and Bible study.

Beginning with a "Lectionary for the Christian Year" published in the Presbyterian *Worshipbook—Services* (1970) for use in The United Presbyterian Church in the U.S.A., the Presbyterian Church U.S., and the Cumberland Presbyterian Church, several other North American denominations have printed adaptations of this system in their own books for weekly use by clergy and congregations. They include The United Methodist Church, The Episcopal Church, the Lutheran Churches, the Disciples of Christ, the United Church of Christ, the United Church of Christ in Canada, and the Anglican Church in Canada. In addition, the Consultation on Church Union has published a popular pamphlet including a "consensus" version of these various editions. The consensus version differs significantly from the Roman Catholic lectionary in displacing readings from the Apocryphal books with passages from the thirty-nine Old Testament books. This has resulted in patterns of ecumenical homiletical preparation groups and parish-wide Bible study sessions. The significance of such Reformation-like activity as a result of a Roman conciliar document should not be lost on students of twentieth-century church history. Surely a significant stirring of the Spirit is here in evidence.

The appearance of this particular volume, SOCIAL THEMES OF THE CHRISTIAN YEAR, which develops the missional implications and themes of the biblical texts included in this lectionary, only carries forward the inevitable relation between unity and mission. As indicated in John 17, the purpose of unity is not unity as such; it is unity in mission. As Karl Barth has pointed out in his ecclesiology, the church does not exist for itself but for its sending. Thus if, in our day, the church is finding a new unity around the table of the Word, that can only be for the sake of its social mission, which is dedicated to serving the unity of all, in justice and freedom.

These considerations require that those churches which are now committed to the use of what may be called an ecumenical lectionary be diligent in their stewardship of this vehicle for the proclamation of the Word of God. To that end, Protestant and Catholic representatives have worked together to produce a minor revision of the lectionary which respects its basic structure but which also responds to certain criticisms of its plan.

The consensus of this revising committee was that a single harmonization of denominational variants should be established and that the principal criticism of the Roman lectionary, namely, its typological use of the Hebrew Bible (or Old Testament) should be addressed. These concerns have resulted in a proposed common text which (1) continues the structures of calendar and three readings; (2) continues the present three-year structure of Gospel pericopes with minor textual revision to accommodate churches that use a Bible in worship rather than a printed lectionary; (3) continues the present New Testament ("Epistle") pericopes with some lengthening and minor textual rearrangement to include contextual materials; and (4) revises the present set of Old Testament lessons for the Sundays after Pentecost to include in Year A a semicontinuous reading of the patriarchal and Mosaic narrative as complementary to the Gospel of Matthew, in Year B a semicontinuous reading of the Davidic narrative as complementary to the Gospel of Mark, and in Year C a semicontinuous reading of the Elijah-Elisha narrative as well as several further prophetic readings as complementary to the Gospel of Luke.

This adaptation was published on a three-year trial basis in 1983 by a working group of the Consultation on Common Texts known as the North American Committee on Calendar and Lectionary. Its chairperson has been Lewis A. Briner, copastor of the First Presbyterian Church of Kalamazoo, Michigan, who was the editor for the lectionary as published in *The Worshipbook*. This effort grew out of an extraordinary gathering in Washington, D.C., in March of 1978, representing all the churches in North America in which the lectionary was being used. During the three-year trial period, Advent 1983 through Pentecost 1986, responses will be gathered by the Consultation on Common Texts and political processes begun to encourage adoption of this *proposed* revision by participating churches, including the Roman Catholic. For users of this volume it should be emphasized that this revision only seriously affects the Old Testament readings for the Sundays after Pentecost—and in that regard, in a direction which is consonant with Prof. James Sanders' particular concerns.

This brings us to Professor Sanders' cautions concerning lectionaries (see the preceding article). The concerns he expresses must be taken seriously not only as the opinion of a leading biblical scholar but also as the serious reflection of a dedicated Christian worshiper. He directs five clearly interrelated criticisms to lectionaries of the Christian year:

1. The dominance of the calendar over the canon.
2. The "typological" tyranny of the New Testament over the Old.
3. The preference for a "Christocentric" over a "theocentric" reading.
4. The confinement of salvation history within the first century of the Christian era.
5. The absence of continuous reading of entire books of the Bible.

It has to be said at the outset that, although the proposed revision of the Consultation on Common Texts does address both (2) and (3), it assumes (1) and (5)—although only to a certain extent. For it does perpetuate the principal structural assumption of the Roman/ecumenical lectionary, namely, the continuous reading of the three Synoptic Gospels in the three years, beginning with the birth narratives in Christmas, the baptism and early ministry in Epiphany, and (after Lent-Easter) the unfolding ministry in the Sundays after Pentecost. It also perpetuates the semicontinuous reading of New Testament epistles during the Sundays after Epiphany and Pentecost. The proposed revision will do the same with Old Testament books on those Sundays.

This analysis uncovers an important aspect of the Christian calendar, namely, that the structure and duration of the church year is actually limited to the approximately six months between the 1st Sunday in Advent and the Day of Pentecost. The Sundays after Pentecost are not integrally part of that year, hence their designation in the Roman calendar as "Sundays of the Year," or "Sundays in Ordinary Time." Those Sundays (well over twenty) are the occasion for the freeing of the canon from the calendar and for the sequential reading of Gospel, Epistles, and (in the proposed revised table) Old Testament. Thus, thematic integration is limited to the Sundays of Advent, Christmas, Lent, and Easter, as well as the days of Epiphany, Pentecost, and Trinity.

Two further considerations (related to each other) must be mentioned in reference to the link between calendar and canon.

First, all Sunday lectionaries in the history of the church have assumed the existence of at least one other lectionary: a daily set of readings. This is known in the Roman tradition as the Daily Office, and in the Episcopal *Book of Common Prayer* it is provided for by the orders of Morning and Evening Prayer. In Reformed history this same biblical-devotional function was accomplished by daily family prayer and Bible reading. In other words, the Sunday corporate reading of the Bible was never meant to carry the whole freight of introducing the biblical story (*his*tory). And even after family Bible study virtually disappeared from among us, the Sunday church school was understood to be the agency to carry that forward. Professor Sanders himself alludes to such a necessity with his reference to the aborted project of the United Presbyterian Youth Program to produce a "theocentric" *daily* lectionary to supplement the weekly lessons for the Lord's Day.

Second, in addition to calendar and canon as determinants of any lectionary system, there is the further factor of the lectionary's cultic context, or liturgical use. For what sort of service is this lectionary ordered? Sanders evaluates it in terms of its contribution to the preaching tradition of the left-wing Protestant Reformation. But this is not the assumption of the lectionary we are discussing. Its assumed context is the un-Protestant (though not un-Reformed) weekly union of Word and Sacrament.

This raises the Christological issue in a new way. However we might debate the need for more theocentric-Christocentric alternation as a theological matter, the cultic context of the Sacrament of Holy Communion (which we Protestants tend to give secondary attention) does emphatically affect the discussion. It also radically changes the history-eschatology discussion which Sanders raises at a number of points without helpful resolution. In what sense, for instance, is the Christ revelation "climactic," or is Christian history simply "till the eschaton, or until . . . history is completed"? Recent liturgical theology emphasizes the character of the Sacrament as proleptic rather than simply historicist. This gives its Christological focus another dimension than that adduced by Sanders in his fourth point.

Both the calendar and the cult of the church are emphatically Christological. That is the reason its most recent effort at lectionary reform is such. That does not imply, ipso facto, that it will be deficient in terms of either creation or eschatology. The latter is intensively dealt with in the Advent lectionary and the former in the Vigil lessons for Easter and Pentecost, which unfortunately do not occur in Protestant worship that ignores those cultic occasions. (The revision by the Consultation on Common Texts provides such lessons as alternatives on those days. It respects however, the lectionary's respect for the Old Testament in not providing pericopes during the season of Easter on the assumption that one should not read Christ's resurrection "back" into the Old Testament, and that the kerygmatic passages of Acts are themselves eloquent enough witnesses to the truth of the Hebrew Bible.)

In conclusion it might be reflected that the reading of the Bible in public worship restores the Scriptures to their primary context as doxological documents, rather than didactic ones. It is precisely this reality to which Sanders points in his description of the annual reading of the Torah in the synagogue. That means that both New and Old Testaments must be read in a different context than simply the literary-historical. The church and its cult are now their "place." Otherwise, as Sanders seems unable to recognize, the Semitic people of God would long ago have accepted the New Testament as "also biblical." This is not to affirm either some "self-serving reading of the Bible" or some thinly veiled anti-Semitism. That most Christological theologian, Karl Barth, declared that "in relation to the Synagogue there can be no real question of 'mission' or of bringing the Gospel. ... The Gentile Christian community of every age and land is a guest in the house of Israel. ... Does this mean that the Christian community has no responsibility to discharge its ministry of witness to the Jews? Not at all! What it does mean is that there can be only one way to fulfil it. To use the expression of Paul of Rom. 11:11, 14, it must make the Synagogue jealous" (*Church Dogmatics,* IV/3/2, pp. 877f.).

My response to Professor Sanders should not imply that lectionary reform is completed. Revisions of the consensus lectionary in the future could result in more canonical coverage. Several expository essays in this volume also suggest how to achieve a faith-forming use of the Old Testament within the consensus lectionary structure. When in the history of the church Catholic and Reforming have we had such a potent instrument and symbol both of our unity in the Word and of our calling to mission?

DEVELOPING A WHOLE PARISH PRAXIS

Dieter T. Hessel

A whole parish praxis can be developed based on the social themes of the Christian year, using this book and other pertinent resources. Steps for planning and Bible study are suggested below.

PLANNING FOR EACH SEASON

Form a planning group or task force that will take the following steps well in advance of the season for which it is responsible. The group involves interested members, the congregation's professional staff, and representatives from committees on worship, education, mission and action, etc. The following is an agenda for a retreat, or for three meetings that take the six steps in pairs. The planning group will want to concentrate on what happens in the Sunday life of the congregation, but should not limit its planning to that weekly time.

1. Scan the current year's cycle of Scripture lessons to comprehend the lectionary's key emphases or clusters of texts for this season of the Christian year. Make use of the article describing a whole approach to the season, as well as other lectionary handbooks and guides. Summarize the story line and the theological-ethical strategy of the season.

2. Note how the Sunday lessons for this year and season reflect basic biblical social themes that bridge the three-year cycle of the lectionary as a whole. Take time to read and ponder selected texts. Identify themes and passages that speak to the concerns of the congregation, that are already part of the congregation's life, or that need to be developed.

3. Read and hear brief summaries of the most pertinent essay(s) about a biblical theme identified in step (2), to gain more appreciation of its theological focus and social thrust. Concentrating on only one of the thematic essays, study a few of the texts on which the essay comments. Keep in mind that all of the themes of the season are likely to be represented in lectionary readings for each year. Yet, in a given year, the parish can entertain only one or two themes of the season.

4. When studying the texts, use a liberating social hermeneutic as sketched below and on pp. 25ff. What questions from our human social situation do we bring to the text(s)? What hopes and anxieties move us? What strange message do we hear, what call to mission gains our attention? In the light of these texts, what aspects of faith development and parish witness shall we emphasize in this season?

5. Think in terms of a creative mix of methods by which the congregation will be engaged in worship-education-action focused on these themes. Plan for adult study of the selected biblical theme(s). Anticipate symbolic actions or aspects of ritual in worship, possible times of educational exposure and study, and occasions for community action or public involvement. Think intergenerationally as well as by existing groupings. What worship, educational, and program resources are available for our use? (Advance homework will be required.)

6. Keeping existing church program clearly in mind, select and schedule appropriate emphases in worship, education, and witness for all age groups, intergenerational gatherings, and committees and organizations of the congregation. Coordinate this planning among groups in the congregation, noting what is happening ecumenically and in larger judicatories of the denomination. Do we want the congregation to gather in any special settings? What steps shall we take to focus parish life as a whole during this season? What are the implications for church school, Bible study, the mission committee's role in worship, or the worship committee's role in education? Write out a brief summary of the plan.

LIBERATING BIBLE STUDY METHOD

Leaders of communal Bible study groups may be guided by this the following summary, without necessarily pursuing each detail or answering each question in exploring how the spirit of a particular text addresses our situation.

1. Begin by experiencing and questioning the text. What is going on in the passage? Comprehend the setting, movement, and actors. Utilize nonverbal, artistic, dramatic, and other expressive techniques. Bring narrative, dialogue, and poetry alive in reading the passage aloud.

2. Explore the human social situation in which we read a biblical passage. What prior commitments do we bring to it? What personal and public realities does it bring to mind? What feelings from inside or outside does it elicit? What experiences of oppression, uncertainty, or apathy do we bring to this reading of the text? What dominant world view or ideology is challenged? Which of our familiar assumptions are questioned? To whom are we listening? Cultivate critical

consciousness by sharing selected quotations of contemporary voices from below, and by summarizing pertinent information about realities of our human social situation.

3. Listen to nuances of the text known through historical-critical scholarship. What is the role of the passage in its biblical book? Summarize the results of exegetical homework concerning structural and literary analysis, historical occasion and sociological setting, theological intention and ethical dynamics. Using several translations, note different renditions of key phrases. Ponder words in the text that annoy you. Consult commentaries about prominent metaphors, key words, and canonical (intrabiblical) links.

4. Note how the passage was probably heard by various groups then, and how different groups tend to hear it now. Suggest parallels of those groups originally addressed by the text, and look for dynamic equivalence (contemporary analogies) to the message and metaphor of the passage. Reassign the cast of characters and our place in the cast. Imagine hearing and discussing this passage in a different cultural setting or situation of powerlessness/power. Draw on the experiences of women, racial and ethnic groups, and Christians in less privileged countries. Share parallel stories of the church's struggle to be faithful today.

Read the passage aloud with inclusive language. Consult other translations, if available, to gain new insights. Draw on the commentaries of base communities, such as *The Gospel in Solentiname* (NOTE: The lectionary committee of the National Council of Churches is preparing an inclusive-language translation of consensus lectionary lessons. For information, write: National Council of Churches, Division of Education and Ministry, Room 704, 475 Riverside Drive New York, N.Y. 10115.)

5. Look for God's action as the baseline for interpretation. What is God doing in the passage? How does God respond to the power/powerlessness of persons mentioned in the text? Think Christologically about any ambiguities that arise: What light is shed by Jesus' radical ministry with nonpersons? Draw out corporate, public, and political meanings of God's action, as well as individual, private, and personal messages.

Contemplate key images found in the text, and consider the implications for life in the world today, utilizing a private journal followed by group discussion. Given the realities of our situation and the movement of the text, to what response in the midst of our history does the Spirit call us?

6. Complete the action/reflection process by highlighting the implications for the church's faithful praxis. Use the text's metaphor in symbolic actions during worship, probe its message in educational sessions, witness to its meaning by engaging in new steps of public

engagement and human service. The congregation in social ministry is the locus for a liberating hermeneutic, particularly as the congregation discerns what is happening in society and participates in the work of the ecumenical church. Conclude with a fresh interpretation of what the text means concretely for the ministering body and its individual members.

NOTES

INTRODUCTION

1. Among the better commentaries on Sunday lessons, see:

Fuller, Reginald H. *Preaching the New Lectionary.* Liturgical Press, 1974.
Proclamation: Aids for Interpreting the Lessons of the Church Year. Fortress
  Press. Fifty-four paperback volumes have been published to date, covering
  the complete three-year cycle twice.
Rice, Charles, ed. *Word and Witness.* Looseleaf notebook with commentary
  and suggestions for worship, issued bimonthly by Sunday Publications,
  Inc., 3003 S. Congress Ave., Lake Worth, Fla. 33461.
Sloyan, Gerard S. *A Commentary on the New Lectionary.* Paulist Press, 1975.

2. Worship suggestions, including prayers and music, appear in *Word and
Witness* (above), and in:

Allen, Horace T. *A Handbook for the Lectionary.* Geneva Press, 1980.
Duck, Ruth C., ed. *Bread for the Journey* (prayers) and *Everflowing Streams*
  (music). Pilgrim Press, 1981. Both books feature inclusive language.
From Ashes to Fire: Services of Worship for Lent and Easter. Abingdon
  Press, 1979.
Kirk, James G. *When We Gather: Prayers for Public Worship* (Year A).
  Geneva Press. Forthcoming.
Seasons of the Gospel: Resources for the Christian Year. Abingdon Press,
  1979.

Educational curricula keyed to the ecumenical lectionary have only begun
to develop; they vary widely in theological depth and learning methods.
Consult:

Alleluia. Combines music with study of lessons and (Lutheran) worship
  forms. Augsburg Publishing House, 426 S. 5th St., Minneapolis, Minn.
  55415.
Christian Education: Shared Approaches, involving most of the major Protestant denominations, has not yet developed a curriculum keyed to the
  lectionary. For advice on how to adapt Shared Approaches to the lectionary cycle, write Church Education Services, Room 1101, 475 Riverside
  Drive, New York, N.Y. 10115.

Living Faith, by the Joint Board of Christian Education of Australia and New
Zealand, 177 Collins St., Melbourne, Australia 3000. Provides minister's
guide and broadly graded materials that link worship, study, and mission
around one lectionary theme per season.

Living the Good News (Episcopal), 600 Gilpin St., Denver, Colo. 80218.

Russell, Joseph P. *Sharing Our Biblical Story: A Guide to Using Liturgical
Readings as the Core of Church and Family Education.* Winston Press,
1979. Gives hints to storytellers of narrative passages.

3. Evaluations of the ecumenical lectionary appear in:

González, Justo and Catherine. *Liberation Preaching.* Abingdon Press, 1980.
Interpretation, Vol. 31, No. 2 (April 1977).
Skudlarek, William. *The Word in Worship.* Abingdon Press, 1981.

4. Justin Martyr, "The First Apology," ch. 67, in *Writings of Justin Martyr,*
tr. by Thomas B. Falls (Christian Heritage, 1948), pp. 106–107.

5. A. Allan McArthur, *The Christian Year and Lectionary Reform* (London:
SCM Press, 1958), pp. 33–34.

I. Advent–Christmas

1. For other aspects of these eschatological texts, see John Gunstone, *Commentary on the New Lectionary,* Vol. I, rev. ed. (London: S.P.C.K., 1979), pp. 65–66.

2. While Isaiah warns of the megalomania of "the mighty man," others look to the dominant male for deliverance in the crises of nation, family, and church: "You will find that when society begins to fall apart spiritually, what we find missing is the mighty man" (Jerry Falwell, *Listen, America!* [Bantam Books, 1980], p. 14).

3. Expressing that hope graphically, Isaiah names one of his sons Shear-jashub, "A remnant shall return." On Israel's "two hopes," see Abraham Heschel, *The Message of the Prophets* (Harper & Row, 1972), pp. 94f.

4. In Deutero-Isaiah we find "the announcement of the new rule of God with its revolutionary implications." Walter Brueggemann, *Living Toward a Vision: Biblical Reflections on Shalom* (United Church Press, 1976), p. 186, selects for an Advent-Christmas lectionary: Isa. 40:1–11; 45:1–7; 54:1–8; 52:7–12; and 42:10–16.

5. This vision portrays "the abandonment of arms in favor of divine judgment as the means of settling disputes between peoples and nations (v. 4)." Everett Tilson, "Homiletical Resources: Exegesis of Isaiah Passages for Advent," *Quarterly Review,* Vol. 1, No. 1 (Fall 1980), p. 11.

6. The inseparability of divine glory *(kabod)* and divine justice *(mishpat)* is a constant in Isaiah and is given forceful expression in this and other Advent texts. Miranda goes further, arguing for their synonymy throughout the Old and New Testaments, with attestation in the Septuagint version of Isa. 61:3 and other parallelisms. See José Porfirio Miranda, *Marx and the Bible: A Critique of the Philosophy of Oppression,* tr. by John Eagleson (Orbis Books, 1974), pp. 232–250.

7. As postexilic editors go on to situate parts of Isa. 11:6, 7, and 9 in 65:25, fresh significance is given to these words in the context of a restored Jewish community.

8. A metaphor and motif for interpreting the biblical narrative and its Christological center is given in Gabriel Fackre, *The Christian Story* (Wm. B. Eerdmans Publishing Co., 1978), pp. 29–39 and 89–111.

9. A. H. Curtis, *The Vision and Mission of Jesus* (Edinburgh: T. & T. Clark, 1954), pp. 12–17, 197–206.

10. P. T. Forsyth struggles profoundly with the relation of God's holiness to God's love in *The Work of Christ* (1910) and *The Cruciality of the Cross* (1909).

11. Josef Jungmann, *The Early Liturgy to the Time of Gregory the Great* (University of Notre Dame Press, 1959), pp. 147–149.

12. See Johannes de Moor, *New Year with Canaanites and Israelites* (Kampen, 1972). Also see Norman H. Snaith, *The Jewish New Year Festival* (London: S.P.C.K., 1948).

13. The Canaanite drama of the death and resurrection of Baal and the role of the goddess Anath in this drama is found on the Ras Shamra tablets. For a translation of the text and an analysis of its influence on the Old Testament, see F. F. Hvidberg, *Weeping and Laughter in the Old Testament* (Leiden: E. J. Brill, 1962).

14. Although the jubilee year may never have been celebrated in ancient Israel exactly as it is described in Leviticus 25, it represents an ideal in Israel of an egalitarian society of free, small landholders and a periodic social revolution to restore this norm. The jubilee idea has also been a continual inspiration in American culture.

15. See Sigmund Mowinckel, *He That Cometh* (Abingdon Press, 1956), pp. 80–95. Crowds waved the *lulab,* or bundle of aromatic branches, in celebration of the king's triumphal procession of reenthronement. They entered into the symbolism of the return of the victorious Davidic king (Zech. 9:9–10).

16. On the Canaanite "Monster of Chaos" (Tiamat) and its adaptation in the Hebrew stories of creation, see Mary K. Wakeman, *God's Battle with the Monster: A Study in Biblical Imagery* (Leiden: E. J. Brill, 1973).

17. See Mowinckel, *He That Cometh,* pp. 96–124.

18. See Hans Conzelmann, "The Mother of Wisdom," in James Robinson (ed.), *The Future of Our Religious Past* (London: SCM Press, 1971). Also see Leonard Swidler, *Biblical Affirmations of Woman* (Westminster Press, 1979), pp. 36–49.

19. Raphael Patai, *The Hebrew Goddess* (KTAV Publishing House, 1967).

II. Epiphany

1. William Barclay, *The Gospel of Luke,* rev. ed. (Westminster Press, 1975), p. 34.

2. Ian Lind, "Blemishes on the Top Banana: A Critical Look at Castle & Cooke," *Multinational Monitor,* July 1981, p. 20.

3. Ibid., p. 11.

4. Frances FitzGerald, "A Reporter at Large: A Disciplined Changing Army," *The New Yorker,* May 18, 1981, p. 60.

5. Dom Helder Câmara, quoted in *The Christian Century,* Sept. 15, 1976.

6. Luise Schottroff, in *Theology Digest,* Vol. 28, No. 2 (Summer 1980). For the German original see: *Evangelische Theologie,* Vol. 39, No. 6 (Nov.–Dec. 1979).

7. Commission on the Churches' Participation in Development, *Towards a Church in Solidarity with the Poor* (Geneva: World Council of Churches, Feb. 1980).

8. John E. Burkhart, *Worship* (Westminster Press, 1982).

9. *The Kingdom on Its Way: Meditations and Music for Mission,* The RISK Book Series (World Council of Churches, 150 Rte. de Ferney, 1211 Geneva 20, Switzerland). Also see *In Accord: Let Us Worship,* by Justo and Catherine González (Friendship Press, 1981).

10. *The Church and Immigration,* Justice Ministries 11–12, 1981 (Institute on the Church in Urban-Industrial Society, 5700 S. Woodlawn, Chicago, Ill. 60637), summarizes denominational policies and models of action by churches.

11. *Journeys to a Dream* is a Doing the Word (CE:SA) resource for younger children. For youth and adults a more detailed list of books, audiovisuals, plays, posters, and music resources is part of the NCC packet *Multi-Cultural Resources Sources* (National Council of Churches, 7th floor, 475 Riverside Drive, New York, N.Y. 10115).

12. *Struggling with People Is Living in Christ* can be ordered from URM-CCA Office, Christian Conference of Asia, 57 Peking Road, 5/F Kowloon, Hong Kong.

13. Amnesty International (594 W. 58th St., New York, N.Y. 10019), works for release of "prisoners of conscience" who are detained for their beliefs, color, ethnic origin, religion, or language, provided they have neither used nor advocated violence. The Church Committee on Human Rights in Asia (1821 W. Cullerton, Chicago, Ill. 60608), publishes *Asian Rights Advocate,* which offers information and action suggestions on behalf of Christian political prisoners in Korea, the Philippines, and Taiwan.

14. Thomas Groome, *Christian Religious Education: Sharing Our Story and Vision* (Harper & Row, 1980).

15. *Circle of Prayer,* Vol. 8, Silver Jubilee Edition; slide set on the Silver Jubilee; and a list of Least Coin projects, are available from Church Women United, Room 812, 475 Riverside Drive, New York, N.Y. 10115.

16. Rome II, a simulation game from New Society Press, 4722 Baltimore Ave., Philadelphia, Pa. 19143.

17. William E. Gibson, and the Eco-Justice Task Force, *A Covenant Group for Lifestyle Assessment* (New York: United Presbyterian Church, Program Agency, 1981). Doris Lee Shettel, *Life-Style Change for Children (and Inter-generational Groups)* (New York: United Presbyterian Church, Program Agency, 1981). Order either or both from Church Education Services, Room 1101, 475 Riverside Drive, New York, N.Y. 10115.

18. *Your Kingdom Come,* Report on the World Conference on Mission and Evangelism, Melbourne, Australia, May 12–25, 1980 (World Council of Churches, 150 Rte. de Ferney, 1211 Geneva 20, Switzerland).

19. Henri Nouwen, "Letting Go of All Things," in *A Matter of Faith: A Study Guide for Churches on the Nuclear Arms Race* (Sojourners, 1309 L Street, N.W., Washington, D.C. 20005), p. 86.

20. For help use David Forrester, *Listening with the Heart: Encountering God in Prayer and Silence* (Paulist Press, 1978).

III. LENT–HOLY WEEK

1. Bertrand Russell, *Power: A New Social Analysis* (W. W. Norton & Co., 1938).

2. Peter Blau, *Inequality and Heterogeneity* (Free Press, 1977), Ch. 1.

3. "The revolution devouring its own children" is the way Vergniaud, the great orator of the Gironde, put it. See Hannah Arendt, *On Revolution* (Viking Press, 1972), p. 42.

4. Blaise Pascal, *Pensées,* Fragment 555; Everyman's Library (E. P. Dutton, 1931).

5. Gerhard von Rad, *Die Theologie des Alten Testaments,* Band II (Munich: Chr. Kaiser Verlag, 1965), p. 381. Translation mine.

6. Reginald Fuller, *The Foundations of New Testament Christology* (Charles Scribner's Sons, 1965); and Paul Lehmann, "The Politics of Easter," in *Dialog,* Vol. 19 (Winter 1980), pp. 39–40.

7. E. E. Cummings, *1 X 1* (Henry Holt & Co., 1944), XIV.

8. See further: Paul Lehmann, *The Transfiguration of Politics* (Harper & Row, 1975), pp. 84–94.

9. Ibid., pp. 91f. See also: Paul Lehmann, *Ideology and Incarnation* (Geneva: John Knox House, 1962), pp. 18ff.; also Rubem Alves, *A Theology of Human Hope* (Corpus Publications, 1969), pp. 85–101.

10. Von Rad, *Die Theologie des Alten Testaments,* Band I (1957), p. 382. Translation mine.

11. J. Christiaan Beker, *Paul the Apostle: The Triumph of God in Thought and Life* (Fortress Press, 1980), p. 160.

12. Cf. Raymond E. Brown, *The Gospel According to John,* Vol. I (Doubleday & Co., 1966), pp. 459–464.

13. See S. G. F. Brandon, *Jesus and the Zealots* (Manchester University Press, 1967); and Oscar Cullmann, *Jesus and the Revolutionaries* (Harper & Row, 1970).

14. W. B. Yeats, *Meditations in Time of Civil War,* 1923.

15. Norman Gottwald, *The Tribes of Yahweh: The Sociology of the Religion of Liberated Israel 1250–1050 B.C.E.* (Orbis Books, 1979), pp. 210–219 and 584ff.

16. Leonard Swidler, *Biblical Affirmations of Woman* (Westminster Press, 1979), pp. 31–34.

17. W. D. Davies, *The Gospel and the Land: Early Christian and Jewish Territorial Doctrine* (University of California Press, 1974), pp. 15–48.

18. See Rosemary Ruether, *Faith and Fratricide: The Theological Roots of Anti-Semitism* (Seabury Press, 1974), pp. 183–225.

19. This view of the relationship of Judaism and Christianity was developed in the famous letters between Eugen Rosenstock-Huessy and Franz Rosenzweig. See Eugen Rosenstock-Huessy, *Judaism Despite Christianity* (University of Alabama Press, 1969). Cf. Paul van Buren, *The Burden of Freedom: Americans and the God of Israel* (Seabury Press, 1976), p. 81.

20. See Rosemary Ruether, *Liberation Theology* (Paulist Press, 1972), regarding feminist, black and Latin-American liberation theologies.

21. See "Ecology and Human Liberation," in Rosemary Ruether, *To Change the World: Christology and Cultural Criticism* (Crossroads Publishing Co., 1981), pp. 57ff.

22. The basic hermeneutical approach of this essay is also one that seeks to do exegesis at the intersection between religious identity (as rooted in Scripture and tradition) and ethical involvement in the context of our present world. Attention to the aspects of "being" and "doing" as interrelated seems to this writer crucial to authentic Christian faith and praxis. Overemphasis on either pole of the Christian life results in distortion. The basic methodology is spelled out fully in Bruce C. Birch and Larry Rasmussen, *Bible and Ethics in the Christian Life* (Augsburg Publishing House, 1976), and applied to a particular set of ethical concerns in Birch and Rasmussen, *The Predicament of the Prosperous* (Westminster Press, 1978).

23. Paul van Buren, *The Burden of Freedom: Americans and the God of Israel* (Seabury Press, 1976).

24. Walter Brueggemann, *The Prophetic Imagination* (Fortress Press, 1978), pp. 16–17.

25. James A. Wharton, "Theology and Ministry in the Hebrew Scriptures," in *A Biblical Basis for Ministry*, ed. by Earl E. Shelp and Ronald Sunderland (Westminster Press, 1981), pp. 17–71.

26. See Brueggemann, *The Prophetic Imagination*, p. 20, for a helpful discussion of the cry of complaint as the first step in prophecy.

27. I have written of these themes in *Singing the Lord's Song: A Study of Isaiah 40–55*, by Bruce C. Birch (United Methodist Church, Board of Global Ministries, 1981).

28. My own work on the character of the covenant community, especially with respect to the concern for the neighbor, is found in greater detail in Birch and Rasmussen, *The Predicament of the Prosperous*, pp. 84–89. I am indebted for the phrase "alternative community" to Walter Brueggemann, *The Prophetic Imagination*. He has greatly sharpened my sense in which covenant community was a radical sociopolitical and religious alternative to Egypt and the other nations that surrounded Israel.

29. James Wharton, "Theology and Ministry in the Hebrew Scriptures," p. 53. Brueggemann, *The Prophetic Imagination*, uses the categories of a "politics of justice" and an "economics of equality."

30. See Bruce C. Birch, "Hunger, Poverty and Biblical Religion," *The Christian Century*, June 11–18, 1975, pp. 593–599, and Ron Sider, *Rich Christians in an Age of Hunger* (Paulist Press, 1977).

31. Walter Harrelson, *The Ten Commandments and Human Rights: Overtures to Biblical Theology* (Fortress Press, 1980), p. 192, lists an analogous decalogue for our own time:

1. Do not have more than a single ultimate allegiance.
2. Do not give ultimate loyalty to any earthly reality.
3. Do not use the power of religion to harm others.
4. Do not treat with contempt the times set aside for rest.
5. Do not treat with contempt members of the family.
6. Do not do violence against fellow human beings.
7. Do not violate the commitment of sexual love.
8. Do not claim the life or goods of others.
9. Do not damage others through misuse of human speech.
10. Do not lust after the life or goods of others.

32. Albert Schweitzer, *The Quest of the Historical Jesus* (Macmillan Co., 1948), pp. 370f.

33. Tissa Balasuriya, *The Eucharist and Human Liberation* (Orbis Books, 1979), pp. 24f.

34. Ibid., p. 25.

35. Frederick Herzog, *Liberation Theology: Liberation in the Light of the Fourth Gospel* (Seabury Press, 1972), p. 176.

36. Friedrich Schleiermacher, *The Christian Faith* (Edinburgh: T. & T. Clark, 1928), p. 33.

37. Gotthold Ephraim Lessing, *Nathan the Wise* (Frederick Ungar Publishing Co., 1955), p. 79.

IV. EASTER

1. The differences and similarities are helpfully presented on a chart by Raymond E. Brown, *The Gospel According to John,* The Anchor Bible, 2 vols. (Doubleday & Co., 1966, 1970), Vol. II, p. 974.

2. Ibid., p. 1013.

3. The RSV translates this sentence, "Greet Andronicus and Junias my kins*men* and my fellow prisoners; they are *men* of note among the apostles, and they were in Christ before me" (emphasis added). The Greek inflected form of Junia is clearly feminine; apparently the translators simply "believed" that only men could have been apostles!

4. For the evidence on Jesus' attitude toward women, see Leonard Swidler, *Biblical Affirmations of Woman.*

5. For reconstructions, see Brown, *The Gospel According to John,* Vol. II, pp. 995–1004; Rudolf Bultmann, *The Gospel of John* (Westminster Press, 1971), pp. 681–689; and, most important, Robert T. Fortna's forthcoming study, *The Evangelist John and His Predecessor.*

6. Fortna's reconstruction (see preceding note) is more complex, but makes possible the same general conclusions. He isolates a core source in which Mary (possibly with others) comes to the tomb, sees it open, runs to tell Peter, who returns with her to the grave, looks in, sees the cloths, and returns home wondering, telling no one. Fortna's analysis of John 20:1–18 has much to commend it: v. 3 ("came out") is singular, suggesting that the beloved disciple has been added; and the beloved disciple's belief (v. 8) stands in contradiction to their not knowing the Scripture (v. 9). But this does not explain Peter's seeing only grave cloths in the tomb, whereas Mary sees angels, or Peter's going home rather than to tell the other disciples, who are, in v. 18, pictured as all in one place together. Perhaps we have to posit three or even more stages of redaction.

7. In the apocryphal New Testament, women are called disciples in the Gospel of Peter 12:50 (Mary Magdalene); in Sophia Jesu Christi (which speaks of seven women who had followed him as disciples); in Pistis Sophia c.96 (Mary Magdalene "will surpass all my disciples and all men who shall receive mysteries of the Ineffable," and she will sit on Christ's right hand); and in the Gospel of Thomas, logion 61 (Salome calls herself Christ's disciple). (See Edgar Hennecke, *New Testament Apocrypha,* ed. by Wilhelm Schneemelcher, Vol. I [Westminster Press, 1963], pp. 186f., 246, 256f., and 298, respectively.)

8. Leonard Swidler's translation (*Biblical Affirmations of Woman*, pp. 310f.). The RSV translates: "for she has been a helper of many and of myself as well," a reading seemingly supported by the Bauer *Greek-English Lexicon* (University of Chicago Press, 1957), which lists only "protectress, patroness, helper" as possible readings. But the definitive Liddell-Scott *Greek-English Lexicon* (Oxford University Press, 1940), which covers all of ancient Greek literature, gives for *prostatēs* the following meanings: one who stands before; leader, chief, administrator; president, presiding officer; guardian, champion, patron. Its feminine form (found in Rom. 16:2), *prostatis,* carries the same nuances.

9. I am indebted for much of this to a discussion at Auburn Theological Seminary in a conference on teaching the Bible, May 1–3, 1981. Professors Elisabeth Fiorenza and Krister Stendahl made particularly acute observations. See also Fiorenza's " 'You are not to be called Father': Early Christian History in a Feminist Perspective," *Cross Currents,* Vol. 29, No. 3 (Fall 1979), pp. 301–323.

10. Hennecker, *New Testament Apocrypha,* Vol. I, pp. 195–196.

11. Ibid., pp. 353–354.

12. Ibid., pp. 342–344. This and the other apocryphal sources bearing on Magdalene's role are helpfully collected and commented on by Swidler, *Biblical Affirmations of Woman,* pp. 200–214.

13. The experience of Israel is formative to biblical consciousness, as is noted in *Liberation Preaching,* by Justo and Catherine González (Abingdon Press, 1980), pp. 16ff. Also see pp. 38ff. for some other cautions for lectionary users.

14. For some liturgical implications see *In Accord: Let Us Worship,* by Justo and Catherine González (Friendship Press, 1981).

15. Among the standard authorities see C. K. Barrett, *The Gospel According to St. John,* 2d ed. (Westminster Press, 1978); Raymond E. Brown, *The Gospel According to John;* Rudolf Bultmann, *The Gospel of John* (Westminster Press, 1971); C. H. Dodd, *The Interpretation of the Fourth Gospel* (Cambridge University Press, 1954); J. L. Martyn, *History and Theology of the Fourth Gospel,* rev. and enlarged (Abingdon Press, 1979).

16. Liberation perspectives have been applied to the Fourth Gospel in Frederick Herzog, *Liberation Theology: Liberation in the Light of the Fourth Gospel* (Seabury Press, 1972), and José Porfirio Miranda, *Being and the Messiah: The Message of St. John* (Orbis Books, 1973).

17. For important application of redaction criticism to the Fourth Gospel, see J. L. Martyn, *History and Theology of the Fourth Gospel,* and R. T. Fortna, *The Gospel of Signs: A Reconstruction of the Narrative Source Underlying the Fourth Gospel* (Cambridge University Press, 1970).

18. C. Lasch, *Culture of Narcissism* (McGraw-Hill Book Co., 1979), and Daniel Yankelovich, *The New Morality* (McGraw-Hill Book Co., 1974).

19. The contributions of Reinhold Niebuhr in *Moral Man and Immoral Society* (Charles Scribner's Sons, 1932); Joseph Haroutunian in *Lust for Power* (Charles Scribner's Sons, 1949); and (more recently, in the context of racist society) Allan Boesak in *Farewell to Innocence* (Orbis Books, 1977), are invaluable analyses, from a Christian perspective, of corrupting power.

20. See Paul Lehmann, *The Transfiguration of Politics* (Harper & Row, 1975), for theological insight into the "political" task of the church.

21. "Christian humanism" is delineated in Joseph Haroutunian's *God with Us* (Westminster Press, 1979) contra present attacks on "humanism in the churches."

22. The Eastern Orthodox Churches' emphasis on martyrdom and suffering is explored in *Martyria Mission,* ed. by Ion Bria (Geneva: World Council of Churches, 1980). The present struggle for survival in most of those churches gives their understanding contemporary relevance.

23. For a defense of this limit to submission to human authority, see John Calvin, *The Institutes of the Christian Religion,* IV. xx. 32.

24. Paul Lehmann, "The Politics of Easter," in *Dialog,* Vol. 19 (Winter 1980), pp. 42–43.

25. See Luke T. Johnson's *Sharing of Possessions, Mandate and Symbol of Faith* (Fortress Press, 1981).

26. Help for this discussion can be found in William Stringfellow's *An Ethic for Christians and Other Aliens in a Strange Land* (Word Books, 1973), especially Chs. 3 and 4.

27. Preface to Dietrich Bonhoeffer, *Letters and Papers from Prison* (Macmillan Co., 1972).

28. See his "Letter from Birmingham Jail" in Martin Luther King, Jr., *Why We Can't Wait* (Harper & Row, 1964).

29. Rosa Parks's refusal to move to the back of the bus started the historic bus boycott. Mrs. Malcolm Peabody and Mrs. John Burgess, both wives of Episcopal bishops, were also jailed in civil rights demonstrations.

30. See Daniel Berrigan, *Ten Commandments for the Long Haul* (Abingdon Press, 1981). See also his *The Trial of the Catonsville Nine* (Beacon Press, 1970). With him in the General Electric plant at King of Prussia, Pennsylvania, were five men and two women, Ann Montgomery and Molly Rush. These Christians risked long prison terms in their protest against the nuclear arms race.

31. For copies of the Freedom Seder, write to Arthur Waskow, c/o Menorah, 1747 Connecticut Ave., N.W., Washington, D.C. 20009.

32. For copies of the Vigil Service for El Salvador, write to Religious Task Force for El Salvador, P.O. Box 12056, Washington, D.C. 20005. Related to this is *So Full of Deep Joy,* songs of the monks of Weston Priory dedicated to Archbishop Romero and the four sisters murdered in El Salvador. It can be ordered from Weston Priory Productions, Weston, Vt. 05161.

V. Pentecost

1. William Greenbaum, "America in Search of a New Ideal: An Essay on the Rise of Pluralism," *Harvard Educational Review,* Vol. 44, No. 3 (August 1974), pp. 411–440.

2. Elisabeth Schüssler Fiorenza, " 'You are not to be called Father': Early Christian History in a Feminist Perspective," *Cross Currents,* Vol. 29, No. 3 (Fall 1979), pp. 301–323.

3. Sabelo Ntwana and Basil Moore, "The Concept of God in Black Theology," in Basil Moore (ed.), *The Challenge of Black Theology in South Africa* (John Knox Press, 1974), pp. 18–28.

4. Ibid., p. 26.

5. Joseph Haroutunian, *God with Us* (Westminster Press, 1979), p. 77.

6. John Meyendorff, "The Holy Spirit as God," in *The Holy Spirit,* ed. by Dow Kirkpatrick (Nashville: Tidings, 1974), pp. 76–89; and Richard Tholin, "The Holy Spirit and the Liberation Movement: The Response of the Church," ibid., pp. 40–75.

7. Quoted in John C. Gager, *Kingdom and Community* (Prentice-Hall, 1975), pp. 130f.

8. *The Charismatic Movement: The World Council of Churches and the Charismatic Movement,* ed. by Arnold Bittlinger (Geneva: World Council of Churches, 1981).

9. José Miranda, *Communism in the Bible* (Orbis Books, 1982), pp. 58–61, also reexamines this abused text from the perspective of Latin American liberation theology.

10. From Jacob of Edessa in his *Epistle to Thomas the Presbyter* as cited in Jaroslav Pelikan, *The Spirit of Eastern Christendom (600–1700)* (University of Chicago Press, 1974), p. 55.

11. See Conrad Boerma, *The Rich, the Poor—and the Bible* (Westminster Press, 1979), p. 57.

12. Martin Hengel, *Property and Riches in the Early Church* (London: SCM Press, 1974), pp. 9–10.

13. Boerma, *The Rich, the Poor—and the Bible.*

14. Exegetical grounds for this contention have been provided in detail by Latin American scholars writing liberation theology. The touchstone volume, Gustavo Gutiérrez's *A Theology of Liberation* (Orbis Books, 1973), remains an important one. But for more guidance to the biblical texts themselves, see Julio de Santa Ana, *Good News to the Poor* (World Council of Churches, 1977).

15. Ernst Käsemann, "The Jesus Tradition as Access to Christian Origins," *Colloquium,* May 1981, p. 9.

16. Gustave Martelet, *The Risen Christ and the Eucharistic World* (Seabury Press, 1976), p. 183.

17. See the work of Norman Perrin, *Rediscovering the Teaching of Jesus* (Harper & Row, 1967), especially the chapter on "The Table-Fellowship of the Kingdom of God," pp. 102ff.

18. William M. Swartley, "Biblical Sources of Stewardship," in Mary Evelyn Jegen and Bruno V. Manno (eds.), *The Earth Is the Lord's: Essays on Stewardship* (Paulist Press, 1978), p. 22.

19. E. F. Schumacher, *Good Work* (Harper & Row, 1979), p. 36.

20. Ibid.

21. Ibid., pp. 34f.

22. Ibid., pp. 35f.

23. *The Global 2000 Report to the President,* a report prepared by the Council on Environmental Quality and the Department of State (Washington, D.C.: U.S. Government Printing Office, 1980), Vol. I, p. 1.

24. Joseph Sittler, *Essays on Nature and Grace* (Fortress Press, 1972), p. 118.

25. Ibid., p. 17.

26. Ibid., p. 120. Emphasis added.

27. Ibid., p. 121.

28. See Justo and Catherine González, *In Accord: Let Us Worship* (Friendship Press, 1981), pp. 27–28, 39–42, for worship aids from Native American sources.

29. *Leader's Guide to People of God, Part Two, Living the Word,* Level 6, Grades 5–7 (published for CE:SA by United Church Press, 1980), p. 28. Also see Arthur Gilbert and Oscar Tarcov, *Your Neighbor Celebrates,* available from the Anti-Defamation League of B'nai B'rith, 315 Lexington Ave., New York, N.Y. 10016.

LECTIONARY CRITIQUE

1. James Barr, *Old and New in Interpretation* (Harper & Row, 1966), pp. 193–200.

2. While there is growing evidence that good portions of the Bible were shaped by the early believing communities out of their own liturgical needs and celebrations, in part shaped by early and different calendars, no lectionary I have seen recognizes this.

On the point of lectionaries' decontextualizing Scripture, there are a few exceptions where clear effort is made to provide a continuous reading—daily and weekly—of the Old Testament, Gospel, and Epistle lessons, with interruptions granted for the major calendar festivals. See, e.g., the *Lutheran Book of Worship* (Augsburg Publishing House, 1978), pp. 179–192.

3. See Barr, *Old and New in Interpretation,* pp. 153f.: "Our approach to the Old Testament is Trinitarian rather than Christological. The direction of thought is from God to Christ, from Father to Son, and not from Christ to God. . . Where we have a Trinitarian structure, we can proceed to a Christological one, so that the Christological is not confined or delimited in any bad sense." Our point is that a Christocentric hermeneutic focuses on God's work as redeemer almost exclusively, whereas a theocentric reading permits an understanding of all phases of God's work.

4. There have been times in the history of Judaism, and perhaps in the crucial first century of the common era, when the Torah has been divided into shorter *parashot* and read through in a three-year cycle. This option is provided even today in a different form.

5. Beginning in James Sanders, *The Old Testament in the Cross* (Harper & Brothers, 1961), but especially in Sanders, *Torah and Canon* (Fortress Press, 1972); see also note 8, below.

6. See Brevard Childs, "The Canonical Shape of the Prophetic Literature," *Interpretation,* Vol. 32 (1978), pp. 46–55; and James Sanders, "Adaptable for Life: the Nature and Function of Canon," in F. M. Cross et al. (eds.), *Magnalia Dei: The Mighty Acts of God: Essays on the Bible and Archaeology in Memory of G. E. Wright* (Doubleday & Co., 1976), pp. 531–560.

7. See James Sanders, "Torah and Christ," *Interpretation,* Vol. 29 (1975), pp. 372–390, and "Hermeneutics," *Interpreter's Dictionary of the Bible, Supplementary Volume* (Abingdon Press, 1976), pp. 402–407.

8. James Sanders, *God Has a Story Too* (Fortress Press, 1979), pp. 1–27. See the excellent article by my former colleague Lloyd Bailey, "The Lectionary in Critical Perspective," *Interpretation,* Vol. 31 (1977), pp. 139–153.